£10

Modern Harpsichord M̶

Modern Harpsichord Makers

JOHN PAUL

LONDON

VICTOR GOLLANCZ LTD

1981

ISBN 0 575 02985 4

Printed in Great Britain at
The Camelot Press Ltd, Southampton

CONTENTS

ACKNOWLEDGEMENTS

This book could not have been written without the extensive co-operation of the makers involved, and my especial thanks are due to them. Some of the chapters were written on the basis of tape-recorded interviews, some with the use of discussion, and some were written by the makers themselves, but all the makers were involved in a great deal of time and effort. It would have been an impossible task to have included every maker in Britain and equally difficult to have done it on the basis of some hypothetical "top twenty". Instead, I have aimed at producing a reasonable cross-section of the makers at present at work. Only one maker approached declined to participate, while four dropped out from pressure of work; in the event this was fortunate as it left a book of balanced size and content. Several people who have helped me have pointed out that the title is misleading and that it should be "Some Modern British Harpsichord Makers". True though this is, I have had to decide that the shorter title is better.

I could not find all the time I needed myself, and the book could not have been written without the help of my brother Denis Paul, who carried out a number of interviews for me. For information on the ageing of wood, I am indebted to Roderick Drew; he is currently engaged on post-graduate studies into acoustics at the Institute of Sound and Vibration Research, Southampton University. I am also grateful for the assistance of Donald Miller, who read the manuscript several times and made valuable suggestions, and to a number of friends who pointed out various mistakes. Those errors which remain, and the laws of authorship require that there must be a number, are my own.

Photo acknowledgements:
The portrait photographs at the head of each chapter are either by the author or by Denis Paul, except that of the Goble family, which is by the *Oxford Mail and Times*, and that of John Barnes, which is by his son, Peter Barnes. Of the pictures in the text, all those in chapters 1 and 3 are by courtesy of the Russell Collection, Edinburgh, except for those on pp. 2, 4, 6, 13, 35, 44, 56, which are by the author. Chapter 2 photographs are by Colin Futcher, Haslemere. Chapter 5 photographs are by Hills Harris, Oxford. Chapter 6 photographs are by courtesy of the London College of Furniture (on pp. 109, 113, 115, and by David Law (p. 110). Chapter 7 photographs are by John Rawson. Chapter 8 photographs are by Reeve Photography, Cambridge. Chapter 9 photographs are by Colin Futcher, Haslemere. Chapter 10 photographs are by Andrew Houston. Chapter 11 photographs are by Royston Morgan (p. 167) and Denis Paul (pp. 168, 170, 173). Chapter 12 photographs are by Stephen Moreton Prichard (pp. 177, 178) and by

courtesy of Whelpdale Maxwell and Codd Ltd. (p. 180). Chapter 13 photographs are by R. L. Mitchell. Chapter 14 photographs are by Robert Davies. Chapter 17 photographs are by Studio 4, Bournemouth. Chapter 19 photographs are by Peter Mactaggart (pp. 250, 253) and Colin Futcher, Haslemere (p. 256). The photographs in chapters 15, 16, 18 and 20 are by the author, except for that on p. 246, which is by Fuller's of Folkestone. The jacket photographs are also by the author, except for the keyboard picture of the Kirckman, which is by courtesy of the Russell Collection, Edinburgh.

AUTHOR'S INTRODUCTORY NOTE

Most of the literature on the subject of the harpsichord and written in English gives sizes and measurements in feet and inches, and I continue to use these units where appropriate while giving metric equivalents if necessary in brackets. Those measurements which have long been standardized in metric measure are given without conversion.

The usual convention is used for defining strings as being at 16ft, 8ft and 4ft pitch. This is organ practice and derives from the actual physical length of the organ pipes; the CC pipe being 16 feet long, the C pipe 8 feet and the c 4 feet long. If middle C is struck and middle C sounds then the strings are at 8ft pitch. If the middle C key sounds the octave above, then the strings are at 4ft pitch while, if the octave below is sounded, they are at 16ft pitch. The convention for indicating in which octave a note falls is not standardized and so I have chosen the most commonly used, as shown below. Each octave is taken as being from C through to B and so on up. Thus the usual five octave harpsichord compass is written FF to f³.

The frequency of notes was given in the past in cycles per second, but cps are now written as Hertz or contracted to Hz. Thus the standard modern, or concert pitch, which used to be defined as A = 440 cps should now be written as a¹ = 440 Hz. Unfortunately this is a little clumsy, so I shall use the simple form of A 440.

CHAPTER 1

✧✧✧

An Introduction to the Harpsichord

The story of the harpsichord is both unique and extraordinary in the way the instrument fell rapidly from favour, was rejected for over a century and then made a return into steadily increasing popularity. It was never entirely forgotten, and there was a small band of collectors and players in the nineteenth century who gave recitals – the names of Carl Engel and A. J. Hipkins come to mind. The real revival started in the twentieth century and came through Arnold Dolmetsch, Wanda Landowska and Violet Gordon-Woodhouse in the first generation. Then came new players, radio and records, and over the past twenty years the harpsichord is again on its way to becoming a familiar instrument in many homes.

The manufacture has changed. In the eighteenth century, the climax of English harpsichord making had become a factory operation, with well-organized production dominated by two firms, Kirckman and Shudi. Today, it is largely a cottage industry, the individual work of one man or a small partnership group. There are only two mini-factories employing between ten and twenty workers. This situation is possibly transitory; if harpsichords become even more popular it would be reasonable to expect that factory production will meet the demand better than individual craftsmen. If this does not happen it will be because economics are not necessarily on the side of the factory. The craftsman competes ably by working in conditions of low overheads, usually in his own home in the country, and by being versatile and giving good service.

Two opposite myths need dispelling about the makers of harpsichords. One is that the factory product is superior because it is made to a high standard of accuracy on precision machinery while the craftsman muddles along in his garage. The other is that the factory product is mediocre because it is made on an assembly line while the craftsman works with a mixture of love and supreme artistry. It should be needless to say that as with all products, there are harpsichords which are good, bad and indifferent, and each should be judged on its merits. Whatever the methods of production, good design and good workmanship should characterize them all.

Although the interest in early music is currently rising, we have no idea whether this will continue or die away. The long-term future of the harpsichord maker is therefore obscure, and it is for this very reason that I want to capture a picture of some of these men and their times in this book. They survive because their instruments are different and, by virtue of that fact, provide customer choice. Some may, in fact must be, better makers than others in certain respects, but I have no intention of judging them or providing a buyers' guide. The purpose of this book is to let them speak for themselves. What I want to discuss in this introduction is the way harpsichords have been made in the past and are being made now, and how these different constructions result in differently toned instruments, so that each maker's methods and opinions can be understood. I shall start by saying that there is no absolute standard of tone against which an instrument can be judged, although most people who judge tone will think that they are assessing objectively. It is purely a matter of personal choice when music lovers consider that one harpsichord sounds better than another, for the appreciation of tone is subjective, within us. Even when there may be wide agreement, a consensus of opinion, there is no certainty about it. It is a fact of psychology that the consensus of opinion, the received view, changes from generation to generation or decade to decade, whether on questions of morals or economics or artistic taste. So in this preamble, while explaining in outline how harpsichords work, I want to point out something of the way different constructions create *different* tone colours, not better or worse.

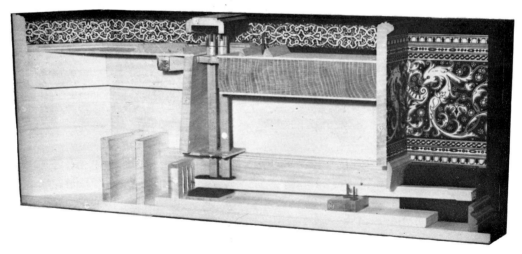

Cutaway model of a harpsichord action at the treble end, showing a key, jacks, and strings stretched between soundboard bridge and wrest plank. (Model made in the Adlam Burnett workshops.)

It is almost entirely the quality of tone colour, using the phrase in the broad sense to include such aspects as attack and clarity as well as timbre, which defines the essence of the instruments which have come down to us. Some of these qualities can be explained and copied while others remain bafflingly mysterious. Every maker understands this and endeavours by experience and insight to penetrate these problems and solve them. In a small way, this book will help to define the state of the art as it is at the moment of writing.

I also hope that I am writing an introduction to the instrument for those who have become interested in the subject but have not yet delved into it. There are some valuable books on the harpsichord, the early piano, on tuning and temperaments, but the best are scholarly works, technical and deeply involved in detail. A brief review of the subject, even if necessarily superficial, may therefore not be unhelpful. We are just beginning to see an explosion of interest, of new knowledge and research, into early music. It is an exciting time both for the instrument maker and for those who play.

The Action

Superficially the harpsichord looks fairly simple; just numbers of the same action component (the jack) repeated over and over. The complications are more obscure, in the hidden details of construction with which the maker must contend. Since I write as a maker I will want to discuss these important aspects, but first we must look at the straightforward mechanics.

The strings, of course, are plucked and this is done from a chromatic keyboard, the standard keyboard common also to piano and organ, of seven natural keys and five accidentals to the octave. Each string has a jack to pluck it, and sometimes more than one. These jacks lie in rows across the instrument, held in position by guides or registers. An instrument with one or two sets of strings will have one or two rows of jacks, but where there are three or four sets of strings it is quite common for there to be an extra row of jacks on one of these sets to give an additional tone colour. It is also common for the disposition of the registers to be split between two keyboards.

The jack, traditionally a flat strip of wood but today sometimes of plastic, rests vertically at the end of each key. The keys are so balanced that when each is depressed by the finger, the jack rises. A plectrum, set near the top of the jack, is positioned just under the string and the moment the jack rises this first catches the string and then lets it go, imparting energy and setting the string vibrating. The plectrum is not fixed to the jack itself, but to a little secondary component, the tongue, also of wood or plastic. This is balanced on a pin and is free to move backward against the pressure of a light spring. The direction of leverage on the tongue is such that the plectrum catches the string when the jack rises but, on the return downward, the tongue moves back so that the plectrum slips past the string. The tongue is therefore an escapement mechanism and, without it, the jack would hang up on the string.

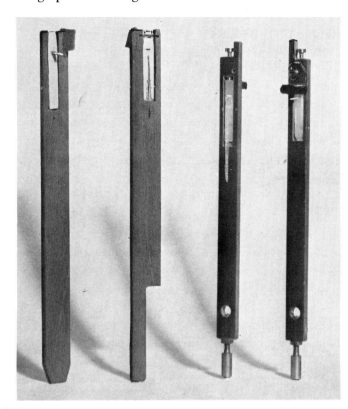

Examples of harpsichord jacks, made by the author. *Left:* wooden jacks after Kirckman, the second being a dogleg. *Right:* modern plastic jacks.

The return of the jack, when the player releases the key, is not quite silent because the plectrum must touch the string in the process of sliding past, and it does this a moment before the damper silences the string. The termination of the note therefore has a little "edge" to it, which merges with the next succeeding sound. At one time the sound of returning plectra was thought to be a fault of the instrument and Arnold Dolmetsch invented an elaborate new jack mechanism in order to eliminate it.

Any reader who has not inspected a jack should find an opportunity to do so, when the action of the escape mechanism will be easily seen.

It will be apparent that the plectra must be accurately positioned in relation to the strings for the plucking action to be uniform, while if the jacks are pulled back away from the strings, the plectra will miss altogether. In simple instruments with one string per note the jacks are permanently located in position with respect to the strings, but, in complex harpsichords, the jack guides are made to move in such a way that the complete row of jacks can be brought into play or taken out again. Because this kind of guide slides in and out, a movement in fact of only a millimetre or two, the guides are sometimes called slides. These slides can be moved into play either by hand stops or pedals, or more rarely by knee levers, but in the earliest instruments the slides themselves projected from the case and the player moved them directly, without any intermediate leverage.

A picture of the simple mechanics of the harpsichord should by now be emerging: an instrument with one, two or three sets of strings and more rarely four, and with either one or two keyboards and very occasionally three. The purpose of the different sets of strings and of the hand stops or the pedals is obviously to provide alternative tone colours; two keyboards either make possible a rapid change of tone or provide a contrast between left hand and right hand. We must now look a little at these alternative tone colours and see how they are achieved.

Tonal Change

Simple instruments with one set of strings will usually be at 8ft pitch and if there are two sets at 8ft pitch they will be described as being in unison, or the instrument will be said to have two 8ft unisons. If there is a set of strings sounding an octave higher this is called the 4ft while a set sounding an octave lower is known as the 16ft.

The harpsichord maker usually endeavours to give these sets of strings a different tone colour so that they can be played separately for tonal contrast but also ensures that they blend and can be played well together. The 4ft, and the 16ft if there is one, will differ in sound from the 8fts almost automatically, as the bridges are of different size and on different parts of the soundboard, while the *scaling* for each may be different. Scaling is something which will be discussed later. It is, however, possible to exaggerate the tonal differences of the 4ft and 16ft by using strings at a different tension. In the case of the 16ft very large tonal changes have been made by using wrapped strings which give a very plummy sound.

The way the strings are stretched across the instrument can be seen in the illustration of the model action. They are held at the far end on hitch pins (one per string), and at the near or keyboard end each string is fixed to a tuning or wrest pin. Turning the wrest pin clockwise with the tuning key tightens the string and raises the pitch. The string passes across two bridges and the length of string between the bridges is called the "speaking length" because this is the section which vibrates and sounds as a note. One bridge is on the soundboard and so conveys the vibrations via the soundboard to the air, the other is on the wrest plank and has acquired the different name of "nut". The wrest plank is always a thick plank of hard wood and the wrest pins are hammered into it sufficiently

The first stages of construction of the body shell of a modern harpsichord, by the author. Made in solid mahogany and oak with a beech wrest plank on a pine bottom.

tightly not to slip. The 4ft strings have their own bridge and nut, and the 8ft strings likewise, but half an inch above the 4ft. If there is a 16ft (now rare) these strings would also be on their own bridge and nut, again half an inch higher, so that there would then be three separate levels of strings.

A very common stop on harpsichords, because it is cheap and simple, is the buff or harp stop which consists of a row of little pieces of buff leather which can be pressed against the strings to mute them. The buff leathers are mounted on a long strip of wood which can be moved by hand or pedal. This strip lies at right angles to the strings close up by the nut and, when it is engaged, each string of the set has its own individual piece of buff leather pressed against it. The buff leather acts as a damper and to work properly must mute only slightly, just enough to take off the top harmonics and leave a clear but modified harp-like tone. If overdone, so that the damping is too heavy, the note becomes quite dead.

The standard practice is to put a buff stop on one 8ft and also on the 16ft if there is one. A quite extraordinary bell-like tone, beautiful but completely unhistorical, is produced by a buffed 16ft plus the 4ft. This can be heard in a number of recordings of the past twenty-five years, but the 16ft now having gone out of fashion it will not be heard so much in the future.

It will be appreciated that, while the individual stops have different tone colours, the combinations are equally important for variations of colour. The individual stops and the combinations also provide the essential variations of loudness, the dynamic contrasts that so distinguish the harpsichord. In the seventeenth and eighteenth centuries the dynamic range would have been used, but not emphasized and not continually changed, as has been the habit in modern professional performance until recent times. The modern harpsichord developed as a rather bland instrument with a uniform tone colour down the compass, while tuning in equal temperament robbed it of key change contrast. Until modern players rediscovered the ability to control the effects they needed by fingering, phrasing and other rhythmic factors, pedals and ease of changing stops provided an alternative. Inevitably they were over-used. Now, with the current fashion for authenticity, we are hearing less harpsichord music played this way.

It was realized by Arnold Dolmetsch that if the plectra were advanced deeper under the string then they would pluck more strongly. This effect is apparent with quill plectra, but works much more strongly with leather, with which a contrasted soft and loud can be produced. The effect is known as half hooking from the fact that the stops can be locked or hooked in two stages. With instruments having a number of pedal stops and half hooking, substantial and continual dynamic changes are possible. Apart, however, from the fact that both the instrument and the way it is played are not historically valid, half hooking has the disadvantage that the strings are not plucked for optimal tonal quality in either position.

[7]

I have now introduced "quill" and "leather" instead of the inclusive word "plectrum". Quill is brilliant, leather is rich and rotund. Leather, of course, is variable in quality, the hardest being almost quill-like, the softest being gentle and harp-like. The difference between these tones is accounted for by the loss of upper partials with leather plectra, due to the very slight damping effect at the moment the leather parts from the string. The best leather is a tough, well-tanned and long-lasting sole-leather, which will be quite strong and brilliant. An oiled strap-leather will be soft and gentle, but wears rapidly. In the late eighteenth century a very soft buffalo leather was experimented with in France, the *peau de buffle*, and this is quiet and delicate. It is not suitable for a main stop but can be very effective if used as a separate register on one of the unisons which has quill as the main stop. The best and traditional quill is that of the pinion feathers of the Corvidores, raven or crow. As there are not enough crows to go round all the harpsichords, it is obvious that substitutes have to be used and quills from other birds are on trial, as well as the plastic, Delrin. In general, leather is rarely used nowadays and current practice is to use quill or Delrin.

The last simple and direct change of tone colour that the maker can introduce is that of plucking proportion, that is, how far down the string between the two bridges the jack is positioned. The theory is that by changing the plucking position various upper partials will be either accentuated or suppressed, and thus the tone from any given string can be made to change quite considerably. The maker has only a small amount of control over the plucking distance. In the treble the slides must fit tightly into the space under the short treble strings, but down in the bass there is more room for choice. The nut can be brought forward close to the registers, or the registers can be swung away from the nut – they do not have to be at right angles to the strings. One stop makes deliberate use of the short plucking distance, the lute stop. For this the strings are plucked very close to the nut, with the effect of a twangy, nasal tone. This stop is usually fitted on two-manual harpsichords, when it must occupy the upper manual. In order to pluck close to the nut a row of jacks runs through the wrest plank, either splitting the wrest plank in half or with every jack of the set having its own mortice in the wrest plank. There is then a second row of jacks set up to pluck this same set of strings at what might be called the "normal" plucking distance. There are two different possible arrangements: the lute and the normal plucking could both be on the upper manual, or the normal plucking could be taken from the lower manual. The makers who fitted lute stops seem always to have provided their manual coupling in the form of the dogleg jack. An analysis of the dispositions of several harpsichords which have lute stops is to be found in Hubbard.[1] He concludes his discussion by saying that these dispositions would be better if the doglegs were replaced by a true manual coupler. I doubt if this would work without altering the balance and depth

[1] Frank Hubbard: *Three Centuries of Harpsichord Making*, pages 156 f.

of touch of the keyboards, and I suspect that the makers who fitted lute stops used the dogleg jack for coupling as their best option.

On a two-manual instrument there has to be some kind of coupling arrangement so that the upper manual jacks can be played from the lower manual. The use of dogleg jacks is the simplest system and as simplicity has great merit there is a lot to be said for it. The dogleg jack has part of the tail cut away to form a step; the bottom of the jack rests on its lower manual key, the step rests on its upper manual key. In this way the relevant key from either manual will play it. The disadvantage of the dogleg is that if it is engaged it has to be engaged on both manuals; it cannot be off one and on the other, so it is not a true coupler.

The other common coupling system is that usually referred to as French. In this system the upper manual can be slid forward so that the upper manual keys come over little pegs projecting from the lower manual keys. In this position, whenever a lower manual key is depressed the peg pushes up the corresponding upper manual key. Thus more physical work has to be done by the player's fingers when the keyboards are coupled, introducing a different sense of touch. Its efficient operation requires the tolerances of the whole system to be made closer than if the coupling is by means of dogleg jacks. There were some variations in German instruments which may be noted. The bottom manual might slide instead of the upper, and, in a cross between both types, a sliding manual has been used to engage a set of dogleg jacks. In this system the jack tails were too short to reach the lower manual keys unless the lower manual was slid so that little blocks of wood on the keys became positioned under the tails.

The two standard 8ft stops will also vary in tone colour, by virtue of their different plucking proportions. There must always be a minimum difference, which is the width of one guide, and some makers have exaggerated this width deliberately. The two 8fts can be separated by the 4ft register; the specification is then indicated as 8 + 4 + 8 while, when they are not separated, it would be shown as 8 + 8 + 4. The interesting harpsichord in the Courtauld Institute has the two 8fts (there is no 4ft) diverging quite widely in the bass.

Some of the possibilities of varying or determining harpsichord tone colour have now been set out, but at the elementary level of describing little more than the tonal effects of the different stops. The real level of understanding the harpsichord and its tonal qualities lies in the materials and methods of construction, which also requires some understanding of harpsichord acoustics.

Many people interested in music will already know that a continuous musical note can be analysed and shown to be built up of a series of pure tones. Usually the lowest tone is the one whose pitch is perceived, and this is called the fundamental or first harmonic. The tone colour is formed by the fundamental being modified by the addition of overtones which are simple arithmetical multiples of the fundamental. These overtones have frequencies which are twice, three times, four times the fundamental, and so on up; they are known as the second, third, fourth . . . harmonics. The colour of any particular note is characterized by the level of intensity of the various harmonics contained in it.

Harpsichord tone colour is much more complex than this simple picture because the note is not continuous. The harmonic content changes, so the tone colour changes as the note progresses; there are also amplitude variations which alter our perception of the tone colour. There is an explosive start to the note, the starting transient, then a gradual dying away, ending sharply with the terminal transient when the damper cuts off the note. The harmonics do not all die at the same rate, the higher partials decay first, which is why the harmonic content changes. Then there are rhythmic amplitude variations which add a vibrant quality or even a rumble to the low notes, and these seem to be due to the way standing wave patterns are set up in the air space of the body and which feed back interference patterns to interact with the main vibrating region of the soundboard and the strings. The picture of a series of harmonics, second, third, fourth, etc., is also not quite true for the harpsichord because some of the upper harmonics may be sharp instead of perfectly in tune.

Changes in design and construction will accent one factor or another in tonal quality. We are beginning to understand these factors, but whether we have sufficient knowledge to design for a particular tonal quality is arguable. In a harpsichord, the whole is greater than the sum total of the parts and the unsolved mystery is the way this subtle concatenation works to produce the magic of an outstanding instrument. It is a salutary fact that makers of the past have produced better instruments on an empirical basis than some of us today with knowledge and intention, but that is no reason for giving up such a search. Wisdom should merely require that we recognize our limitations.

The Soundboard

The soundboard is the heart of the instrument and an understanding of the part it plays is of such great importance that it must be looked at closely. The soundboard is often incorrectly described as an amplifier. An amplifier is a device to increase the strength of a signal or vibration, but a soundboard does not do this. Rather, it makes the vibrations of the strings available to the air and it is therefore a radiator, a matching device between string and air. An analogy could be a transformer which matches electric load to supply. Any apparent amplification that takes place is partly the effect of the efficient transfer of energy and partly the fact that the amount of energy in the string is used more quickly.

The relationships between the different parts of vibrating systems, either electrical or acoustical, are considered technically in terms of impedance, which can be regarded as a resistance which varies with frequency. It is not necessary in a simple explanation to produce the formulae for working out impedance, and I propose anyway to discuss the subject in more everyday terms. It is, however, useful to know the effects of impedance where there are junctions between vibrating systems. In a harpsichord there are two principal junctions to consider. In the string to bridge-cum-soundboard junction the impedances must match so that the vibrations flow through. The other junction is at the surrounding edge of the soundboard where it fits the case rim. If the impedances of the soundboard and case are a reasonable match, some sound vibrations will flow into the case, while if there is a mis-match there will be reflection back into the soundboard. The effect of different ways of making the case and, more importantly, the effect of the use of different woods, affects the tone by virtue of the impedance match between soundboard and case plus, of course, the effects of resonance and absorption in the woods on either side of the boundary. This needs to be remembered when looking at the different types of traditional construction.

Most books on physics show a vibrating string as stretched between two fixed points with nodes (places of nil movement) occurring at both ends, while the antinodes or points of maximum displacement occur along the length of the string. At the actual moment of plucking, the plucking point is the site of the largest antinode. In a harpsichord the string is stretched between two bridges, that on the wrest plank and that on the soundboard, and obviously if the soundboard is to be flexible and capable of vibrating in sympathy with the string then the point where the string crosses the bridge is not an absolutely fixed point and not the perfect node of theory. Thus the string/soundboard complex vibrates as a whole, and it is too simple to describe the system as the strings vibrating and the soundboard conveying sound, as if they were separate entities.

It will be apparent, in fact, that for a musical instrument to work, the node must not fall on the bridge pin for, if by definition the node is the point of nil movement, no motion could be conveyed to the bridge. The node in practice must fall a little in front of, or behind the bridge pin, and where it falls depends on the phase relationship between the vibrating string and the vibrating bridge. Now, this relationship is a fluctuating one, because the bridge is receiving energy both from the string and also in the form of reflected waves coming back from the soundboard rim and these two wave sources do not synchronize. If the position of the node fluctuates, the wavelength is altering and thus the pitch; there is a slight and rapid pitch variation which is heard as a vibrant quality, and this forms an important contribution to the richness of the bass quality in a good instrument. Another, and possibly even more important effect of the wholeness of the vibrating system is that the resonance peaks of the soundboard reflect back into the string and so play an important part in determining the mixture of fundamental and harmonics, and therefore the tonal quality of the instrument.

There is a conflict between the need for the bridge to be rigid, so that the string can vibrate at maximum efficiency, and for the soundboard to be flexible in order to convey the vibrations to the air, and this conflict sets the narrow limits within which the soundboard must be constructed. If a harpsichord soundboard were thick and solid and the bridge heavy, as with a piano, the string could vibrate near the theoretical optimum but the soundboard would draw off the energy slowly. Such a combination would give a low-intensity initial transient and a long sustaining tone of rather rich, thick quality. If an extremely flexible board were made with the intention of maximizing sound transfer, the bridge might be so lacking in rigidity that the string would hardly vibrate at all. It will be appreciated that this is another way of saying that the impedance of the bridge/soundboard complex must match that of the string.

These acoustic facts, and the use of wood for soundboards, puts a limit on variations of board thickness which is normally a tenth or an eighth of an inch (2·5 to 3·0 mm). The wood is usually spruce or a close relative and textbooks on pianos state that spruce is chosen because it is strong and flexible and has the highest rate of transmission of sound. As early makers used spruce without any means of measuring these qualities it is obvious that they chose it experimentally and because they liked the tone. The measurements of the physical properties which have been made in modern times throw little light on the tonal qualities of spruce but they do indicate that it is one of the most efficient woods as a radiator of sound. Efficiency is directly related to the velocity of soundwaves along the grain and inversely related to the density and the calculated figure for spruce can be shown to be high.

In Northern Europe the woods of choice were and still are the Common or Norway spruce (*Picea abies*, earlier known as *Picea excelsa*), and the Silver fir (*Abies alba*). Both of these woods have been identified in old soundboards and today both are sold indifferently under the trade name of "Swiss pine". They cannot be told apart by a simple visual inspection, although they can be identified microscopically. Trees grown at high altitude are chosen for soundboard wood, as the growth is then close and even, both desirable qualities. The best soundboard wood comes from the Alps and the Carpathians. A well defined selection process by experienced buyers enables high quality soundboard wood to be available to the trade. In North America, Sitka spruce is used extensively for pianos and harpsichords.

An interesting exception to the use of spruce is that Italian harpsichords were frequently made of cypress (the Common cypress of the Mediterranean, *Cupressus sempervirens*), this wood being used for both the casework and the soundboard. Cypress is so

The underside of a modern harp-sichord soundboard by the author, showing the jointed spruce con-struction, belly bars also of spruce, and the 4 ft hitch rail of beech.

different in appearance from spruce that it would hardly occur to an experienced North European maker to try it, and it is not until one hears an Italian harpsichord that it is apparent how marvellous a soundboard wood it is. The moral of this is that there may be other, quite unexpected woods which should be tried for soundboards. In fact I do know of experiments on these lines but have not been able to judge them. High altitude spruce was available in Italy as it was used in Cremona for violin making, and it is recorded in a proportion of Italian harpsichords. It is obvious the makers had a choice, but we do not know why they made the choice they did. It may have been nothing more than that spruce was expensive or not generally traded. The problem of transporting materials long distances was a factor that we nowadays fail to appreciate. The widest use of cypress for Italian soundboards occurred in the earliest instruments, spruce becoming more common in late ones, and this could very well have been an effect of improving communications.

The soundboard is barred underneath, that is, it has bars of wood glued to the underside, and the commonest way these were placed in the past can be seen in the illustration. How the bars came to be put on in this way is something of a mystery, and at first sight quite irrational. If the barring on a modern piano is examined, it will be seen that it serves an obviously rational purpose. The bars are regularly spaced and go right across the board, at right angles to the grain, providing upward support against the downbearing of the strings, equalizing the speed of sound across the grain and preventing the board from warping. This type of barring on a piano was introduced between the years 1815 and 1820, and before that time pianos had harpsichord barring.

Most harpsichord bars are in a group in the corner area away from the bridge, so that the board is barred across one half underneath, while there are other bars (the bridges) on the other half on the top side. This unequal strain should be a certain recipe for warping, and it must be a miracle that all harpsichord boards do not warp automatically.

The longest of the corner bars is traditionally called the cut-off bar and this name gives a clue as to why barring developed. The tone must have been found to improve if the vibrating area of the soundboard was reduced. In fact, the result is not to cut off and deaden the corner of the board, but rather to divide the board into two halves which have different ranges of resonant frequency, one high and one low. I have experimented by making a harpsichord without soundboard bars, instead limiting the area by bringing the rim across diagonally where the cut-off bar would normally go (something that has been found on a few early instruments) and the tonal result was poor. The acoustic interaction between the barred and unbarred parts of the board must be highly important to harpsichord tone. Of great importance is the degree of thickness and solidity of the bars. A glance at the illustration of the underneath of a soundboard shows that while the cut-off bar divides the board into a main resonating area and a subsidiary, more rigid, area, the main resonating area is again divided by the 4ft hitch rail, so that there is an 8ft area and a 4ft area. The 4ft hitch rail (sometimes called the *boudin*) is a mechanical necessity but, obviously, makers recognized the acoustic effect of having it there, for some instruments have a bigger rail than would be needed for just holding the 4ft strings. There are instruments in which a large boudin is partnered by a heavy cut-off bar; it is possible to look at this as giving rigidity to the whole board or alternatively as being intended to strongly separate the 8ft and 4ft. Such a board should give a rather dry tone, while a lightly barred soundboard would tend to be more singing and sonorous. But it is unwise to make too close an estimate of tonal effects from variations in one component because there are too many other factors involved. My own instinct is not to keep the soundboard too tight, so that the boudin is small, while I keep the cut-off bar back from the 4ft bridge. A rich, vibrant tone is usually my aim, and this is a contributing factor.

It is important to mention that a number of early harpsichords do have barring going right under the bridge. The Sodi design is heavily barred, just like a modern piano, and the effect should be to increase the sustaining power. Some French instruments not only have the full corner cut-off system but also an additional two or more bars going under the bridge. It must be assumed that these bars have the function of helping to keep the board flat, but the suggestion has been made that in some cases they are the later addition of restorers and not the work of the maker.

Soundboards that are tapered in thickness are common, and it is extremely interesting that tapering is always reported as being thinning in the treble area. But, on the contrary, I have restored a very late harpsichord with the board thinner in the bass, which is also true of every early grand piano I have restored. Perhaps the intention of early makers in thinning the treble was to compensate for the smaller surface area of this part, where it is cramped by the return of the curved side. The physics of the subject indicate two opposite requirements for the bass area, a need to thin the board to make it more efficient as a transmitter of the low frequencies and a need to thicken it to match the impedance of the bass strings. Thus makers would have felt that there were no positive indications of what they should do. My own practice is to compromise by thinning the soundboard in the bass area but making the bass end of the bridge heavier and taller. More important, in my view, is the practice of tapering the thickness of the board so that it is thicker under the bridge and fined off a little to the rim and to the boudin. This is necessary to give the right degree of flexibility to the board.

The instrument maker is dependent on an important quality of the wood and wire he uses, their elasticity, for it is this property which makes vibration possible. Equally important is damping, the property which makes vibrations die away. Wood and wire have the property of internal damping, sometimes called internal friction, which results in vibrations being converted into heat within the material. It will be apparent, for example, that an instrument made with wood which has high damping qualities would be quiet and dull. The effect of internal damping is for the most part proportional to frequency and thus the result is the reduction of the higher harmonics. Woods vary in their damping factor and it should not be thought that woods with low damping are necessarily best for musical instruments. It is obvious, though, that non-traditional woods should be tried out with care before they are used. By happy chance, wooden instruments in general produce tones which suit our hearing, neither too harsh nor too soft. Particular instruments vary in tone for a multitude of reasons; internal damping is an important one which at the moment goes unmeasured but which should prove an interesting area for research.

The Effects of Age

In examining any old wooden instrument, whether in admiration or in consideration as a model, the effect of age on tone is always doubtful. It has to be recognized that here is a subject on which there is a lot of opinion and little fact. There is a widespread belief that age improves tone and this belief is especially attached to old instruments which have a high value. Unfortunately little positive research has been done on the subject, largely because owners of valuable instruments are reluctant to have pieces of them cut away for examination. Research, too, is concerned with measurable effects and tonal quality is not something which is directly measurable.

Wood must alter with age, otherwise it would last for ever but, provided it is kept in stable conditions free of insect or fungal attack, it will last for a very long time, certainly for thousands of years. Thus two or three hundred years in the life of an instrument may be too short a time to show much effect from ageing.

There have been reports that an exact copy of an old violin will be heavier than an original. This is not something that has been properly investigated but, before assuming that the old wood has lost substance and that in some way such a loss is related to tone, it needs to be said that the reason may be nothing more than normal variations in the density of different pieces of wood of the same species. Nevertheless, wood will lose substance with age, and one at least of the reasons for this happening can be linked to tone. Wood contains a number of constituents known as extractives which are volatile and will therefore leave the wood. The presence of these extractives contributes to the damping factor, meaning that they absorb sound, so that when they are lost the wood becomes more resonant. The seasoning process of wood is largely concerned with the removal of extractives so that the bulk of them should already have gone before an instrument is

AN INTRODUCTION TO THE HARPSICHORD

made; it is possible though that in the course of a couple of hundred years the further loss of extractives may be significant.

Substance is also lost from wood as a result of the effect of ultra-violet (UV) light and from oxidation. As far as instruments are concerned the effect of UV must be considered minor. UV breaks the bonds in the lignin molecule but as instruments are kept indoors and UV cannot anyway penetrate beneath the surface layer, the effect in practice is usually that of damage to a microscopically thin surface layer, noticed as a lack of adhesion of the varnish or polish, which will then flake off.

Changes in the colour of wood are well known and, as a general rule, UV bleaches wood and oxidation darkens it. Spruce turns dark with age and the effect of oxidation, the slow burning away of the wood. In time, wood will completely burn away, in the way that paper will turn brown and disintegrate. I have not traced any report of the rate at which oxidation of wood takes place and it must be sufficient to say here that it is slow but, in terms of hundreds of years, it could be significant. The effect is one that could no doubt be hastened for research purposes by keeping samples of wood in pure oxygen.

Although a clear link has not been established between tone and chemical changes related to ageing, one physical difference between old and new soundboard wood has been reported. This is that old wood absorbs fewer low frequencies but more of the higher frequencies. The effect on tone, other things being equal, is that an old instrument will be louder but more mellow. If we think about it, this is the sort of change we must expect: a change in frequency response so that there may be more or less top or bottom or a different peak of resonance, or perhaps a change in the velocity of sound propagation which will actually again show up as a change in resonance. There are not going to be any extraordinary changes with time that will produce some mysterious and marvellous tonal quality which was not there before. Tonal quality is intimately bound up with resonance peaks that accentuate some harmonics at the expense of others, noticeable because the human ear is so responsive to small changes in harmonic content.

It has been suggested that tone will be improved by playing an instrument over a period of time, but there have been no logical reasons put forward in explanation which can be related to the modern understanding of wood physics. To have an effect, the vibrational energy (which is very small) would have to alter the linkage between the molecules of the cellulose and lignin, or alter the molecular structure itself. However, time itself, principally through slow oxidation, will bring about such changes. Many players, who pick up an instrument untouched for a long time, observe that the tone apparently improves after a few days' playing. What probably happens when they do so, is that they remember and accept the tone and also bring to the instrument the minute adaptations of technique which bring out the best in it.

The Scaling

The bridge determines the length of the strings, and the shape of the curve of the bridge on the soundboard is set by the maker to allow the string lengths to increase from the treble down to the bass. The way the lengths increase is called the *scale* but the word is also used by way of a shorthand description of the scale of the whole instrument by giving the length of one string, the 8ft string of c^2. The majority of old instruments had a c^2 scale lying between 10 inches and 14 inches and, as a very general rule, Italian harpsichords had short scaling, 10 to 12 inches, and North European instruments a longer scale between 12 and 14 inches. It is an acoustic fact of vibrating strings that if c^2 is 10 inches long, a string 5 inches long at the same diameter and tension sounds c^3, one 20 inches long sounds c^1 (middle C) and strings of 40 inches and 80 inches sound the next two C's down. A scale in which each octave length doubles is referred to as a just scale. In the extreme bass, strings of the order of 80 inches or more would make the instrument over long, so these strings are shortened to come within a reasonable case size and made thicker to compensate. If string lengths are doubled for each octave and kept at the same tension, this means that the same gauge wire would be used throughout except for the shortened strings in the bottom octave but, in practice, the strings are thickened steadily down the scale, thus resulting in changes of tension through the instrument. Early makers obviously intended the tension to be graduated smoothly down the scale, although, as they did not always position their bridges with great accuracy, this result was not always achieved. A graduated tension gives a change of tone down the compass, contributing to life and brilliance, but at some expense to tuning stability.

The scale that makers chose depended intimately on the pitch to which the instrument was to be tuned and the wire they were using. These are variables which have to be defined before it is possible to make a really close replica but at the moment we have definitions of them in only general terms. Very little early wire has survived and our knowledge of early pitch is fragmentary.

Musical Pitch

The word pitch has several meanings; one is the level of a sound up or down a scale; another, the audible sensation of a given frequency of sound. The meaning is more specific when used to refer to the pitch to which an instrument is tuned. We have now an internationally agreed pitch, accepted at a conference in London in 1939, at $a^1 = 440$ Hertz. This conference defined the frequency of the note a^1, the A above middle C, as having 440 vibrations per second, or Hertz. For simplicity, we will from now on refer to it as A 440. Since the beginning of the century pitch had been settling down to near A 440, but if we go back a hundred years more to 1800 the level of pitch was very indefinite, while to define the pitches of two or three hundred years ago becomes difficult. We know a number of pitches with considerable accuracy from fixed pitch instruments and the rare tuning fork, but not enough to produce a chart of early pitch over the whole of Europe. One of the few eighteenth-century tuning forks to have survived and which is associated with a harpsichord maker is that of Pascal Taskin, at A 409.

Pitch varied because the human voice varied – and on the whole the voice held pitch down – and because instruments varied in the pitch which suited them; autocratic rulers with military bands under their command tended to raise pitch. The unifying influence was the musician who travelled. It was not until the widespread use of the tuning fork, say from 1800 onward, that there was a trend to standardization and even then it was local as each country set its own standard. The history of musical pitch was investigated thoroughly for the first time by A. J. Ellis,[1] a hundred years ago, while a new monograph has just appeared by Arthur Mendel.[2]

Ellis arrived at the conclusion that in spite of variations in pitch during the seventeenth and eighteenth centuries, there was a general consensus or level at about A 420 plus or minus a few Hertz. Mendel regards the evidence for this as inadequate and thus throws the whole question open again. In the meantime, the musical world had come to accept the idea of a consistent old pitch and harpsichord makers have taken to making their instruments to a pitch which is an equal tempered semitone below 440 – A 415 to the nearest whole number. If the concept of a definite old pitch is accepted, this is the most sensible figure to choose, as it makes transposing practicable. It is also a reasonable compromise as the evidence still suggests that eighteenth-century pitch stayed within the overall limits of A 400/440. From the point of view of the listener I think it makes very little difference whether music is played at 440 or 415, as most of us do not have a sufficiently acute sense of pitch to feel that either is right or wrong. There are occasional problems for singers at modern pitch, but we are concerned in this book with the problems of harpsichord makers. If a harpsichord copy is tuned to an arbitrarily chosen pitch with no certainty as to what was the original pitch, then the string tension and tone may be quite wrong. The question of string tension and tone is intimately connected with the metallurgy of the wire and here makers are having to choose or even guess on evidence which is still being researched.

The Strings

Both iron (or steel) and brass wire are used for stringing harpsichords, and the diameter will usually start at around 0·20 mm in the treble and end up at bottom FF at 0·75 mm thick. The tension on each string will lie between the average limits of 2·5 to 5·0 kg (5 to 10 lbs), the bass strings at a higher tension than the treble. If iron wire is too thick it gives a

[1] A. J. Ellis: "On the History of Musical Pitch". In *Journal of the (Royal) Society of Arts*, 28 (1880) and 29 (1881).
[2] Arthur Mendel: *Pitch in Western Music since 1500*. Bärenreiter Kassel, Basel and London.

false quality in a harpsichord and for this reason the bass is usually strung with brass wire. The point at which brass changes to iron will often show a change of colour; my view is that makers in general do not carry the brass high enough and that if the cross-over point is taken further up the compass then the tone colour change is lessened. However, the point of change is limited both by the scale length and by the breaking strain of brass wire.

There is some interesting research in progress on early music wire; it is unfortunately incomplete but I will endeavour to give as clear a picture as possible of the state of knowledge at the time of writing. As many of the references overlap, they are listed together.[1]

The early written records about the harpsichord are delightfully vague when describing the type of wire used. The descriptive references simply divide it into white, yellow, red and copper. White wire is very obviously iron and yellow is brass; red and copper are terms a little more obscure. There is a modern usage of the terms yellow brass and red brass which indicate differently proportioned alloys of copper and zinc: yellow has a ratio between 60/40 and 70/30 while red lies between 80/20 and 90/10. The probability is that the early terms red and copper both originally applied to a high copper, low zinc brass; it is unlikely that "copper" meant pure copper, which would have been too soft. The current picture is that red brass was used for the bottom few notes, then yellow brass for most of the bass, with iron in the tenor and treble. The use of all-brass stringing in Italian harpsichords will be discussed later. There is a possibility that red wire meant bronze, the alloy of copper and tin, and a number of makers believe this to be so. There is no positive evidence, but certainly I know of no reports of old bronze wire being found, and the analysis reports of red wire have all shown it to be a low zinc brass. Plain bronze wire is not available in Britain, although I have been informed that it is available and used in the USA. Phosphor bronze wire, which is readily available, is a wire harder than brass and has a slightly higher breaking point. In my opinion, and in that of a number of makers whose opinion I value, phosphor bronze has poor tonal qualities in a harpsichord, although it is not unsuccessful in a clavichord.

[1] Wm. R. Thomas and J. J. K. Rhodes: "The String Scales of Italian Harpsichords". In *Galpin Society Journal*, XX (1967).

Wm. R. Thomas and J. J. K. Rhodes: "Harpsichords and the Art of Wire-drawing". In *The Organ Yearbook*, vol. X (1979).

Grant O'Brien: "Some principles of 18th Century Harpsichord Stringing and their Application". In *The Organ Yearbook*, vol. XI (1980).

Scott Odell and Martha Goodway: *Harpsichord Wire of the 17th and 18th Centuries*. American Institute for Conservation of Historic and Artistic Works.

I am also indebted to Professor Anthony Simpson of the School of Engineering and Applied Sciences, Sussex University, and to Malcolm Rose for preliminary analytical data on early wire, which will be published in due course. With another colleague, Derek Slater (a metallurgist), Malcolm Rose is now preparing a specification for the drawing of wrought iron music wire, and it is hoped that this will be available for sale some time in 1981.

Until a few years ago the only wire available to modern harpsichord makers was steel piano wire (in thin gauges of course) and brass spring wire. It has long been appreciated that modern wire differed from early wire, but it is only recently that methods of accurate analysis have made possible the proper examination of wire and also only recently that makers have doubted the sense of using piano wire.

The tonal colour of an instrument starts with the vibrating string so that the quality of the wire to be used could be one of the most important things to get right. The problems have been those of accurately dating old samples, of analysing them and of the high cost of obtaining trial quantities of wire made to specification.

Some explanation of terms and of the history of wire may be useful, but must be given with a word of warning. The names of the alloys of common metals have been, and are used, in differing ways so that the terminology is not precise. Iron is the pure metal, although the term is also used when it is impure and not specifically alloyed. Steel, as the word is used here, is carbon steel, while all the other steels, with which we are not concerned, are alloy steels. Carbon steel is iron to which has been added a small amount of carbon. A low carbon steel, containing about 0·25 per cent carbon, is mild steel, much stronger than iron and used for constructional work. High carbon steel, containing up to 1·0 per cent carbon, is used for making all kinds of edged tools, springs, and also piano wire. The effect of the tiny amount of carbon (which is in the form of iron carbide) depends on the way it is distributed within the crystalline structure of the iron, and this is modified by heat treatment. Heating to a high temperature and quenching leaves the carbide so very finely dispersed that it may be considered in solution in the iron and in this state the steel is hard. Quenching also brings about a change in the shape of the atomic lattice. Conversely, heating and then cooling slowly anneals the steel and makes it soft; annealing causes the atomic lattice to revert and produces comparatively large carbide precipitates and in this state the carbon has a minimal hardening effect on the iron. The exact degree of hardness is controlled by the method of heat treatment. Carbon steel is usually first heated and quenched at room temperature, an operation which makes it glass hard, and then re-heated to a lower temperature and again quenched in the partial annealing operation known as tempering. Modern piano wire is treated in one operation by being heated to 900°C and then quenched in a bath of molten lead.

Another effect which needs understanding is work-hardening. All metals, and this includes brass and iron as well as carbon steel, will work-harden. If a metal is stressed in any way, such as by being pulled, it passes through three stages. The first is known as the elastic region and in this state the metal stretches but returns to its original length on release. If greater stress is applied the stage of plastic deformation follows and in this state the metal is permanently stretched, becoming progressively harder and more brittle.

Once the elastic region has been thus extended, the metal will behave elastically at a higher stress. The final stage, as more stress is applied, is that of fracture. Therefore, to work-harden a metal it must be stressed towards its breaking point. Wire is work-hardened both when it is pulled through dies and if it is pulled to a sufficiently high tension in an instrument. Modern piano wire is not only heat-hardened but is also work-hardened by being drawn, and the end product has a very high elasticity and tensile strength, at the cost of being somewhat brittle.

Carbon steel as we know it today dates from when Bessemer, in Victorian times, developed his process for first purifying pig iron and then adding a controlled amount of carbon. Modern piano wire dates from this period. In the early days of the ferrous industries the only types of iron available were cast iron (the brittle and impure product straight from the blast furnace), wrought iron (the same material purified by hammering, soft, ductile and thus suitable for making wire), and "steel" which meant wrought iron which had been case hardened, an operation in which red-hot iron is baked in carbon to give it a hard skin. A primitive carbon steel was made towards the end of the harpsichord period, when in 1740 Huntsman produced the first homogeneous steel by melting bars of case-hardened iron, but this does not seem to have been used in music wire.

Analysis so far carried out on old iron wire shows that it was remarkably pure, with a minute carbon content – as low as 0·01 per cent – and it was free of sulphur. This means that it was smelted from a high grade ore and then wrought with great skill and care. As more samples are examined and more analytical reports are published the picture may change. I have seen several mentions of early wire containing up to 1·0 per cent carbon but these were not accompanied by precise analytical statements and so for the moment they must be regarded as doubtful. The probability is that the bulk of old iron wire was soft and relatively pure because it would then have been a consistently easy material to draw. Using this material, wire makers then proceeded to harden it as well as they could by the drawing process. The improvement of both dies and the drawing technique resulted in wire getting harder and stronger, and piano wire as late as 1860 (a date just before steel wire came into use) has been found to be much harder than harpsichord wire, although metallurgically very similar.

It can now be seen that the most readily observable difference between modern piano wire and old harpsichord wire is that the former is both heat-hardened and work-hardened and so is very hard, while the latter is only work-hardened in the drawing and so is much softer. The breaking strain of old iron wire is also much lower than that of modern steel. The belief that relative hardness was the important factor in the difference between old iron and modern steel wire led to the introduction of several modern soft wires, two of which, one American, one British, are still available. These wires are of modern carbon steel which has been annealed and then cold drawn so that they are work-hardened only, in a comparable way to old iron wire. There is no precise and easy metallurgical definition of such wire; one supplier describes it as high carbon iron and the other as soft steel. Both terms are probably reasonable.

Obviously, this wire is not an exact analogue of old wire, and continuing research will be necessary to find out whether it could be bettered. It is possible that a true soft-iron wire would go out of tune more quickly and at the same time have no better tone. The tone of iron wire is darker, more sombre, than steel, but the difference is most noticed in the tenor while the tonal quality in the treble is similar.

Analysis of early brass wire shows it to have been a roughly 70/30 alloy for yellow and a 90/10 for red, with practically all samples having a 0·1 per cent inclusion of minor impurities, mostly of lead or iron or both. These were probably natural impurities, not added intentionally, and are unlikely to have had any noticeable effect on the wire. The indications are that early brass wire was more ductile and had a higher breaking strain capacity than modern wire. The difference is most likely due to the fact that modern brass wire is not designed for harpsichords but for making piano springs. It has a little too much zinc in it and has been hard drawn to the point where it tends to be brittle. A modern American brass music-wire has recently been produced which has a higher breaking strain than the English spring brass wire and first trials indicate that it may be much better.

It has been shown, with a reasonable degree of probability, that early makers scaled their harpsichords so that the wire was stretched close to the breaking point. At first sight this seems an odd thing to have done as it was bound to result in the trouble of having to replace broken strings. They did so, of course, for the simple empirical reason that they liked the tone. One reason which has been put forward as a possible explanation of the improvement of tone with high tension is that the upper harmonics tend to be sharp instead of exactly in tune with the fundamental. This effect is known as upper partial in-harmonicity and has been studied mostly in piano tone experiments. It has been shown that the effect is least in long, thin and highly stressed strings. Harpsichord strings are, however, so thin anyway that the effect is slight whether they are highly stressed or merely strongly stressed.

There are other explanations. The tone may improve simply because further hardening takes place in the instrument as the wire stretches on settling to tune, but this begs the question of the relationship between hardness (and all the other qualities of wire) and tone. The answer possibly lies in the fact that changes in grain structure during work-hardening affect the phenomenon known as internal damping, the way upper partials are reduced by the internal friction of the grain structure when under elastic stress. There are research projects on these problems being undertaken at a number of universities so that positive information should be available to us within a few years.

This very brief review shows that we cannot be sure that we are stringing our harpsichords with wire which is adequately comparable to old wire, and our lack of knowledge of old pitch shows that we do not know if we are putting the right tension on that wire. In this respect the state of the art is a long way from being authentic. Makers are therefore building instruments on assumptions which may be proved wrong. I do not think it matters; we must do our work to the best of our ability and make instruments which are acceptable to those who wish to buy them. Research is a continuous process and its findings are influencing us all the time, but we have to make the instruments of today on the basis of today's research, not on that of tomorrow. We also need to remember that while it is interesting to have reasonable answers to every question, in the

An anonymous Italian harpsichord of *c.* 1600, the instrument of cypress in an outer case with painted decoration. It is in largely original condition, although the music desk is modern and the keyboard has been altered. (In the Russell Collection, Edinburgh.)

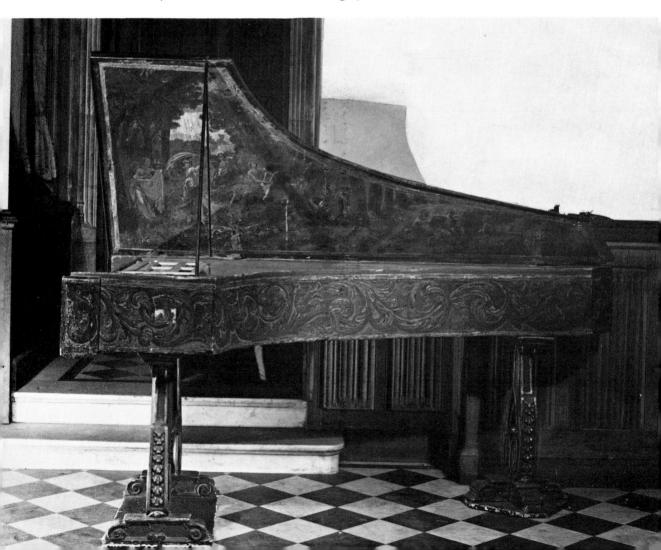

long run we are concerned with the subjective impressions of tonal quality. More than anything else, the solutions of physics applied to musical instruments are there to help us repeat qualities that people like.

The Case and Italian Instruments

Case design is a major single factor in the differences which exist between instruments, and it is useful to review this while looking at the main types of harpsichord. The concept of different schools of harpsichord making is now giving way to the recognition that the history of the instrument cannot be so easily simplified, but as an introduction it has great merit.

The earliest harpsichords still extant are Italian, and it is possible that the instrument was originally developed in Italy. Early Italian harpsichords are of a fairly consistent pattern, although this has been brought about to some extent by rebuilding, which obscures the early development.[1] The compass was close to four octaves and although very early instruments often had only one 8ft, or sometimes an 8 + 4 specification, over the period as a whole the usual stringing was 8 + 8. These harpsichords differ from the North European tradition in that they are extremely lightly built, rather like violins, and that the casework and soundboard are usually made from the same resonant wood, cypress. With bottom boards often no more than three-eighths of an inch thick and sides little more than an eighth, the whole instrument is one with the soundboard and is so light and responsive that the energy is drawn quickly from the strings, giving a rapid and sharp initial transient and little follow through.

Quite a number of Italian style harpsichords are currently being made, but these copies lack certainty about how the originals were strung, or to what pitch. Suggestions have been made that there were various pitches in common use, by which is meant that there were various nominal pitches, for there would have been local variations due to the impossibility of setting pitch accurately in those days. The evidence for whether different pitches coexisted for which transposing instruments were necessary (analogous to the Ruckers transposing keyboards) or whether pitch started low and steadily rose, is too complex to be discussed here. The most important question is how the instruments were strung in relation to the pitch. We have already seen that harpsichords may have been strung to the highest possible tension, and if we knew the breaking point of old wire sufficiently accurately, the pitch could reasonably be inferred as being just below that point. The North European scale of 13 to 14 inches relates closely to the known pitches, but the short Italian scale of 10 to 11 inches, if strung with iron wire, does not. Then an early treatise was found to contain the information that harpsichords scaled at below 11 inches should be strung with brass wire, and this matched the knowledge that brass wire

[1] John Barnes: "The Specious Uniformity of Italian Harpsichords". In *Keyboard Instruments*, ed. Edwin M. Ripin.

was highly stressed at a 10 inch scale when pulled up to A 420/440. As a result it has now become common practice to string Italian copies with brass wire right through the compass. An Italian harpsichord with a scale lying between 9·5 and 10 inches can be strung throughout with brass wire and pulled up easily to A 415 or even A 440. At these tensions the thinner brass strings from middle C upward are hardly more than a semitone from breaking point. Breakage can be common and obviously it is necessary to tune with care, but this is a small price to pay for an instrument which sounds marvellously better than a similar one with iron or steel strings. John Barnes,[1] in a monograph on the subject, considers that Italian pitch rose steadily to reach a level which was close to the modern A 440, and that all Italian harpsichords should be strung with brass wire, those with longer scales being pitched lower. If this opinion becomes generally accepted the result will be interesting, as it will no longer be possible to string Italians which have scales of more than 10 inches with iron or steel wire and pull them up high.

Later Italian harpsichords, those from the eighteenth century, show a much heavier construction and a compass growing to five octaves, with a higher proportion of spruce soundboards, but those with which I am familiar retain the cypress soundboard and the short scale suitable for brass wire pulled up to a high pitch. There is a very special quality in the combination of cypress board and brass wire that marks off the Italian instrument as quite apart from North European harpsichords.

In spite of the delicate structure, Italian harpsichords do not often show signs of warping. The weak point of the harpsichord is the action gap combined with the curved side corner and it is at this point that warping will usually occur. Italian instruments which are built on a baseboard running the whole length have sufficient strength to carry the stress past the weak area.

The cypress wood was usually left quite plain but the instruments were fitted into a second, outer case, which was often considerably ornamented. This can be designated as the "separate case" construction; later instruments have the normal North European integral case construction in which the lid is attached to the instrument itself and so forms its own "box".

Flemish Construction

A different and important school of harpsichord making developed in the Low Countries during the seventeenth century, principally in Antwerp, the instruments of the Ruckers family being the best known today. Here the compass started to grow, the 4ft was added and the second manual introduced, firstly at a different pitch for transposing purposes, but later in the modern manner for contrasting colour. The Ruckers instruments are currently regarded as among the most important we have. I would agree, in spite of

[1] John Barnes: "The Stringing of Italian Harpsichords". Monograph given at the Internationale Arbeitstagung des Instituts für Aufführungspraxis der Hochschule für Musik und darstellende Kunst in Graz (1971).

the fact that the attribution to Ruckers is in some cases unsure. The majority still extant are those which have undergone *ravalement*, that is, enlargement and rebuilding and as such are cross-breeds, with a great deal of life and vitality, but are not wholly Ruckers. To try to pin down the Ruckers quality (and also that of the other early Flemish makers), I would suggest looking at the construction. It is pointless, as has been done, to look for derivation and discuss whether the designs evolved from an Italian basis; the construction, the woods, the wire, are different. Nevertheless, they do stand halfway between early Italian lightness and the fully developed North European instruments of the late eighteenth century. The rim-wood thickness is almost halfway between the two extremes, and the wood itself has neither the resonant quality of cypress nor the reflective quality of oak. Poplar was the normal construction wood and this was also used for the soundboard bars. Generally, it can be said that the softwoods (such as pine, spruce and fir) are resonant and the hardwoods (the deciduous trees) are not, but poplar and lime, and to some extent sycamore, are deciduous hardwoods which combine softwood characteristics with moderate hardwood strength. I like to classify such instruments as having semi-solid cases, resonant and radiating, although not to the extent of Italian instruments. The string tension is moderately high and the scale long, approaching 14 inches. One needs a long scale to have room right up in the treble for the 4ft bridge. Some of the soundboards have been found to be exceptionally thin but this does not seem to have been a consistent factor and so it is probably not representative. Exceptional thinness is of no special value, certainly of no value which would offset the problems of fragility which go with it. I have restored an instrument with a board $\frac{1}{16}$ inch thick and could find nothing special or valuable about the tone.

The real Ruckers, those which have not been rebuilt, are smaller than those which have undergone *ravalement* and this means that the resonant frequency of the case would be higher, so that one would expect them to have a less sonorous bass than the late instruments and a more important tenor. Unfortunately, I do not have enough experience of the genuine instrument to be qualified to judge them, but they are generally regarded as superior to their contemporaries. As the men who were engaged in re-building Ruckers, the Blanchets and Taskin for example, constructed their own harpsichords on closely similar lines, it would be reasonable to expect that all would have tonal qualities in common. Remarkably, those Ruckers that I know are quite unlike the classical French instrument, the tone is breath-taking and envelops the listener in a brilliant tapestry of sound; the French instruments by comparison are much dryer.

It is difficult to estimate the trading conditions under which the Ruckers family worked. Antwerp and part of the Low Countries were under Spanish occupation, resisted by the free protestant north. Periods of war, resistance and blockade were interwoven with periods of treaty-agreed stability. On the whole a good deal of their production must have been exported for them to have prospered, and this seems to have been what happened. The stressful political situation must have made the age a little unsure of itself for some of the decoration must be regarded as a very overdone mixture. The run-of-the-mill instruments, however, have a simple, cheap and delightful finish consisting of nothing more than block-printed paper stuck on the inside of the cases, the outsides being painted.

The classical period of the Flemish harpsichord had ended by the last quarter of the seventeenth century, but the Ruckers instruments continued to be rebuilt, or faked, for another century; a remarkable tribute, according to the way one looks at it, either to Ruckers' quality or to the ability of fashion to persuade otherwise hard-headed people to part with their money. Antwerp ceased to be an important centre, but the Dulckens, father and son, should be mentioned. Several important Dulcken instruments are currently copied, the best known being the large two-manual of 1745 in the Smithsonian Institution.

French Makers

Late French construction was certainly influenced by the Ruckers tradition. We have seen that the Ruckers instruments were so highly thought of in France in the eighteenth

Single-manual harpsichord by Joannes Ruckers, 1637. This is a *ravalement* instrument, enlarged in the eighteenth century; the keyboard and painted case decoration dates from this time, while there has also been some modern restoration. (In the Russell Collection, Edinburgh.)

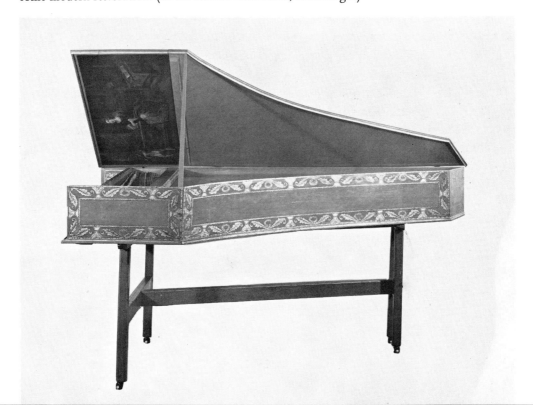

Two-manual harpsichord by Pascal Taskin, 1769. One of the most
copied of early instruments, the original is decorated in lacquer with
gold leaf banding, the soundboard with flower painting in water colour.
(In the Russell Collection, Edinburgh.)

century that there was a flourishing business in rebuilding and enlarging old Ruckers
harpsichords. The Blanchet family was heavily engaged in this business, and they were
followed by Taskin, a Blanchet apprentice who married his late master's widow. Many
of the Ruckers which have come down to us have been transformed from their rather
crude, early construction to elegant late-French instruments. Some of these enlarged instruments are not Ruckers at all and must be regarded as spurious, although it would be
better to look on them as genuine late French. The enlarging must have altered the
character, and not much of the original wood remained. Blanchet and Taskin were
highly competent makers, and they not only rebuilt these old instruments to quite a large

extent in the Ruckers manner (apart from the decoration, which is contemporary) but they built their own instruments in the same tradition.

The structure is substantially the same. The bentside bracing is stronger and placed at a better angle to give support but the system is unchanged. The same woods were used, lime, poplar and pine generally, but everything is scaled up; thicker sections, the compass enlarged of course, the bridges heavier. The scaling is virtually the same, lying between 13 and 14 inches. The much larger body-cavity should and does give a noble resonance. One would expect a much grander sound from a late French harpsichord but I am not sure if it is always there, due perhaps to modern voicing. When late French instruments were first copied the essential characteristic was thought to be the light touch and in pursuit of this aim the plectra may have been too fine, with a resulting thin, wiry sound. They should be capable of a sharp clarity *and* of a lush richness.

Germany

Too few German harpsichords have survived for them to be discussed on any sort of national school basis. The Dulcken family, of course, was from Hesse, but they worked in Antwerp and Brussels and so are regarded as Flemish. The most interesting instruments, because they are so remarkable and extraordinary, are those of Hieronymus Hass. Their size, complexity and quality have given them a status which is perhaps unjustified, as they are completely outside the mainstream of North European tradition and they cannot even be related to the work of other German makers.

Hieronymus Hass made very large harpsichords with a 16ft of unique design, in which the 16ft bridge was on a separate soundboard from the 8ft and 4ft, thus taking the 16ft weight from the main soundboard area. He even went so far, in a complex design, as to fit a 2ft stop and a third manual. These large instruments with the 16ft need to be considered because they were an influence on modern makers but, unfortunately, instead of the design being copied as it was, modern instruments of this general type were kept down somewhat in size and the 16ft bridge was placed on the same soundboard area as the 8ft and 4ft. In many cases the 16ft bridge was combined with the 8ft bridge so that the scaling was too short, while the rigid and heavy bridge killed all the flexibility which is so necessary for fluid tone. While saying that the Hass design is superior to that of the average modern concert harpsichord with 16ft, the Hass has the drawback that the 16ft soundboard area is small for the function it has to perform. The compromises that have to be made in designing any harpsichord with 16ft reinforce my own preference for the simple 8 + 8 + 4 specification. There is one very important single manual of 1764 by Johann Hass, son of Hieronymus, in the Russell Collection; this has a specification of five octaves FF–f^3, 8 + 8 + 4 + buff.

Single-manual harpsichord by J. A. Hass, 1764, an important instrument which is believed to have belonged to Mozart. It is finished in a mahogany veneer, cut to a herringbone pattern; the legs are modern. (In the Russell Collection, Edinburgh.)

England

Harpsichord makers in different countries drew on the experience of earlier generations or picked up ideas from imported instruments and developed them, except possibly in Italy, where a fairly consistent pattern of design was adhered to. Harpsichord makers were inventive, continually improving, changing, chasing up blind alleys and, here and there, attempting to change the harpsichord into the piano. The climax of inventive design can reasonably be attributed to the middle-eighteenth-century makers, principally Kirckman and Shudi. These English makers built to a cabinet-making tradition that used highly decorative veneers laid in panels edged either with a line or a patterned banding, and framed with cross banding. The carcass wood for this veneering was often oak, braced with pine battens, and these instruments are described as having solid-case construction.

In Italian and Flemish instruments the casework is light and resonant, and virtually an extension of the soundboard so that it contributes to the sound transmission to the air. Solid cases have very little resonance but a fair degree of internal damping, and the effect

Two-manual harpsichord by Jacob Kirckman, 1755. A fine example of the fully developed English harpsichord, with elaborate marquetry decoration. (In the Russell Collection, Edinburgh.)

of this construction on tone depends on a critical effect in the relationship between the soundboard and the rim to which it is glued. If the rim is sufficiently hard and rigid then soundboard vibrations do not travel into it from the soundboard but are reflected back from the edge, so that the soundboard is the only transmitting medium to the air. If, however, the vibrations do travel into the case they will be absorbed and lost in the wood. In practice, some of the upper partials are lost in this way so that these instruments are a little less brilliant, more mellow, than those of the continental tradition. The late English makers who used oak in their rims, a very reflective wood, exhibit in my view the solid-case quality at its best. Oak is reflective because it is dense; reflection occurs when there is a sharp change of impedance such as is brought about by a change of density at a boundary. Quite a number of modern instruments were developed from solid case originals and in some the cases were further strengthened by the use of additional wood bracings without an acoustic understanding of what was being done. Such modern harpsichords, made up to the 1960s, can exhibit quite a considerable upper partial loss and have a rich, organ-like quality.

The best known of the eighteenth-century English makers is Jacob Kirckman, who learned his art when apprenticed to Tabel; Burkat Tschudi had already served his time under the same master. Kirckman's harpsichords are beautifully made, with a marvellous eighteenth-century drawing-room tone, but a number of them have warped. His baseboards were in two sections which met just in line with the weak join of the curved side and the jack-guide gap, a method of construction which was unfortunately asking for trouble. Kirckman harpsichords had a number of features that we should note. The rim was usually of oak, and the shape wider than continental instruments. The soundboard area was therefore more open, especially in the tail, and he placed his bridges as far as possible in the centre of the vibrating space. This gives a very rich and sonorous quality. His rather heavy stringing contributed both to this quality and to the tendency to warping. He used dogleg jacks as a means of coupling the two manuals, and front guide-pins on the keys, in the manner of modern pianos. So many Kirckmans have survived that it is apparent he had a well organized factory production.

Like Taskin, Kirckman married his master's widow and so inherited the business, but carried on under his own name. Burkat Tschudi set up on his own, and partly anglicized his name to Shudi. In turn he had a famous apprentice, John Broadwood, who married Shudi's daughter and in due course took over that business. John Broadwood took scientific advice on the construction of his instruments, one part of which was to the effect that there should be an even plucking proportion down the scale and this, in my opinion, made them dull. The same advice, applied to pianos and combined with their exceptional quality of construction, was exactly right and made the reputation of the firm.

The Spinet and Virginal

The harpsichord has always existed in several forms and it is tempting to think of the two simplest, the spinet and virginal, as the poor relations, the cheap domestic version, in the way that the piano market is now shared between the grand and the upright. In eighteenth-century England this was true of the wing spinet and the harpsichord. The place of the virginal, which was an instrument of the seventeenth century and earlier, is not quite so clear, and it may have been preferred to the harpsichord. To start with, the usage of the name has changed, as virginal was then the common term for all plucked instruments. It is equally correct, by the way, to say either virginal or virginals. It is not known whether the plural started as the name of the double instrument, and there were of course two kinds of double instrument, the two-manual harpsichord and the mother-and-child virginals (see Glossary). The term "pair of virginals" was certainly used by Pepys to mean a single instrument. The great group of composers whom we refer to as the English Virginalists are just as likely to have composed at and for the harpsichord. We hear of Queen Elizabeth, who was very fond of music, as playing the virginals and her Italian polygonal instrument is preserved in the Victoria and Albert Museum. We do not know if this was her favourite; indeed she probably had a large number of both harpsichords and virginals if the inventory of her father's instruments is any guide. Let us say, at any rate, that to many ears today the virginal is better suited to playing virginal music than the harpsichord and the reason for this is understandable. The contemporary harpsichords were more than likely Italian instruments with a simple 8 + 8 disposition which would have had many characteristics in common with the virginal. Certainly, the classical eighteenth-century harpsichord is nearly as unsuitable for virginal music as the piano.

The English virginal of the seventeenth century had the rectangular shape of the Flemish instrument so well known from pictures of Dutch interiors. Flemish virginals, and especially those of the Ruckers family, were often made with the keyboard on the right so as to pluck the strings fairly centrally, and the name "muselar" was given to these. The resulting tone is low in the even harmonics, and this tone is peculiar to the virginal, as central plucking is not possible on a harpsichord. English virginals are different in having the keyboard on the left, so plucking close to the bridge. The characteristic tone of the virginal is, however, more derived from the rectangular shape and the fact that (usually) both bridges are on the soundboard, whereas the harpsichord has one of its bridges, the nut, on the wrest plank. Soundboards do not vibrate as a whole but in discrete sections; these vibration patterns are controlled by the shape of the board and the source of the sound waves, that is the section of bridge which is responding to the string stimulus. Two sources of sound are fed into the virginal board from opposite ends, which in conjunction with the rectangular shape of the board, results in a pattern of vibration quite unlike the harpsichord. To these differences must be added the fact that the cavity volume under the virginal board is relatively tiny.

The virginal has a small compass, usually between $3\frac{1}{2}$ and $4\frac{1}{4}$ octaves, and only one set of strings. It was common for instruments of the time to be played standing, or from a high stool, as can be seen in many Dutch paintings, and the virginal is therefore often set on a relatively high trestle.

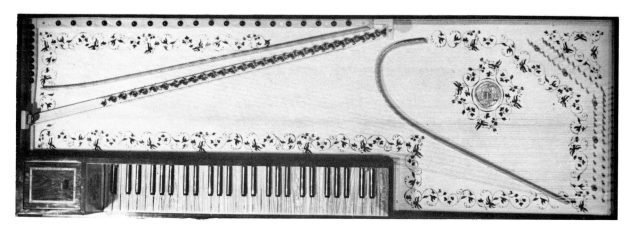

Soundboard view of a virginal by the author, showing the oil painted arabesque decoration. A modern, original design, but influenced by the Stephen Keene of 1668 in the Russell Collection.

By the eighteenth century the virginal had been replaced in England by the spinet, a miniature harpsichord with one set of strings and no stops, in which the shape had been distorted to take up less room. Instead of the keyboard being at right-angles to the long side, in the spinet it is at a more acute angle, giving the instrument a narrow wing shape. Spinets usually had the same compass as contemporary harpsichords, but it was common for the late, five octave compass to extend from GG to g³, instead of the harpsichord FF to f³. Both the spinet and virginal are made by modern makers and still excellently serve the function of small and not too expensive domestic harpsichords.

In Italy the virginal was usually made in a many sided form instead of the rectangular shape of the north. The same light construction of cypress wood was used as for Italian harpsichords, and they have the same small compass. Rather confusingly, the Italian virginal was often known as a spinet. It is best to call the English instrument a wing or transverse spinet and to refer to those made in Italy as polygonal virginals.

Research and Tone

Now that we have looked at various aspects of harpsichord construction and glanced, however briefly, at some of the salient features of early designs, it may be useful to consider the extent to which acoustic knowledge affects copying and even new design. As I have shown, the acoustics of harpsichord tone are known fairly clearly in outline. The material of the string and the conditions under which it vibrates gives an initial pattern of fundamental and harmonics. This is modified by the natural resonances of the soundboard and case, which accentuate some of the string harmonics at the expense of others while, overall, there is an attenuation of the upper harmonics caused by the internal damping of both wood and wire. To this picture must be added the aural effect of the amplitude envelope of the vibrations and the possible result, which I have not yet seen quantified, of the frequency modulation of the nominal pitch of any note brought about by the displaced node effect of the vibrating bridge.

Research in acoustics consists of putting figures on measurable effects and then making statements about these results in terms of tonal qualities. The work which is currently being done is mostly on wire: its metallurgy, its vibrational behaviour at various points on the stress curve, and the internal damping factor. This is the work which will have the most immediate impact on harpsichord construction, for it will either result in new wire being drawn, or it will confirm that currently available wire is satisfactory — and certainly the soft steel and brass wire from the USA is extremely good.

Can research give us any more information which would enable us to make better copies than we do already? At the moment one thing we know for certain is that no two instruments made the same way sound exactly alike. The reason is that apparently similar pieces of wood will have slightly different densities, speed of wave propagation, etc., and therefore differing resonant characteristics.

Thus, although it is possible to buy very exact plans of quite a large number of outstanding early instruments, making a copy may or may not produce exactly the tonal qualities to be expected. It should be possible for research to give us additional information, in terms of, say, bridge impedance, soundboard and cavity resonance and soundboard damping, which would make repeatable the quality of every instrument. For example, research into violins has shown that tone is good when the prime resonant frequencies of the body and cavity coincide with the frequencies of two or more of the unstopped strings. A violin maker who has the necessary measuring equipment can tune his resonances to achieve this result. It seems to open up the possibility of every cheap factory violin being as good as a Stradivarius.

Whether this sort of information will become available and whether harpsichord makers will take advantage of it, it may be best not to predict. I like to think that instrument making is an artistic and creative enterprise which requires something more than straight technical knowledge. I have access to absorption curves for all the pigments I use, but unfortunately it makes me a no better painter; on the other hand, modern chemistry ensures that the paint I put down stays stuck. Thus I am inclined to hope that as knowledge accumulates, we will take from it as much as we want and no more. I am a great believer in every harpsichord sounding different.

The Rose

The rose is a decorated soundhole, but the soundhole function has disappeared (if indeed it ever existed), while the decoration remains. The acoustic function of a hole in the soundboard would be to raise the resonant frequency of the column of air contained in the body cavity, but the size of the hole in relation to the size of the body is too small to have any recognizable effect. The hole was probably copied from the hand-held stringed instruments; whether early makers had an acoustic intention we do not know, but it stayed as a decorative feature. The hole was covered with a perforated disc of some kind, finely cut parchment or veneer, carved in more solid wood, or cast in metal, and the rose is this actual disc, not the hole. If the soundboard was painted, then the painting flowed round the soundhole, to emphasize it.

The Antwerp guild, to which the instrument makers of that town belonged, required each maker to place his distinctive sign or emblem on every instrument he made, and they must have decided to use the rose for the purpose. They frequently chose a design which included their initials, a practice that spread and continued long after the disappearance of the guilds, and is continued by modern makers. North European roses were usually cast in a lead alloy and covered with gold leaf, but I have seen some late English roses which were cast in brass. The roses of modern makers differ as much as ever they did in the past, being variously of plastic, metal or wood and either of a geometrical pattern or a design containing the maker's initials. When I was endeavouring to design mine, a friend pointed out that there were heraldic symbols for my name which fitted happily together. I cast my roses in either bronze or zinc, and use the method devised by Bronze Age men to cast their axe heads, which happens to be very simple.

The Clavichord

Although this book is largely about modern harpsichord makers, it is not entirely about harpsichords, as many of these makers also produce clavichords and fortepianos. The clavichord is assumed to have grown from the monochord, which would give it an ancient history. Pythagoras used the monochord to evaluate the relationship between pitch and string length and tension, and in this form it consists of a piece of wire stretched across two bridges. The addition, probably in late mediaeval or early renaissance times, of a key that struck the string and of a soundboard under one bridge, made possible the sounding of a note to set the pitch for singing. The translation of the keyed monochord into the clavichord would have been a simple one of adding more strings and more keys.

It is the simplest of all keyboard instruments, the most beautiful to hear, the most difficult to design and, probably, the most difficult to play. It is shaped like a virginal but with the soundboard on the right and not across the whole box; in both instruments the strings are stretched almost at right angles to the keys. The action comprises nothing more than a piece of brass, stuck in the end of the key lever, which hits the string when the key is depressed. Called the tangent, this brass hammer most nearly resembles the tip of the blade of a screwdriver. The strings are interwoven with cloth or soft felt to the left of the tangents. Thus, as the strings are permanently damped, there is no need for any mechanical damper. When a tangent strikes a string, it does two things: it excites the string into vibration and also acts as a temporary bridge for as long as the key is held down. Thus the tangent divides the string into two halves, a dead, damped length to the left and a speaking or vibrating length to the right. When the tangent falls back, at the moment the key is released, the whole length is damped by the felt and the note ceases.

The clavichord is very, very quiet and for this reason: it will be remembered, in my earlier definition, a vibrating string was described as being stretched between two bridges, the vibrations occurring along the length of the string while the two bridges were (nominally) points of nil vibration or nodes. The tangent itself forms one of the two bridges in a clavichord, the other being the normal soundboard bridge. Thus, when the tangent strikes a string it not only sends a shock wave down it to set it vibrating, but it immediately forms a node at the point of impact, limiting the amount of energy which is transferred to the string.

If the judgement of a musical instrument rested on the volume of sound it produced the clavichord would be regarded as ludicrously inefficient, but it combines two exceptional advantages, simplicity and a marvellously beautiful tone. There are a number of special characteristics which define the clavichord. There is the richness and complexity of the tone due to the great number of harmonics; the range of piano and forte within its quiet limits; the clarity in part playing, for every note stands out with a thread-like clearness; the particular quality of Bebung, in which it is unique. The sustaining power is poor and this is no doubt the reason for the clarity of articulation – an advantage, in fact.

It cannot ever be used for performance except solo, in a quiet room, and with a very small audience. It has been amplified and played in a small hall and also recorded, but not with great success. It is too easy to amplify the quiet mechanical noise of playing. A friend tells me that the joy of playing it is at midnight, when the world is sleeping and I cannot improve on this description.

Bebung, translated literally as "quivering", is the vibrato which can be applied to the notes of a clavichord. I have described it as unique to the clavichord; in fact it has been made to work on a harpsichord but, in my view, artificially and ineffectively. If the key is over depressed on the clavichord then the tangent stretches the string and raises the pitch; if this is done with rapid finger pressure then Bebung results. Not, it should be noted, by trying to flex the key sideways. Bebung has a very special quality for marking off a single sustained note before a pause. One cannot play chords with it and its use is restricted to the upper register; I cannot remember it coming in the left hand. It should be used rarely so that its painful cry catches the imagination.

It will be apparent that if the keys are over-depressed for any reason the pitch will change and the instrument sound out of tune. Thus the player must learn always to obtain exactly the right depth of touch. The clavichord has a great range of *piano* and *forte*, in spite of the quiet maximum, but changes in volume must be achieved with the same depth of touch. A *forte* requires striking the keys with speed and force but without exceeding that proper depth. Late clavichord keys usually descend an eighth of an inch before the tangent touches the string, while the depth available for Bebung is about $\frac{3}{8}$ of an inch.

The clavichord comes in several forms, fretted and fret-free, large and small, and with steel or brass strings, and some of these alternatives pose important considerations of design. The instrument was made initially fretted and small – small enough to be carried under one arm – and it grew steadily larger until, some time after 1800, in competition with the piano, gross instruments seven feet or longer were made. These were German or Scandinavian instruments and were never made in this country; in fact there is very little evidence of clavichords being made at all, here, during the historical period, although they must have been.

Fretted clavichords have more than one note to a string (or pairs of strings where they are double strung). As the tangents mark off the speaking length of the string, more than one tangent can mark off more than one speaking length, so that one string, or pair, can serve more than one key. Naturally, one cannot play both keys together on one course and different systems of fretting will bar different music from being played. One fretting method is to use one string for two adjacent semitones, so that in theory there are half as many courses as keys; but in practice fretting cannot be carried right down into the bass. The advantages of fretting are speed of tuning (fewer strings to tune), low bridge loading and so a soundboard which is freer to vibrate, with less tension on the case.

Clavichords are made with single or paired strings per note, and occasionally with extra strings in the bass tuned to 4ft pitch. Two strings per note do not make the instrument noticeably louder, but they make a big difference to the tone. Phase differences between the two strings impart an especially lovely tone, so that, in my own opinion, single strung clavichords are of little value. Arnold Dolmetsch used to tune his clavichords with the two strings imperceptibly apart in pitch to give a special quality he liked. One can also add a little savour to the tone by omitting the felt which normally dampens the dead lengths of strings between the bridge and the tuning pins. In any other instrument, doing this would add dissonances, but in the clavichord it imparts a gentle extra fragrance.

The strings can be steel or brass, or possibly other copper alloys. As with harpsichords, clavichords with brass wire must be strung to an approximately ten inch scale. This presents design limitations on very large instruments which have been overcome by using steel wire, but unfortunately steel wire gives a very unpleasant clunk in the starting transient of the note. I prefer brass wire for clavichords, and I would rate beryllium copper next and nearly as good, with the added advantage of a higher breaking strain. Phosphor bronze is quite good but with no advantage over brass so there is not much point in using it. I doubt if clavichords would be made nowadays with steel wire; such instruments were mistakes of the early nineteenth century.

The design problems can be understood by looking at the plan picture of a clavichord (below), which is a photograph of the Hass of 1763 in the Russell Collection of the University of Edinburgh. It will be seen that the soundboard must encroach on the

Soundboard view of the large clavichord by J. A. Hass, 1763, showing the flower painted soundboard. The natural key finish is of tortoiseshell, while the accidentals are capped with mother-of-pearl. (In the Russell Collection, Edinburgh.)

keyboard area in order to allow free soundboard space to the left of the bridge. How cramped this is can be judged from the fact that the speaking length of a top f^3 string must not be longer than about 9 cm (tuning to a pitch of A 415) while the curve of the bridge comes even closer to the edge an octave lower. The practical limit of the compass is f^3 with brass strings. As a maker, I prefer to go up only to d^3 but many players would no doubt rather have the extra notes. The top keys are cranked to the left to allow the sound-board more room, but there is a limit to the amount this can be done and, anyway, the string-length limitation means that shifting the keys will pull the bridge after them. There are some old instruments in which the necessary soundboard area was provided by taking the soundboard over the keys, on a soundboard rim which is a flying arch; it seems a good idea, but I feel the rim then lacks the necessary rigidity.

The soundboard must be of reasonable size. The large Hass illustrated is magnificently balanced for size of soundboard and free soundboard area but at the cost of a longer scale of $11\frac{1}{4}$ inches. The compass is the full one of FF–f^3 and it will only pull up to about a whole tone below A 440, i.e. A 392. If such an instrument was wanted at either modern pitch or A 415 it would be necessary to compromise by shortening the scale and omitting one or two of the top notes.

The design requirements for balancing the keys is that the finger pressure both for Bebung and for the general "feel" of the touch must be as even as possible. The treble strings are stiffer than the bass, but the tangents come nearer the centre of the strings, while in the bass the tangent might come only one tenth from the end. The ideal balance will vary according to the tension of the strings and their elasticities, which in turn will depend on the gauge and material of the wire which the maker has chosen. If one makes any departure from copying an old instrument it is necessary to make repeated experiments to get the balance right again.

The clavichord is not an instrument for public performance but rather one for private pleasure. The very quiet volume makes it difficult to record, but techniques have improved and I have heard a few good records. It should not be light heartedly bought by an amateur just beginning to explore early music and for whom a small harpsichord would be more appropriate. The controlled touch means difficulties for the beginner, but the discipline necessary is not a disadvantage to any player moving to another instrument.

The Fortepiano

The makers of harpsichords have always shown a tendency to experiment, and inventing the piano was the self-imposed task of several of them. Bartolommeo Cristofori, harp-sichord maker at one time in the employ of the Medici family, succeeded first. A visitor who saw Cristofori in 1709 recorded that he had by then made three or possibly four pianos, so it may be assumed that he had been working on the problem since about the turn of the century.

The problem he was endeavouring to solve was not how to invent the piano, but how to make an "expressive harpsichord" with a graded volume control at the tips of the player's fingers. He still regarded his instrument as a harpsichord and in fact called it "gravicembalo col piano e forte", harpsichord with soft and loud. It is with hindsight that we look back and see that he had invented a completely new instrument. What is more, he invented it nearly perfectly, although as we shall see it did not fulfil the function he intended.

It is often thought that the modern piano has developed through a mass of inventions to something quite different from the first instruments, but this is not really so. The modern piano is just the same as an early piano but there is more of it. The prime qualities which go to making a piano which works are: a hammer which is projected towards the string by a lever linked to the key, with a power which is proportional to the impact of the player's finger; an arrangement whereby the hammer is freed from the lever a moment before striking the string so that it flies free that last distance, while the lever moves out of the way (the escapement); an arrangement whereby the hammer is caught after rebounding from the string so that it does not bounce about until the residual energy is used up (the check); a separate damper which stops the string vibrating as soon as the key is released; and finally the lever/hammer/escapement link must be capable of immediate re-engagement so as to allow quick repetition of the note. All of these qualities were efficiently worked out in Cristofori's later design. Cristofori was, of course, a maker of Italian harpsichords, the most lightly constructed of all. He matched the fragility of his strings with fragile hammer heads, which were little circles of parchment or paper capped with leather patches. His instruments were still really harpsichords with soft and loud, but they were not very well appreciated and people went on playing ordinary harpsichords. Indeed, considered as harpsichords they were failures. They may have had the "expressive" qualities of soft and loud that the age was beginning to need in a keyboard instrument, but they lacked the power and sonority and tonal qualities of the harpsichord. They were thin and weak, and were so little thought of that several were converted into ordinary harpsichords.

It is surprising that the piano did not die with this failure, and it was over a generation before the piano was suddenly accepted and began to be made in quantity. The need for a harpsichord with soft and loud was felt, but when it arrived it added nothing to harpsichord music. It had to grow in reality closer to the piano we know for composers to write piano music for it, and until there was piano music there was no demand for pianos. That pianos continued to be made and improved was due to the efforts of other makers after Cristofori, men such as Gottfried Silbermann. We may assume that Silbermann strung his instruments more heavily because the harpsichord tradition in the north was heavier. Once the need for heavier strings and stronger actions was recognized and composers were writing for it, the piano was suddenly successful and, in the course of another generation, ousted the harpsichord. Pianos became instruments in their own right with the demand created by the music of the first major piano composers, J. C. and C. P. E. Bach, followed of course in overlapping succession by Haydn, Mozart and Beethoven.

The arrival of the piano coincided with the first stirrings of "romantic" influences in art and literature. Tonal concepts and musical styles were changing at the same time as instruments were changing. It needs to be recognized that there was no simple cause and effect which can be stated as: "the piano was invented and composers therefore started to write for it". The century was in a ferment of change, artistic, economic and political, of which the growth of the piano and piano music were a tiny part.

Production started in earnest in England in the 1760s when J. C. Bach took up residence in London at the same time as a number of German piano makers who were refugees from the Seven Years War. The industry started with the square piano, a little instrument in the shape of the clavichord, which at first had a primitive action lacking an escapement; the grand piano was not made on a regular basis until about 1770. I have restored grand pianos spreading over the whole period of English development from 1770 to 1870 and am therefore able to review their development. The English grand grew from the English harpsichord, with an action that was virtually that of Cristofori. This action came to England via Silbermann and the refugee German piano makers, although as we shall see, a different action came to the fore in Austria. The most successful maker was John Broadwood, already established as a harpsichord maker with his father-in-law, Shudi. The work of other makers hardly differed from his. The cases were exactly the same in appearance as those of English harpsichords: square cheeks, cross-banded and inlaid; partly solid mahogany, partly veneered on oak, with pine bottoms and bracings, and harpsichord soundboards with the typical cut-off bar system. Almost from the start they had three strings per note, dampers on damper-jacks which could be raised together via a pedal, and a true *una corda*. This is something which has been partly lost in the modern piano, and a sad loss too; piano music through to Beethoven needs it in its original form and we no longer hear it as it was intended. There were three strings per note right through to the bass (which was brass strung) and a keyboard shift pedal which could make the hammers strike all three strings, or two, or one. The action was stronger than the Viennese, giving a more powerful dynamic range. The hammer heads were covered in leather, either sheep or doe skin, giving a harder tone than modern felt. The action came to be known as the English action and was so successful that it remained in general use for over a hundred years.

The early English grand piano sprang into being fully fledged, or so it seems, for there is very little evidence of experiment or change for the first fifty years. There were

An early English grand piano, *c.* 1802, by Muzio Clementi. In cross-banded mahogany, inlaid with a box-wood line, the nameboard in satinwood with flower painted decoration. (Author's collection.)

unimportant changes, which one can use for dating purposes, such as an enlarged compass and, at the end of this period, the disappearance of the stand and its replacement with turned legs and a lyre to hold the pedals. It seems as if the piano took a new turning for reasons of external technology, although this cannot be a fully adequate explanation. The demands of composers, above all Beethoven, must have had something to do with it. The Appassionata Sonata is twenty years ahead of the piano at which it was composed. The English piano started to change rapidly just after 1815, the year of Waterloo. As we have seen in our own time, the return to peace brought a surge of new manufacturing techniques which had been forged in war, and these in turn threw up new designs.

From 1815 the piano became heavier with stronger strings and by 1820 harpsichord soundboard barring had given way to modern cross-barring. The internal structure became steadily strengthened; first, two metal bars appeared in the treble, bracing the curved corner to the wrest plank in an endeavour to stop the corner from bending. This was not sufficient and more bars were added, both above and below the soundboard, until in 1827 there arrived Broadwood's new patent full metal frame, virtually modern in technology. At the same time as Broadwoods introduced the full metal frame they dramatically altered the appearance of their pianos: the square cheeks and the inlaid and cross-banded classical look disappeared and was replaced by a plain instrument with a roll front. In the space of almost exactly ten years the instrument developed from being a hammer harpsichord with soft and loud to the modern piano. That may be exaggeration for the sake of effect – there was still a little way to go before the piano was completely modern. Three more changes were still to be introduced: Erard's double escapement, invented in 1821 but not in common use for years; the fully cast-iron frame; and the use of felt to cover the hammer heads instead of leather. The first two of these changes were directly due to heavier stringing: the cast-iron frame to take the strain, while the single escapement had grown too slow, with the heavier hammers, to give a fast repeat. Even if it is wrong to choose the year 1827 as a bench mark in the history of the piano, the changes that occurred close to that year are remarkable. All the grands I have restored that were made before this date were warped, while none afterwards have suffered; so it was close to 1827 that a fundamental problem was overcome. The deaths of Beethoven and of George IV, the Regency king, occurred within a year of each other and, even if Victoria's reign was still ten years away, the Victorian piano had arrived, and the fortepiano passed away.

Parallel with the grand, there developed the smaller domestic instrument, the "square", and then, around 1800, the upright piano was invented. Since modern makers have not considered this instrument suitable to copy, it does not have a place in this discussion. Most of the early pianos now copied are Viennese which has resulted in a regrettable tendency for the use of the term fortepiano to be limited to meaning the early Viennese grand. But possibly the term serves a useful purpose, for the Viennese instrument was quite different from the early English grand. The qualities of the Viennese instrument are especially relevant when we consider that the most important composers for the piano during this period were also central European. The technical differences of the Viennese piano can be described easily. The hammer is attached to the key, on a hinge called the kapsel; the English action keeps the key and hammer quite separate. The hammer is thrown upward when the key is depressed because the tail of the hammer shaft is held in a notch which is part of the key-frame. The action is much lighter than the English, and the strings lighter also. The attachment of the hammer to the key gives a quite different touch; the action seems to be much more part of the player's fingers, so that there is a sense of direct communication with the strings; a halfway instrument, almost, between the clavichord and the early English grand.

Mozart was an admirer of Stein, perhaps the most important maker of his time, and there is a frequently quoted letter he wrote to his father after a visit to Stein's workshop. In this he describes Stein's method of subjecting his soundboards to all weathers, so that if they are going to split and crack they will do so and get it over with, and can be mended before they are glued into the case. Stein, a good businessman, had obviously found a superb advertising gambit with which to impress his customers; but soundboards have in fact very little tendency to split, however they are treated, until they are locked into the rim; before this they can expand and contract freely.

The Viennese fortepiano had qualities which deserve the recognition of being copied. It did not develop other than marginally, and was eventually swept away by the Victorian piano, which in Austria, as in the rest of Europe, grew from the English grand. I would hesitate to call it a superior instrument to its English relation but it was different and that difference was important; both have their several qualities in which we can take delight.

Tuning and Temperaments

Music can be regarded as sound organized in a way that is enjoyable, and tuning and temperaments form the vital framework for it. A digression into this subject is necessary because the playing of early music in early temperaments is becoming a very important part of our musical heritage, and keyboard music will be at the forefront of this new wave. We are now, and will be hearing more harpsichord music played in early temperaments, and at the same time amateur players are finding that these temperaments are easier to tune than modern equal temperament.

The newcomer to the subject is likely to find all its ramifications of daunting complexity, and there is space here for only a simplified outline. In thus compressing an important part of a thousand or more years of musical history a number of corners will have to be cut, for which I hope the expert will forgive me. The history of tuning and temperament is that of a number of changes brought about by men whose intention was either to improve or perfect a system. Not long ago the received opinion would have been that with our modern equal temperament we had arrived at the best possible system. Now, we can see that there is no such thing as the best possible system. Rather, as music developed, the tuning or temperament suited the then contemporary music; to play it now in a different temperament reduces its value. The recognition of this simple fact is prompting the return of early temperaments; the practicality of choosing the right one may be a little more difficult.

It would be a self-obvious statement that music has developed to suit human auditory pleasure, but both music and instrument-tuning have changed and developed within the limits of human hearing. Tuning and how tuning relates to the beauty of keyboard music is a necessary background to the understanding of temperament.

There is a spectrum of sound our ears can hear and the definition of any pure note from that spectrum is given by its frequency, measured in vibrations per second, or Hertz. It is a trait of human hearing that we find pleasurable, and regard as consonant, any two notes played together whose frequencies bear a simple mathematical relationship to each other. Examples are: the octave $(1 : 2)$, the fifth $(2 : 3)$, the fourth $(3 : 4)$ and the major third $(4 : 5)$. If these intervals, as they are called, are sufficiently out of tune, we find their combination to be unpleasant, and we call it dissonant. These are the most important intervals in understanding tuning and it should be noted that the fourth and fifth are intimately related: if we take two notes an octave apart, the fifth up from one is the fourth down from the other, and vice versa. The ratios of the other intervals can be found in the glossary, as can also various detailed definitions which would complicate the easy reading of these pages. The intervals can be most clearly demonstrated in the key of C set out on the treble stave.

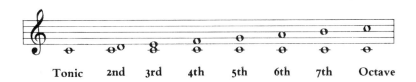

Tonic   2nd   3rd   4th   5th   6th   7th   Octave

The problems in tuning arise when an attempt is made to fit the intervals together and to do so on a keyboard which is restricted to twelve notes to the octave. The most commonly quoted example, and the most important to know, is that no number of fifths added together will ever equal any number of octaves. They come fairly close if twelve fifths are related to seven octaves; the difference is a small one known as the comma of Pythagoras; it is equal to about a quarter of a semitone.

With an instrument of flexible pitch such as a violin, or with the human voice, notes can be altered according to their context, so that it is possible to make the intervals perfect, true or just. These are all synonyms meaning that the interval is exactly in tune. For example, notes of 440 Hertz and 880 Hertz form a perfect octave. The human voice by itself cannot of course sing two notes together, but two notes sung (or played) in succession make an interval just as much as two voices simultaneously singing two different notes. (They are called melodic and harmonic intervals, respectively.) Keyboard instruments are naturally fixed in pitch. If we set out to tune a piano or harpsichord using pure intervals, it would not be long before we found that we had created other intervals which were very impure, or dissonant. Some kind of compromise is necessary, in which various intervals are slightly mis-tuned, so that most of the intervals are accommodated at an acceptable level. These systems of mis-tuning are known as systems of tuning or, more properly, temperaments. To temper is to soften or moderate, and in tuning it means to moderate dissonances by spreading them more equably.

When an interval is gradually mis-tuned, it does not become immediately dissonant. Our ears tolerate a certain amount of tempering and a tiny error is accepted as true. Further mis-tuning is heard as a distinct colour, not necessarily unpleasant, but a point is reached when the tonal quality is positively dissonant. The temperaments that we use, combine different mixtures of pure, off-pure and, sometimes, dissonant intervals, but we can generalize and say that the octave is always tuned pure and that if the fourths and fifths are pure, it is at the expense of the thirds and vice versa.

European music as it is today is based on tonality, the concept of twelve major and minor keys. It grew from Greek music, which was modal, its structure built round a series of scales each of which had a different tone/semitone sequence. The number of modes was extended in the Middle Ages but some were theoretical and in practice only a few modes were used, these becoming fewer until in the end only two were left, which we know now as the major and minor scales. Our keyboard was almost certainly developed for the organ and for accompanying liturgical music which was based on the modes. Tuning in the Middle Ages was Pythagorean, a system which gradually failed in practice when all the accidentals had been added to the keyboard. The simple intervals already listed are harmonic, which is to say that they are harmonious to our hearing. Pythagorean fourths and fifths are the same as the harmonic fourths and fifths, but the thirds have a more complex ratio and are rough; they differ from the harmonic thirds by nearly a quarter of a semitone. I have seen it suggested that the dogmatism of theory dominated the pleasures of consonance. This judgement, however, may be that of a later age which fails to recognize the musical taste of the time. In the context of the music, which is polyphonic, the thirds are not dissonant; they have a harsh, strong quality against which the pure fifths stand out sweetly. It is also possible that we are incorrect in assuming that the thirds were sung to the Pythagorean interval; they could easily have been sung pure in the sense that we use the word, and certainly singers today would find it difficult to sing the interval of the Pythagorean third.

Music developed away from modality when it became secular and when it became harmonic, that is, when it developed a chordal structure. There were a number of parallel developments which reached fruition probably between 1500 and 1600. The organ became a musical instrument in its own right, instead of a simple accompaniment to chant; the harpsichord appeared; the key system of tonality and modulation grew from modality, harmony required acceptance of the simple harmonic intervals, and modulation with harmonic intervals required a suitable system of tuning. Although it was possible to temper Pythagorean tuning, the first modern temperament for the keyboard was meantone.

There are a number of meantone temperaments but the "classical" one, and the most important, is usually regarded as that of Pietro Aron, the $\frac{1}{4}$ comma meantone, which was published in 1523. The Aron meantone gives eight perfect or very good major thirds and four unusable ones, while the fourths and fifths tend to be rough. It solved the problem of how to modulate from key to key while keeping the intervals as consonant as possible by pushing dissonances into remote keys. These dissonances were known as "wolf intervals" from their painful howling quality but, provided composers avoided them, meantone modulation had a smooth and even quality. Within the limitations which it imposes on the composer, meantone has intervals which are closer to just than later temperaments. Composers soon felt the need to extend these limits and one way it was found possible was by making instruments with extra keys, so as to provide both sharps and flats; the chromatic keyboard, of course, does not distinguish between sharps and flats. There was some variation in method but the most common, to judge by surviving instruments, was to split the E♭ to give also a D♯ and the G♯ to give also an A♭. This was not done throughout the compass but, usually, in the middle two octaves. The sharp was cut in half, the back section raised slightly and, out of sight, these two halves became two key levers with their own jacks and strings.

It is difficult to decide how long meantone lasted; there was certainly a great deal of overlap between temperaments, and change was slow. Organ tuning is an expensive process, so organ music was the last to resist change. One should also question how meantone was defined in the past. Every textbook refers to organs still being tuned to meantone after 1850, but textbooks copy each other and possibly "meantone", to the Victorians, had become an embracing term for "old" temperaments, including unequal, unrestricted temperaments. Certainly, harpsichords ceased to have divided accidentals before 1700, and the fact that by this time modulation through all the keys was possible, suggests a change away from meantone at this earlier date. A number of new temperaments were evolved from around 1650, by mathematicians and theorists such as Mersenne and Werkmeister, composers such as Rameau and, probably, J. S. Bach — although he left no system written down — and, in the piano era, men like Kirnberger, Bach's pupil. These temperaments were built with the new intention of designing unrestricted temperaments (that is, temperaments in which it is possible to modulate through all the twenty-four keys), while also providing changes of key colour. As great a consonance as possible was provided in the keys close to C, while the intervals were allowed to grow a little rough in the more remote keys. The changes of colour which occur with modulation require perception and acceptance but, once the ear has come to recognize key difference, the contrasts stand out with a shaft of illumination. These temperaments are likely to be an acquired taste for the present generation because keyboards so tempered are not part of our normal background.

Bach defined his "48" as being for the well-tempered clavier. We do not at the moment have a definitive term for these temperaments. "Good" temperaments and "Well-tempered" tunings have been suggested; we will have to wait and see what common usage takes to itself.

From around 1800 equal temperament, our common modern temperament, came into use. Until recently many standard works speak of equal temperament as the ideal, obvious solution to the temperament problem and towards which earlier generations had been groping. This is not so; equal temperament was known, in fact was used for fretted instruments, it being the most practical way to place the frets. Equal temperament was rejected because it contained no key-change quality and also because the thirds are rough, a characteristic especially noticeable in brilliant instruments such as the harpsichord. Equal temperament came into use when times were right for it, which was when the smoother voiced Victorian piano had arrived.

In equal temperament, all the intervals except the octave, which is perfect, have a slight error and the error of each interval is the same in every key, which is why there is no key colour change. All the semitones are equally spaced and, as there are twelve semitones to the octave, the equal tempered semitone is defined as having that proportional increase of frequency which, re-duplicated twelve times over, will effect a doubling. This factor is the twelfth root of two, or, to say it another way, if we multiply the frequency of any note by the twelfth root of two (worked out to an adequate degree of accuracy this is 1·059), we obtain the frequency of the next note up and we can do this repeatedly until we obtain the frequency of every semitone.

A substantial number of historical temperaments have come down to us, some of which have been in common use while others were academic exercises. The problem is that composers of the past took their temperaments for granted and did not record which they were using. The date of a composition and its harmonic construction will sometimes give an immediate indication while, in other cases, extensive scholarship will be required to unravel a composer's intention. An example of what is being done in research can be found in the article "Bach's keyboard temperament" by John Barnes[1] in which he explores the internal evidence to be found in the distribution of the intervals in the "48", and on the basis of this makes suggestions as to the temperament Bach might have used.

Both for the listener and the player this is a new area. For the listener there is today the pleasure of hearing some of our most distinguished harpsichordists playing in unequal temperament, although regrettably usually failing to indicate in the programme notes which one. The amateur harpsichordist who can tune, can easily explore this fascinating area for himself. There are now several books giving practical tuning instructions, and many of the old temperaments are easier to tune than equal temperament. For an amateur who tunes with an electronic tuner designed for equal temperament, a number of unequal temperaments can be tuned by setting in the necessary cent deviations, tables for which are given in the book by Murray Barbour.[2] The electronic tuner is a tool of great value for the beginner, and should not be despised.

Amateurs who are new to the harpsichord should not be afraid of learning to tune. Harpsichords do not stay in tune very long so it is a useful accomplishment. A small instrument such as a virginal can be tuned in perhaps twenty minutes, less with experience, and this is not much time to find every few weeks.

Harpsichords go out of tune because of changes in atmospheric humidity, to which they are sensitive. They are best kept away from fires, radiators or windows and, ideally, should not be kept in a south facing room where variable sunshine will cause rapid changes of temperature and humidity.

Modern British Makers and the Historical Tradition

In modern times Erard and Pleyel, working in Paris, were the first to make harpsichords, but in this country Arnold Dolmetsch was the motive force and was so important that I have asked Dr Carl Dolmetsch to write about his father in the next chapter. In those years

[1] John Barnes: "Bach's Keyboard Temperament". In *Early Music*, vol. 7, no. 2 (April 1979).
[2] Murray Barbour: *Tuning and Temperaments*.

Henry Tull was in the piano business and also made a small number of early keyboard instruments on the side as a personal interest. The revival did not really get on its way until just before and just after the Second World War and the makers who were active in this period were Robert Goble (still working and, in his seventies, the doyen of modern makers), Hugh Gough (moved to the USA), Alec Hodsdon (now retired) and Thomas Goff (now dead).

Thomas Goff was not a maker in business; he was a wealthy and dedicated amateur in the old sense of the word, a lover of his art. He was an inspirer of anecdotes, aristocratic in many ways, a private man whom I never met and of whom I cannot now form a true image. He trained as a barrister, although he may have practised little. It is said that he heard Violet Gordon-Woodhouse play the harpsichord one evening and never went back to his chambers, but started his new career of harpsichord making, which dominated the rest of his life. He employed a cabinet maker, J. C. Cobby, and set about making large two-manual concert harpsichords. These instruments can be described as Pleyel-derived, in Kirckman cases, beautifully veneered and cross banded – no doubt the work of Cobby. They had an aluminium frame, pedal operated stops and a $16 + 8 + 8 + 4$ specification. The tone was not very powerful but rich and lovely and much admired. As a young maker I tried to emulate it, and in fact the work of Tom Goff had a considerable influence on the post-war English harpsichord scene. This was due both to the excellence of the instruments and to the fact that the demand for them exceeded supply. He made less than twenty harpsichords and parted with about half of them, although he did make and sell more clavichords, probably about fifty.

Thomas Goff died a disappointed man. He had set out to design the perfect harpsichord, an impractical task comparable to trying to paint the perfect picture. He succeeded in producing the finest work in his generation, but by the end of his life the fashion in harpsichords had changed and there was a new establishment which derided his work.

The interesting thing about the first sixty or seventy years of twentieth-century harpsichord making is the way it departed from historical origins and has been dragged back, during the past ten or fifteen years, into a mould of authenticity, a pendulum swing both strong and sudden. This swing has been ascribed to the influence of Frank Hubbard's *Three Centuries of Harpsichord Making* which was published in 1965. But it was in the air before then, probably due to the influence of Hubbard, and also to that of his partner, William Dowd. However, the influence of individual men on wider affairs is often only that of catalyst and I prefer to stand back and try to observe history in perspective and to recognize the way opinions will swing through society or whole sections of it. The reasons behind these trends can often be simply and logically explained; the reasons why large numbers of people suddenly accept that logic, and act on it almost in unison, are more mysterious and outside my province.

The first twentieth-century harpsichord to be made in England was Arnold Dolmetsch's "Green" harpsichord, known thus because it is painted in that colour on the outside. It was actually made in 1896 but we can stretch those few years without too great a lack of precision. The firm of Pleyel was already making harpsichords in Paris and these were known and heard in England.

Arnold Dolmetsch was struggling, against immense odds, against a largely indifferent public and against a hostile musical establishment, to establish the principle that early music should be played in the way the composer knew, on the instruments the composer knew. Yet his very first harpsichord contained two innovations which, although they had been known before, had not been fully realized and made to work properly. These were half hooking and pedal operation of the stops. Pascal Taskin had invented a form of half hooking, and also knee levers as an improvement on hand operated stops. Arnold Dolmetsch owned a harpsichord rebuilt by Taskin and he had found Taskin's knee levers highly impractical. (This instrument is now in the Russell Collection; Dolmetsch believed it to be a Couchet but it has now been identified as a Goermans.) In fact, he rebuilt this instrument with pedals, after making the "Green" harpsichord. He ingeniously fitted the "Green" harpsichord with piano-type pedals and made these to half-hook. Was he the purist that we think or not? We learn from his biographer (Margaret Campbell) that one critic at least had already compared Pleyel's piano-derived harpsichord unfavourably with Dolmetsch's own restored Kirckman, and here he was starting out on a similar path to Pleyel.

The explanation is, I think, that Dolmetsch was a child of his time, thrusting and inventive. He was a superb craftsman and a perfectionist, who was committed to proving to the opposition that he was right. The attitude of the musical establishment was that the harpsichord was all very well in its place, which was the museum, while the piano had superseded it because it was demonstrably better. Dolmetsch was a practical musician who found that pedals and half hooking suited him, a choice we should respect, but he also felt it necessary to improve the harpsichord in order to get it accepted at all. In fact, what was wrong with the harpsichord was not so much that it needed improving, but that the twentieth century could not accept it as it was.

The view, and one that seemed perfectly true until a few years ago, was that the harpsichord had steadily developed and improved throughout its history only to be cut short by the piano. When it was re-introduced it would carry on where it left off, again steadily developing. Thus Dolmetsch developed the harpsichord quite naturally and without recognizing the inconsistency of what he was doing.

The harpsichord was developed by all who touched it. We all did it. In the 1950s I was inventing forms of structure that I later found to have been invented by Arnold Dolmetsch twenty years before, when he was seventy.

The rise and fall of the 16ft register is a piece of harpsichord history that almost deserves a chapter to itself. A few harpsichords with 16ft have come down to us from the eighteenth century, notably those by Hass, but they were patently an exception to the general tradition of the whole of the early period of making. The revival of the instrument in the twentieth century accelerated in a period of heady expansion which had its roots in Victorian self-confidence, a time when anything bigger and more complex was better. It was an era that spanned the giant liner, the skyscraper, Megalopolis as an ideal city, and is perhaps now ending as we wonder about Concorde. The harpsichord with 16ft and a row of seven or eight pedals had the absurd appeal of a motor car with power steering and little buttons to raise and lower the windows. It was wrong for the very simple reason that the essence of the harpsichord is clarity, and the 16ft smoothed it all over with a sort of muddy diapason. The designation of some of these instruments as "Bach models" by modern German makers was made on inadequate evidence and it is unfortunate that the prestige of some of the makers was a contributory factor in the widespread adoption of the instrument as a type. The realization, from the sixties onward that the old harpsichords stored in museums and silent for so long, sounded *better* than these modern "Bach models", marked a new phase in harpsichord construction and the end of the 16ft era.

The early history of the harpsichord can now be seen in proper perspective. It did develop, and early makers were inventive and constructive and seldom content to make instruments all their lives in the way that they had been taught as apprentices. The history of other musical instruments shows a period of invention and change until a plateau level is reached, after which design is stabilized, only very small modifications being introduced from then on. Changes which go too far result in a new instrument, the spiral of change that resulted in the pianoforte.

The harpsichord reached this stage of plateau development in the hundred years between 1650 and 1750. The flurry of inventive activity which came after that was not normal development but the frenzied activity of a threatened industry that was fighting for its life against the piano. This must have been recognized if only subconsciously by modern makers because the Venetian swell and the machine stop did not come into use again. I think it would be true to say that the majority of modern harpsichord making, after a confused period of thrashing about looking for a modern identity, is back at the plateau level. The excesses of some modern inventions have been recognized as unnecessary, and those makers who are now producing "modern" instruments are for the most part working close to classical designs with only minor experimental changes which may or may not prove to be advantageous.

History has a way of marching along and leaving side alleys which go nowhere. We will find in due course which of the modern innovations are worth keeping and which will be discarded. My own feeling is that most will go, but I have a strong regard for the adjusting screw on the jack, which I find too useful to do without. I also regard the body structure as needing careful thought before it is copied. Too many harpsichords of the past have bent and too many of the present will bend for lack of proper knowledge of structure strength.

Apart from the makers of "modern" instruments, there are those who are making harpsichords in the way that went on in the past but putting their own idiosyncratic stamp on them – derived instruments. Others again are copyists, taking a masterpiece that appeals to them and copying it as exactly and carefully as they are capable. Some makers have chosen the path that suits them and stuck to it, others make instruments in more than one group. No doubt posterity will decide that it likes some of our instruments better than others and direct some to museums, some to bonfires and some to continued use.

There is no practical sense in my trying to guess that future. I would prefer to put the present into a clearer perspective. There is at the moment a cult in early music, complete with high priests and acolytes who regard harpsichord making and makers of the first half of the century rather as sheep that went astray. I see us all (common humanity that is, not makers in particular) as sheep who flock in random directions all the time. Just now we live in a confused and unstable culture with no sense of direction at all, and this has a great deal to do with the harpsichord revival. We are harking back with nostalgia to the cultures of the past.

What is certain is that all life is change and that harpsichords will change. The harpsichord literature sets very small limits on that change, but it is apparent that the best makers of today are making small changes. It would be surprising if it were otherwise. There is here a body of very competent men, the nature of whose work requires ego, drive and creativity. It is impossible to imagine that they could submerge their personalities for all their working lives in a humble posture before the master craftsmen of the past.

This moment, then, when change is slight, a pause for breath, is an excellent one in which to capture something of the lives of a few of the men who are making harpsichords today. They have in common only that they make harpsichords, although the majority share also a surprising factor: they were educated in another discipline and came to making by chance. There are those who are motivated by a driving creativity; others are dominated by a vision that they can make the perfect instrument. Others again are entrepreneurs seeking profit, but whether this looms large or small it is an aspect none dare ignore entirely or bankruptcy will loom. Each will have something to say about why he makes his instruments the way he does and why he thinks his way is best. I use "he" and "his" provisionally because this is one of the male dominated strongholds which is only just beginning to fall to women.

I also hope that I am writing for the future, that when we are all gone and our instruments remain, some future reader will gain from a backward glance at us. How welcome it would be to have a little self-analysis from some of the old makers we now regard as important; how unwelcome perhaps if we knew which of us is going to be esteemed in the future.

Cast metal rose with painted surround from an
instrument by the author.

CHAPTER 2

Dr Carl Dolmetsch, CBE

ARNOLD DOLMETSCH AND THE HARPSICHORD REVIVAL

Jesses, the house in Haslemere which Arnold Dolmetsch bought in 1917, is still the family home. It is large, Victorian, beautifully kept, filled with instruments, the walls covered with paintings and photographs of the past. It is not, however, a segment of times gone by, for the Dolmetsches have been occupied with music for generations and they still are; the house is as alive as ever with musical activity. Adjacent is the building which was once the workshop and is now a miniature museum, filled both with precious old instruments and with examples of the work of Arnold Dolmetsch. The present workshop is in another part of Haslemere.

If one visits Jesses, as I did, at the same time as reading the recent biography of Arnold by Margaret Campbell, and re-reading the earlier *Recollections* by Mabel Dolmetsch, the effect of both seeing his work and knowing the difficulties under which it was produced is overwhelming. There is the feeling that early pioneer work will be crude, feeling its way. It is not, design and craftsmanship are superb.

It is probably still too early to define fully the influence of this remarkable man. One is baulked by the sheer range of abilities; I can recognize the technical competence, the inventive ability, the craftsmanship; but that he was also an exceptional musician and musicologist puts him in a class apart. His influence on modern harpsichord making has been most direct through the number of pupils who have studied at Haslemere and carried his standards all over the world. The many inventive improvements to the harpsichord may or may not have a lasting impact — at the moment the tide of opinion is against them and they will need to be viewed in the greater perspective of a future time. The dominant influence of Arnold Dolmetsch will, I think, ultimately be regarded as the way he altered our musical life by restoring to it the wide range of early music. He was the man who did the real work, without the reward, and most probably it was a rôle he would have preferred to being a second-generation establishment figure. The gravestone epitaph of Violet Gordon-Woodhouse (who was his devoted pupil for many years), that her genius brought the dead music of the past to life, should really have been his.

The failure which comes to the pioneer can be seen in Arnold Dolmetsch's pianos, of which he made several, starting around 1900. He hated the large concert grand and decided to build fortepianos as an alternative. These were not the early Viennese instruments which we tend now to define as fortepianos, but were based on the English grand of *c.* 1820, and can be described as his idealization of a late Beethoven instrument. They did not find a market, for the simple reason that they were seventy years ahead of the demand for fortepianos. Yet that eventual demand stemmed more from the work of Dolmetsch himself than from any other single person. Being before one's time and yet creating that time, is both the tragedy and the triumph of the pioneer — and this is the epitome of Arnold Dolmetsch's life.

DR CARL DOLMETSCH:

The harpsichord is so firmly re-established as an indispensable part of today's musical scene that only the older generations among us can recall a time when it was regarded as a curiosity, whether loved, hated or greeted with indifference. During my childhood and the years up to the Second World War, it was still necessary to campaign for the harpsichord to be used in performances of music written for it, solo and continuo, in place of the piano, which then seemed impossible to dislodge from its usurping position.

The genius and pioneering fervour of Arnold Dolmetsch in so many realms of instrument making, combined with the authentic performance of a wide spectrum of early music, is too well known to need re-emphasis here. None the less, since it was my privilege to live with him, to learn from him and to be closely involved in many aspects of his work, I claim a special qualification to record for posterity the unique and vital rôle he played in the renaissance of the harpsichord. Anyone wishing to study in greater detail Dolmetsch's many-faceted contribution to the world of music is recommended to read Margaret Campbell's biography, *Dolmetsch: The Man and His Work* (Hamish Hamilton, 1975).

Arnold Dolmetsch tuning an octavina in the music room at Jesses,
c. 1938.

My own participation was by no means confined solely to the research, production and playing of the recorder, with which instrument I have for so long been closely identified. My involvement with my father's harpsichord-building activities began when I spent much of my time in the workshops as a child. Like my elder brother and sisters before me, I was initially entrusted with simple tasks, like the bushing, rounding and weighting of keys, stamping out felt washers, etc. In due course, we were all promoted to more delicate work on harpsichord actions, such as fitting tongues within jacks and jacks into their slots; and finally came the skilled cutting of leather and quill plectra.

During my late teens, I served an apprenticeship on the construction side at my father's direction, under the mature craftsmen who then headed his harpsichord department, just as he had done when a boy in his father's and grandfather's piano and organ-building workshops. It was mainly from Bernard Unwin and Reginald Brown (an uncle of Andrew Douglas) that I acquired the use of tools the hard way, with plane, hand-saw and chisel, before I was allowed access to any of the machines.

Although Arnold Dolmetsch was passionately devoted to the use of hand tools to express his artistic skill, he was none the less a realist who scorned futile expenditure of time and energy working with hand tools on operations which could be performed with more accuracy and speed by machines. When it was either impossible or too costly to purchase the exact type of equipment needed for his specialized purposes, he would himself design and build not only the machines, but also the jigs required in conjunction with them. Among many such was a very adaptable machine for covering strings to any required length; the cores of gut, silk, steel or brass were wound with copper, brass, silver and even gold wire. This was among the many machines I learnt to operate and I remember to this day the concentration and dexterity needed to handle the finer gauges of copper wire, often running two strands side-by-side. All too frequently, one of them would break, or lumps would form if the guiding stick momentarily failed to move at the exact speed required to follow the fine spiral created by the two fragile wires as they gradually covered the string length.

Arnold Dolmetsch's devotion to authenticity was neither blind nor pedantic and he saw no merit in the perpetuation of faults or limitations in many of the early instruments from which he learnt his craft, much as he admired their undoubted good qualities. By nature a creative artist as opposed to an imitator, Dolmetsch began by restoring and studying fine instruments by early makers. Then, in the same spirit as a Stradivarius learning from an Amati, he designed and built his own models, their tone and reliability often surpassing those which had served as his inspiration.

Over the years, since his death in 1940, I have pursued this same policy, believing as he did that there is little merit in the sterile imitation so much in vogue today. To stifle some creative contribution, skill or modern resource, which could bring about an improvement in resonance, purity of sound or increased mechanical efficiency, would be to me a complete negation of the rightful evolution of any instrument. The whole history of the harpsichord, from its psaltery beginnings to the elaborate instruments of Kirckman, Broadwood and Hass, is built on a series of innovations all along the line. Why should this natural process be arrested in the twentieth century? Is not such a policy bound to achieve the same fatal results as before, and for exactly the same reasons? Arnold Dolmetsch always claimed that he was merely continuing the process of evolution from the point where it had been left by earlier makers. Had they succeeded in overcoming the main limitations of their day, the harpsichord would probably never have become extinct. The opportunity of solving these problems while remaining true to the essential character of the instrument is once more open to us and, indeed, a new approach is obligatory if the harpsichord is to enjoy more than a limited revival or to be a mere historical exercise.

The reason for the rapid progress and acceptance of the piano in the eighteenth and nineteenth centuries was that it provided very seductively some of the more robust qualities which keyboard players had for so long sought in vain from the harpsichord, even though the piano obviously lacked the harpsichord's clear, incisive sound, wide spectrum of tone-colour and the ability to blend unobtrusively with other instruments. A survey of the short-comings which eighteenth-century makers were striving to overcome will help to explain the policies which guided Arnold Dolmetsch's work in his later years. It will become clear that he did, in fact, solve many of the problems, though the significance of his vital contribution to the present-day renaissance is yet to receive the widespread recognition it deserves. One of the main obstacles to the harpsichord's reinstatement at a time when the public's appetite for massive sound was at its peak, was the fact that the harpsichord was less powerful than the piano; it was therefore too readily assumed that the harpsichord's volume of tone was inadequate to fill large concert halls, or to hold its own against "louder" instruments. This judgement was perpetuated mostly by people unaware of the true potential of a fine harpsichord, and was often the result of unhappy experiences with ill-restored or badly regulated instruments in an age when there were very few craftsmen with the knowledge and skill to restore old harpsichords to proper playing order.

The First New Harpsichords

It was in this setting that makers like Pleyel and Erard produced their first harpsichords, their principal aims being to increase volume of tone, to conquer public prejudice and to meet the needs of players like Landowska and her following for the performance of concertos with orchestra by Bach and Haydn, for instance. Unfortunately, all these first modern makers, French and German alike, were primarily piano builders, with the result that while their craftsmanship was above reproach, the frames and cases of their harpsichords were thick, heavy and lacking in the natural resonance required for plucked instruments. Their immediate remedy for this deficiency was to increase the strength of the plucking agent, which only resulted in a louder, more explosive sound of short duration, combined with a very heavy touch. Other piano characteristics were excessively thick soundboards and thick strings at great tension – admirable features for a percussive instrument, but death to a plucking harpsichord.

Running parallel to, but in complete contrast with, these earnest but ponderous endeavours, Arnold Dolmetsch was acquiring his knowledge of harpsichord building and technology by restoring fine examples of harpsichords, virginals, spinets and clavichords by English, French, German, Italian and Flemish makers of the sixteenth to eighteenth centuries. His first object always was to restore a mute or maimed instrument to its original playing order for use in his own concerts. As the restoration progressed, his affection for an instrument would grow and he would tend to hold on to a newly-restored gem for as long as his precarious financial position permitted, in order that its beauty of sound could be shared with his loyal audiences. Whenever possible, such vital features as original soundboards were preserved, though when ravages of time, climate and woodworm necessitated replacement, he would always adhere scrupulously to the measurements of the prototype. He took particular note of their thinness, average one-tenth of an inch as against the quarter of an inch in the piano soundboards with which he was familiar in his youth. Dolmetsch was amazed at the relative "feather" lightness of the frames and casework in early harpsichords, especially Flemish and Italian examples, the latter in particular relying on an outer case for protection. He soon found that the timbre and overall resonance of a harpsichord depend on more than the strings and soundboard alone; he discovered that the entire instrument must vibrate freely. He also learnt that there is far greater strength in flexibility than in rigidity. Possessed of this knowledge, coupled with his genius for design and a standard of professional craftsmanship second to none, Dolmetsch was able to produce harpsichords which combined lightness of touch with considerable volume and length of resonance.

Dolmetsch achieved sophisticated mechanical efficiency and remarkably silent working of all moving parts. To this end, jacks had always to fit perfectly in their slots; points of contact, with the key at one end and the jack rail at the other, were lined with felt; even the slots within the jacks were padded with leather to prevent the tongues clicking on their return from plucking the strings. Just as thoroughly, every point of contact where keys or coupler might have produced an extraneous noise was meticulously lined or bushed with felt. Some mechanical noises may indeed be historically authentic, but they possess neither musical value nor charm and can but retard the acceptance of early keyboard instruments by the discerning professional musician of today.

Susceptibility to atmospheric changes and the consequent inability of many early harp-sichords to hold in tune, even for the duration of a single concert, posed a problem which Dolmetsch was determined to overcome. Accounts exist of eighteenth-century concerts where a second harpsichord was kept back-stage to replace the one in use when it had gone out of tune in the heat of the auditorium.

When planning the construction of his harpsichord frames, Dolmetsch took careful note of the stress points in order to counter them with strong, flexible, yet light struts of resonant wood. Thus, with frames built entirely of wood, he produced a whole range of keyboard instruments, including clavichords, with the finest record in history for remaining in tune. The large concert harpsichords designed during his association with

Chickerings of Boston (1905–1911), Gaveau of Paris (1911–1914) and subsequently in Haslemere (1917 onwards) stand to this day as examples of his genius, having remained in fine structural and playing order with no more than the lightest maintenance. In the course of concert-touring on both sides of the Atlantic, in Australia and New Zealand, it has been my pleasure on innumerable occasions to use these greatly cherished instruments, proudly loaned by their owners.

My father also designed models of various shapes and sizes between the double-manual harpsichord and the tiny octavina spinet. They were all devised to meet some everyday practical need such as space or portability. One of the most successful – which remains in the front rank of popularity to this day – was a triangular instrument with a 5-octave compass and, initially, two pedals controlling a harp stop and crescendo achieved by moving slides. It is of 8ft register and has a clear tone of sufficient volume to fill any recital hall. This model was designed in 1915, when we were living in Hampstead and needed to travel in the box-like taxis of the day. One such instrument has been invaluable to me in the giving of literally thousands of concerts over many years. The procedure is to tune the harpsichord the day before leaving for a tour, loading it into my car for an early departure the next day. From this point on, it spends every night in the car, come rain, frost or snow. It is unloaded and reloaded twice or three times a day for school concerts and again in the evening for a public recital. The initial tuning usually lasts for a tour of ten to fifteen days; the all-time record was a tour of twenty-four concerts – Yorkshire, Cheshire and Lancashire on one tuning! However, even this good-tempered harpsichord would rebel if left in a parked car in full sunshine.

For overseas touring, where travelling is mostly by air, I have evolved a tuning strategy adapted to arctic conditions in Alaska, desert heat in Southern California, humidity in Florida and Colombia and, hottest of all, 115°F in Melbourne. On these tours we use a very small model, a spinet-shaped harpsichord built in 1953 to my specification by my brother-in-law, Leslie Ward.

After my preliminary experiments with stringing on an octavina-spinet, this slightly larger innovation proved that it is possible to have an instrument weighing no more than 41 lbs, comprising a compass of $4\frac{1}{2}$ octaves at 8ft register (commencing at cello C), producing a volume of tone sufficient to fill any hall suited to chamber music. It is fitted with a hand-operated harp stop. This model has been reproduced in hundreds, but I own the prototype which has flown thousands of miles and is, I claim, the most travelled keyboard instrument in the world. I have learned to overcome extremes of humid heat by tuning the harpsichord a calculated amount above pitch to enable me to play the recorder comfortably at the same pitch as my accompanying instrument.

Although my father disliked the heavy rigid cast-metal frames of pianos and some

The "Green" harpsichord, Arnold Dolmetsch's first harpsichord, made in 1896. Soundboard and lid painting by Helen Coombe (later Mrs Roger Fry), lettering by Herbert Horne, nameboard and inside rim painting by Selwyn Image.

modern harpsichords, he was not entirely averse to the use of metal as a means of achieving greater tuning stability, provided this could be combined with lightness, flexibility and resonance. In 1929 he began to explore the possibilities then available. Aluminium could not at that time be welded; duralumin could be welded but this too proved impracticable at the time; he finally decided to use light steel struts, bent to shape and welded together in a beautiful "web", much lighter than any cast-iron frame. On this strong, resilient structure could be built a correspondingly light, freely vibrating case, no different in outer appearance from an all-wood harpsichord. Several large double-keyboard instruments incorporating this type of frame were built between 1930 and 1939, including the first BBC harpsichord in 1931. All the steel frames were produced in the Dolmetsch workshops at Beechside, Haslemere; there is an example in my music-room today, as sound structurally as when it was completed in 1933.

Stringing and Scaling

Given a basis of structural resilience and stability, the type of strings and scaling still play an important rôle in the capacity of a harpsichord to remain in tune. This involves the subtle relationship between length, weight and tension of the strings required to give the desired pitch of each note. The material of which the strings are made is also a critical factor; both iron and brass were used in the past, but both have their disadvantages. My father established – and I have since proved unequivocally under the practical conditions of my concert giving – that modern high-grade steel strings hold their pitch incomparably better than brass; they also last much longer because crystallization develops in brass in a relatively short time. One capacity in which brass strings have continued to be used in Dolmetsch harpsichords is in the upper range of the 16ft stop; here, at low tension, they give a beautiful clarinet timbre. Nevertheless, the first stop to go out of tune is invariably the 16ft.

When steel is used for an 8ft stop and the lower octaves are reached, the strings are foreshortened and it would be tempting to change over to brass, which readily supplies at this point a fuller, more substantial sound than could be obtained by merely increasing the gauge of steel wire. Unfortunately, these brass strings are the very ones which do not hold in tune under concert conditions. Dolmetsch solved the problem by using a steel core, covered with copper wire. During my long experience of tuning, I have invariably found that from the point where the copper-covered steel strings begin and the plain steel ceases there is the greatest pitch stability of all. I merely report this as a fact, without attempting to supply the scientific explanation which undoubtedly exists.

Standardized Jacks

An examination of the jacks in many early harpsichords – and some modern replicas – reveals considerable lack of uniformity in standards of workmanship and mechanical efficiency. In earlier years the fact that some notes repeated reliably while others became mute or misfired tended to give the harpsichord an undeservedly bad name and encouraged pianists to prefer playing harpsichord music on their more "dependable" pianos. Very early in his career, Arnold Dolmetsch revolutionized a somewhat haphazard situation by standardizing the traditional jack. One of the first essentials to absolute uniformity was the judicious use of machines and jigs in operations where they clearly surpassed the hand-tool. Equally essential was his skill in cutting leathers and quills with a razor-sharp knife to the exact shape and thickness required to obtain quality and tone, plus ensuring that notes would repeat reliably almost indefinitely. For the plectra, he used only the finest grade leather combining the right degree of hardness, pliability and durability; a set of well-cut leathers should last for at least twenty years and for the playing of millions of notes. For his quill plectra, quality had also to be of the highest order and, during the 1880s, he made friends with keepers at London Zoo in order to obtain ravens' quills at moulting time. He conformed to tradition in using pearwood for jacks and holly for the tongues within the jacks; lime for the keys; beech for the bridges and wrest plank; spruce for the soundboard, etc. Equally traditional was his careful selection of hogs' bristles of just the required strength to act as springs holding and returning the tongues to their forward plucking position. Whereas strings are relatively short-lived Dolmetsch declared that hogs' bristles would "last for ever".

During the late 1940s, Leslie Ward originated a Diokon plastic jack to the traditional pattern, but incorporating a screw mechanism to control the volume. In combination with metal slides, this has overcome the old problem of jacks sticking in their slots when damp, or working too freely and noisily in dry conditions. Wooden tongues are equally susceptible to atmospheric change and this hazard too was disposed of by using plastic material. Since they are not in direct contact with strings, plastic jacks have no effect on quality of tone; the type of material used for the plectra, however, does have a tremendous effect on the tone. Good leather has no equal, but natural quill has been very effectively replaced by Delrin, which is more durable and less brittle than natural quill.

During the early years of the modern harpsichord movement, the trend was all in favour of pedals and, in general, European and American makers were in agreement. However, in recent years, heated controversy has developed over pedals versus hand stops. An exaggerated adherence to less important aspects of authenticity has been accompanied by a masochistic return to unnecessary limitations; this is analogous to limiting the motorist to veteran cars, which certainly have their charms on the London–Brighton annual run, but are hardly practical in terms of trouble-free motoring on modern roads.

In its simplest form, the harpsichord has neither hand stops nor pedals to effect changes of tone colour or volume, though, quite apart from registration, much more can be achieved on a single stop by a sensitive touch and musicianly phrasing than is usually conceded even today: how often are we treated to the purely mechanical style of playing which I call the "treadle-machine".

As the developing harpsichord acquired additional sets of strings and variety of tone colour, mechanical means had to be devised to bring these into play. First among them were hand stops and knee levers. Unfortunately, the same hands had to operate the stops as were playing the keys; this proved distracting to the player and severely restricting to his resources in registration. Not surprisingly, eighteenth-century makers realized that idle feet could be made to relieve the hands of extraneous duties. Although makers began to provide their harpsichords with pedals, and invented ingenious mechanisms for their functioning, they had not achieved complete liberation from hand stops before the harpsichord became extinct.

During his time with Chickerings, Arnold Dolmetsch took over and completed the old makers' task where they had been forced to abandon it. In Boston, he produced the first all-pedal double keyboard harpsichords and established a basic pattern of registration which he continued to produce with evolutionary modifications when he was working with Gaveau in Paris and, later, in Haslemere. These models had four sets of strings and seven (later eight) pedals, with a specification on the lower keyboard of 16 + 8 + 4 with buff stops on the 16ft and 8ft; on the upper keyboard a lute register and a normal 8ft, both plucking the same set of strings, with a buff stop as well. Both manuals could be coupled. Each action was brought into play by a slide moving the jacks closer to the strings and it was possible therefore to obtain individual gradation of sound, from zero to maximum, on any set of strings. There were also half stops to the four principal pedals and by employing the many constituents in a variety of combinations, it was possible to obtain over ninety permutations of sound.

Sixteen Foot, Past and Present

Although 16ft stops had existed in a number of eighteenth-century harpsichords, including one owned by J. S. Bach, it was Arnold Dolmetsch who established that, by the judicious scaling and weighting of the lower strings with copper covering, it was possible to have the 16ft and 8ft strings at the same lengths and to accommodate them on the same bridges, without the necessity for a separate soundboard and auxiliary bridges.

Another refinement introduced from 1926 on, but (sadly) discontinued after my father's death, was a means of producing vibrato on the upper keyboard in a manner resembling *Bebung* on the clavichord. The principle consists of a leather-capped dowel impinging on the string at a point between the hitch pin and the tuning pin. At its lower end, the dowel rests on the key, reaching the string through a hole in the wrest plank. After the note has sounded, the finger can pulsate the key at the player's discretion producing an individual vibrato, as on the clavichord. The effect can be very expressive, especially when a solo line – as in the slow movement of Bach's Italian Concerto – is played with vibrato on the upper keyboard, while accompanied by the muted sound of a harp stop on the lower. There is a harpsichord incorporating this device in my music room in Haslemere. All these resources are there for the player to use or ignore at will. As Arnold

[67]

Dolmetsch remarked to a dissenting Viennese harpsichordist: "You don't like it? Don't put your foot on it!"

Many of the harpsichord's most faithful devotees are, none the less, not entirely happy with the basic plucking principle of the traditional jack which, even at its best, is not wholly scientific. For example, there is no organized escapement. When the plectrum has engaged and is lifting the string, a form of haphazard escapement occurs, due in part to the tongue and its spring giving way and also to the string itself rolling off the bending plectrum. An additional problem is that the plectrum, on its return from plucking, collides briefly with the still vibrating string, resulting in a short buzz which mars the purity of tone. These problems had baffled harpsichord makers for centuries and engaged Dolmetsch's serious attention since 1908. One effect of this second touching of the string was that it prevented the harpsichord having a damper-raising pedal, so integral a part of the piano's resources; such a resource would have been a great asset in providing added resonance in the playing of arpeggios, also in music calling for the crossing of hands or sustaining in the bass. In 1924 Arnold Dolmetsch devised an ingenious type of jack where the plectrum did not touch the string a second time; but this first effort proved too complex to put into production.

Invention of a New Action

In March 1925, a "flash of inspiration" (to quote his own words) revealed to him an entirely new plucking principle. An experimental model worked to perfection and an entire action was fitted to a virginals; in 1928, a large concert harpsichord was equipped with the new action. The principle is one of indirect plucking and it incorporates a controlled escapement. Put another way – the plectrum itself is plucked by the jack and released while the string is resting on it; when the jack escapes, both the plectrum and the string return simultaneously to their original positions, leaving the string to vibrate freely. Fundamentally, a string is plucked by being pulled out of its course and allowed to spring back. The plucking agent (finger or plectrum) normally crosses to the other side of the string; with Dolmetsch's new action, this principle remains the same but the plectrum returns whence it came without crossing or touching the string again. The resulting pluck feels exactly the same to the player's finger and sounds exactly the same to the listener's ear.

My father had once owned a Taskin harpsichord equipped with a sustainin device which allowed the sound to continue after the fingers had left the keys. He found it effective in the playing of wide-ranging arpeggios and in sustaining the bass when the hands crossed. But notes could not be repeated while the pedal was down because, while

Clavichord in English walnut, made by Arnold Dolmetsch in 1937.

the dampers were still clear of the strings, the jacks had not yet returned the whole way to their starting positions.

My brother, Rudolph Dolmetsch, used a "new action" harpsichord for some of his Columbia recordings during the 1930s, notably in a sonata in D major by Scarlatti (D.B. 1100), Handel's Passacaille in G minor (D.B. 1322) and "The King's Hunt" by John Bull (D.B. 5713) played on a new action spinet. Copies of these 10-inch 78s may still be obtainable in collectors' markets. A number of large harpsichords incorporating welded metal frames, new action, sustaining pedal and *ad lib* vibrato, were completed and delivered right up to the outbreak of war in 1939. My father assigned to me the responsibility of mounting and regulating the actions in these new harpsichords, with our valued assistant Andrew Douglas.

[69]

All the costly experimentation connected with these achievements, plus the obtaining of patents in England, France, Germany and America, were severely inhibited by want of financial support in the days before the manufacture of early instruments had become the profitable pursuit it now is for so many the world over, thanks largely to Arnold Dolmetsch's pioneering sacrifices.

One of the biggest obstacles to the new actions being widely adopted was the lack of specialized knowledge and skill outside Haslemere to maintain and regulate them, often thousands of miles away – an argument that had been levied against the adoption of the piano during the eighteenth century! Largely because of this and also for financial considerations, production of the new action was not resumed when harpsichord building re-commenced in the Dolmetsch workshops after the war.

Decoration

Dolmetsch attached great importance to his instruments being decorative in design and he favoured such refinements as crossbanding and inlay, averring that an instrument which was ugly in appearance was unlikely to be beautiful in sound. Among many decorative woods he used for case work, his prime favourite was English walnut; to a lesser degree, he also favoured lacquered cases, paintings on soundboards as well as inside the lids. Well-known artists such as Roger Fry ordered harpsichords "in the white" intending to apply their own decorations; my father was not always in sympathy with the style of these decorations, needless to say! His very first large harpsichord, built in 1896 at the suggestion of William Morris and destined for the Arts and Crafts Exhibition Society's exhibition at Burlington House, was a highly ornate instrument. The underside of the lid and the soundboard were decorated with flowers and musical motifs by Helen Coombe (later Mrs Roger Fry), while the inside of the case was embellished in a refined, less ostentatious style by Selwyn Image. Herbert Horne, eminent reformer of Roman lettering, was responsible for the nameboard and motto inside the lid. Horne laid down a standard of lettering which my father employed to the end of his life. For lettering on polished wood, Dolmetsch always used real gold leaf as he did also for mouldings.

Painting in Tempera

From 1918 onwards, Mabel Dolmetsch (my mother) made an exhaustive study of painting in tempera, a process employing white of egg as a medium, popular during the Italian Renaissance. She herself ground the natural colours on glass with a pestle; she would arrange flowers from the garden gracefully on the soundboard within the spaces either side of the bridge and then reproduce them in tempera, adding a bee here or a butterfly there, as it took her fancy. Many fine examples of her artistry survive in harpsichords, spinets and, especially, clavichords. It is always possible to deduce in which season she was working by the varieties of flowers captured in her paintings.

The Spread of Dolmetsch's Influence

While the approach of nineteenth-century French harpsichord makers was from the concept of the piano, Dolmetsch's influence on twentieth-century English, American and, later, German makers was far stronger. It developed gradually and naturally through makers who had studied and worked with him, such as Robert Goble and Hugh Gough; others who admired his work learnt from him indirectly by studying his instruments. Today, when there are more English makers than can be kept track of who recognize the importance of light, resonant construction, it should be remembered that Arnold Dolmetsch held the line virtually alone for some fifty years.

Apart from the continuous effect of the export of his English-made harpsichords to America, his impact on the American scene was in two main stages; the first came from the series of fine concert harpsichords he produced in Boston early this century, most of them still in sound playing condition and highly prized by their owners. Ralph Kirkpatrick still plays on the harpsichord which Arnold Dolmetsch made at this period for Busoni. The second stage resulted from John Challis' term of intensive study in Haslemere (1926–1930), after which he established workshops successively in Ypsilanti, Detroit and New York. America now abounds not only with pupils of Challis – such as William Dowd and Rutkowsky – but with pupils of pupils *ad infinitum*. Many are now pursuing lines of their own, possibly unaware of their indirect indebtedness to Arnold Dolmetsch's pioneering work. Harpsichord building in Germany gained great impetus during the 1920s and 1930s, stemming largely from the influence of the early Haslemere Festivals (founded 1925), patronized extensively by German musicians and craftsmen. The Landowska school of playing on heavily constructed French instruments had initially influenced the first modern German makers to produce massive piano-style harpsichords. The all-important turning point came when Dr Hans Neupert, of the famous firm of J. C. Neupert, became keenly interested in Dolmetsch's "Paris model" concert harpsichord. Particular tribute should here be paid to Dr Neupert, the first to introduce an altogether lighter, more resonant style of construction to the German scene. He also used pedals in preference to hand stops and introduced innovations of his own, including new designs of jack.

It has long been customary to speak of "the harpsichord" as though referring to one instrument, overlooking the wide diversity in shape, size, resources and quality of workmanship existing within the family, ancient and modern. Given this licence, the modern maker should feel encouraged not to cramp his style and work within unnecessary limitations, but to be adventurous and to give his imagination full scope in such matters as design, tone quality and mechanical efficiency. While retaining a profound respect for the genius of his predecessors, the modern maker should feel free to introduce modifications and improvements which, wisely employed, can enhance the vitality of his work and ensure that "the harpsichord" is accorded its rightful place as a musical resource of the future. Today's ideal should surely be to profit from the best of both worlds.

Dr Dolmetsch directs the Haslemere Festival from his home at Jesses, Grayswood Road, Haslemere, and is also artistic director of the Dolmetsch Summer School at Chichester.

CHAPTER 3

John Barnes

The majority of harpsichords currently being made in this country are either copies of, or are fairly closely derived from, important early instruments. Some of the makers in this book are making copies of instruments that they have personally restored while others have had the opportunity to inspect closely and to measure their chosen original, but the

majority of copies are now made from published plans. A report on the availability of such plans should not only be of use to amateur and professional builders but also to players wishing to commission an instrument or wondering what instrument would suit them.

I could not have found anyone more suitable than John Barnes to write this chapter. I first met him thirty years ago, when he was hardly more than a schoolboy, his first clavichord recently made and so precious to him that he carried it everywhere; his enthusiasm is undiminished today. For the past twelve years he has been Curator of the Russell Collection at Edinburgh University: his tasks there have been those of restoration, of maintaining the instruments that are in playing order and preparing them for occasional public concerts in the building where they are housed. He has also been involved with the drawings sold by the Collection and this he regards as probably the most important aspect of the work of the Russell Collection. His large Victorian home in Edinburgh holds a substantial collection of his own, two dozen square pianos, ten grand pianos, and several very important plucked instruments, including a single-manual Dulcken, a two-manual Kirckman, an Italian harpsichord by Gregori and an English spinet. John Barnes has made valuable contributions to a number of areas of research and his publications are listed in the bibliography. At the moment he is collaborating with Richard Loucks in the preparation of a book on the design and construction of clavichords.

The plans which are discussed here are all full-scale drawings; some of these will be on paper and some on dimensionally stable plastic, and they include all necessary measurements. The collections are, variously, privately owned and in museums and conservatoires and colleges of music. The method used to display the information is to list the instruments in date order under virginals, spinets, harpsichords, clavichords and pianos, each entry being coded to indicate the collection it is in.

JOHN BARNES:

In the modern world, people who depend on others for the designs of things they make, presumably do so because they cannot produce better designs themselves. Whether the production occurs with or without the consent of the originator of the design, the copyist is usually counted to be inferior in status to the designer. It therefore surprises and even annoys people to find what is apparently an inversion of natural order among builders of harpsichords, virginals, spinets, clavichords and early pianos. The people who make copies feel themselves superior to those who design their own instruments. A brief account of the history of the revival of interest in old instruments is necessary to understand how this has come about and the extent to which the attitude is justified.

The making of harpsichords ceased about 1800 and was resumed some 90 years later, an interval of time sufficient to break the thread of any living tradition. Those who revived the harpsichord were, of course, conscious of the transformation of the piano in those 90 years, from a wooden frame instrument of 5 or $5\frac{1}{2}$ octaves with a simple action to the louder, more robust and more stable 7-octave instrument with an iron frame and a double escapement action. Inevitably, the development of the piano suggested "improvements" which found their way into new harpsichords.

Since that time, the makers and players of harpsichords have learned, step by step, a great deal about the instrument's history, with the result that the first revival harpsichords no longer seem to be quite what their makers intended. We see them nowadays as ingenious, well-built and mostly reliable but quite unsuited for the performance of old music. Nevertheless, their characteristics made good sense in the context of the powerful prejudice the instrument met in the early days of the revival. In order to impress the pianist, the harpsichordist needed to be able to do things which were impossible on the piano. Playing in three octaves at once and rapidly changing the tone colours were obviously valuable weapons for winning the ensuing battle.

The harpsichord has now regained its natural place in our contemporary musical life as an instrument for the performance of music of its own period. This period, however, covers three centuries, during which the harpsichord changed considerably. It is therefore acknowledged nowadays that sixteenth- and seventeenth-century harpsichord music was written for instruments with a different combination of qualities from that found in the late eighteenth century. It is obvious that sixteenth-century harpsichords were not large enough for some music written in the eighteenth century, but it is also true that eighteenth-century harpsichords somewhat distort the performance of the music of earlier centuries. This is the justification of the modern interest in designs of harpsichords from different periods.

The present situation does not, of course, satisfy everyone. Some players still prefer the kind of harpsichord which was developed during the early years of the revival and is still being made, with thick soundboard barred across the bridges, 16ft stop with wrapped strings, leather plectra and a touch heavy enough to make pianists feel at home. There exists, also, some important modern music written for harpsichords of this type, most of which, fortunately, transfers satisfactorily to the traditional harpsichords of suitable size. If present trends continue, the revival type of harpsichord will soon have declined in popularity to the point at which commercial production is no longer possible, and it will then be only a matter of time before it will be difficult to find well-maintained examples for public performances.

Sooner or later a maker is asked what kinds of harpsichord he has built. He then finds an answer like "Taskin 1769" or "Dulcken 1745" is convenient and concise. What matters to the performer is that the tradition in which the instrument is made is appropriate to the music he wishes to perform, within such practical compromises as he is obliged to accept. This means that the Stehlin of 1760 (H30) might be just as good as the Taskin of 1769 (H33) or that the van den Elsche of 1767 (H31) might be as suitable as the Dulcken of 1745 (H24), and there is nothing inherently wrong in combining the designs of several makers working in the same tradition. It also means that anything in a design that does not affect the performer, performance and audience can be altered if there are advantages in doing so.

This gives ample freedom for instrument makers to develop their individuality, but there are many modern makers who realistically see themselves as novices compared with a particular historical maker. Who can blame them, then, for setting themselves the task of copying a particular historical instrument, believing that they will learn by it? They may be taking historical accuracy further than is strictly necessary but a performer and customer will often prefer that they err in this direction and avoid alterations which could later have unforeseen consequences or which simply spoil the artistic or historical ambience he is conscientiously trying to create.

The commonest reservation concerning the copying of old instruments is that by so doing the maker will also copy some fatal flaw in the original design. This fear is quite irrational. The vast majority of our surviving historical harpsichords are still in existence because they were well designed and executed, and any damage that has taken place is usually the result of hard wear, abuse or adverse conditions of storage. The old makers aimed to build instruments with good tonal and mechanical properties which were as robust and stable as possible and no more expensive than necessary. Those aims are still valid, and modern technology and materials have given to harpsichord making hardly anything of value. This explains why an accurate reproduction of an old design can usually compete on equal terms with a harpsichord incorporating the best improvements a modern maker can devise.

If a maker is following a drawing, it is important that he can trust it to give him reliable information about the original state of the instrument he is copying. He may, of course, want to reproduce an altered state, especially if the original has been altered by an important builder (for example, the reputed Goermans of 1764 (H32), rebuilt by Taskin), but if a suitable unaltered instrument is available it is more likely to be characteristic of its period. The Grimaldi of 1697 in its original state (H20), for example, is very similar to the altered state of the Baffo of 1575 (H4), probably because the alteration was made around 1700, but the Grimaldi is more likely to represent a typical Italian harpsichord of *c.* 1700. In general a builder should check the background information supplied with a drawing, writing to the source if necessary, and he will probably find that the most trustworthy drawings come from museums or private sources which have specialized organological knowledge. The three leading museums for keyboard research at present are the Germanisches Nationalmuseum, the Smithsonian Institution and the Russell Collection.

The draughtsman producing an instrument-drawing has many of the same responsibilities as the editor of an old musical manuscript. An editor may have to weigh whether the composition really was by the apparent composer, or whether some of the accidentals were inserted by another hand. He will have to decide what advice should be given, if any, on pitch, tempo, timbre, phrasing and style. These problems, which are well understood in connection with the production of *Urtext* performing editions, have close parallels with the problems of drawing historical instruments.

In order to be comparable with a good *Urtext*, an instrument-drawing should give:

1. Reliable information concerning the original state,

Virginal by Stephen Keene, 1668. The case is of oak with painted and gilt decoration, while the stand is modern. (In the Russell Collection, Edinburgh.)

2. Information from other similar instruments when parts of the original are missing (e.g. jacks),
3. The internal structure from evidence of X-rays or restoration work,
4. A complete list of materials from which the original was made,
5. Soundboard thicknesses, preferably in a dozen or more places.

The best instruments for copying tend to be:

1. Those typical of their period, especially if the period was musically fruitful,
2. Those that have survived in reasonable condition, and, if possible, are now in playing order,

3. Those which have not been altered or whose history of alterations is understood,
4. Those which have been measured inside and for which accurate soundboard thicknesses are available,
5. Those with a respected identity or a name which is becoming fashionable (since most instruments have to be sold).

Makers will often wish to alter details to increase the usefulness or versatility of a design, the commonest alteration being an increase in compass. Such details were somewhat flexible in most periods, and changes can often be made without sacrificing the essential character of the original.

There are interesting differences between Italian and Flemish instruments which apply both to virginals and harpsichords. The Italians built lightly, simply and robustly, and a traditionally-made Italian copy with boxslides and hardwood key levers should continue to function reliably until its key facings are severely worn. Italian jacks are short compared with Flemish, so they can afford to be thick without being too heavy. This makes the Italian box guide practicable, since the jacks can be trusted to remain straight. Mechanically, the Flemish instruments are more delicate, though a careful owner will find them reliable. While Italian instruments are lightly built, anyone who lifts a large Italian harpsichord in its outer case will find that the total weight is sometimes more than that of a Flemish of the same size. Italian integral construction, which was used from about 1650 as an alternative to having a separate case, involves less total work and less total weight. Italian inner instruments by themselves are too vulnerable for hard use without the protection of their cases. Outer cases give the impression of being made by a lower class of workman, and the acceptance of the obvious advantages of integral construction was probably retarded by a socially prescribed division of labour.

Musically, the Italian taste seems to have been for a muscular sinuous sound while the Flemish taste was for fullness and colour, something like the aural equivalent, respectively, of an acanthus and a tulip. Both kinds of instrument have attractions, and the regional schools of building of the seventeenth and eighteenth centuries drew on both traditions.

Virginals

The typical Italian virginal was pentagonal, decorated with delicate mouldings and protected by a separate outer case which was usually painted. Up to c. 1600, Italian virginals usually had a C/E $-$ f^3 compass (those instruments listed as V1, V2 and V3 have probably had a change of compass) and a c^2 string length of about 11 to 13·5 inches (280 mm to 340 mm). During the seventeenth century this gradually gave way to a C/E–c^3 compass (an example is V9) and c^2 lengths of 9·5 to 10·5 inches (240 mm to 270 mm). This is a unique example of a later compass being smaller than an earlier one, and no one has yet discovered precisely why this happened, but my own view is that a change of pitch, possibly a gradual one, was involved, and that the pitch of any fairly typical Italian instrument should be derived on the assumption that brass strings were used close to breaking point.

Italian virginals use plucking positions roughly similar to harpsichords, but there are two distinct versions of the Flemish virginal, one of which (the muselar) plucks near the middle of the strings and has a most distinctive voice, hollow and throaty. V7 is an example of this kind of instrument, with the keyboard well to the right of centre, a familiar sight from three of Vermeer's most famous paintings. V4 and V5 are smaller virginals, plucking in a more conventional position and intended for higher pitch than normal. The Flemish makers are known to have used iron wire, but V5 can be converted to modern pitch by the simple expedient of using brass wire instead. V5 would be a good choice for someone making a first instrument.

English virginals owe much to the kind of Flemish virginal which plucks near the ends of the strings with the keyboard to the left of centre. V6 is an early and V8 a late example, both exhibiting the English tendency to chromatic bass octaves at a time when Continental instruments usually had short octaves.

Spinets

By turning the virginal string band upside down, someone created the spinet, possibly Zenti in Italy about 1630. Spinets have an attractive shape with a bentside like a harpsichord, and by 1670 the virginal shape had become old-fashioned. S1 is a typical early English spinet of walnut with a marquetry panel on the nameboard, S2 is from a generation later, after English keyboards had changed from black to white and the compass had reached 5 octaves, while S3 is a spinet from a respected Paris maker.

Harpsichords

Italian harpsichords followed the same pattern of development regarding compass and string scaling as Italian virginals, and could be of either integral construction or with separate outer cases, but a distinctive feature of the sixteenth century was that some harpsichords originally had only one unison register (H2) and some had one unison and one octave (H3 and H4) resembling the contemporary Flemish harpsichords in this respect. These instruments were usually brought up to date later by converting them to the usual Italian seventeenth- and eighteenth-century specification of two unisons, often with keyboard changes designed to reduce the scale to that of a c^2 of about 10 inches (250 mm) so that brass strings would reach eighteenth-century pitch. H17 and H22 are of integral construction, while the others are the more usual kind with separate cases.

Large clavichord by J. A. Hass, 1763. Elaborately decorated, this has a chinoiserie lacquered exterior with an oil painted scene on the inside of the lid. The soundboard view of this instrument is shown on page 40. (In the Russell Collection, Edinburgh.)

Throughout the seventeenth and eighteenth centuries the Ruckers family of Antwerp (including Joannes Couchet, nephew of Joannes Ruckers) had a great reputation. The family made single-manual harpsichords of various sizes and pitches (H7, H9–11 and H14) and double-manual harpsichords arranged to give two of the various pitches in common use in the one instrument (H8). These were transposing harpsichords, the lower manual displaced to the left of the upper, so as to play a fourth below it. When the needs of music changed, many of these harpsichords were rebuilt, the two manuals brought into alignment at the same pitch, so that they became expressive doubles.

The eighteenth-century Flemish harpsichords developed the Ruckers tradition, Dulcken's speciality being the double thickness bentside (presumably to give extra strength) and all having bass strings rather longer than most of their foreign contemporaries (H24, H25, H27, H31, H35 and H36). Delin's speciality was the making of upright harpsichords (H28).

During the seventeenth and eighteenth centuries, regional schools developed in Germany (H23), England (H21 and H37) and France. The regional school which has been copied the most has been the French, and this is reflected in the number of drawings of French instruments which are now available (H15, H26, H29, H30, H32 and H33). Some Italian influence is detectable in these three schools until about 1720, when the dominant influence became the Flemish school.

A recurring practical problem with harpsichords is that of making do with only one for a varied repertory; either for a public recital covering early and late harpsichord music or for home practising by those who do not have room or money for more than one harpsichord. The designs most favoured at present for this purpose are those of Taskin and Dulcken. Taskin is favoured because of the lush sonority of his bass register and the general attraction of his tone colour, and Dulcken because of a classical and somewhat neutral quality which seems to give it a genuine versatility. The Taskin design is splendid for French music and attractive for other periods, but its sonority is not ideal for the virginalists, or for Bach or Scarlatti. Dulcken's design has less immediate attraction, particularly for French music, but it has a benefit for the composers whose colour is written into the score (e.g. Scarlatti) or whose strength is in contrapuntal writing (e.g. Bach). A less colourful alternative to Taskin is one of the French makers of a generation earlier, e.g. Hemsch (H29). French harpsichords usually have three rows of jacks but a few were fitted with a fourth row with buffalo hide plectra for special effects which became popular after about 1750 (H26 and H32).

Clavichords

Most of the surviving old clavichords are unpretentious, anonymous fretted instruments which were probably made for less than half the price of a virginal. They are very portable and easy to maintain, advantages which compensate somewhat for the quietness of the tone. Their popularity was largely confined to Scandinavia, the German speaking regions, Italy and Iberia, where they were always valued for developing a good keyboard touch. During the eighteenth century the German clavichord developed into a responsive instrument and its devotees remained loyal until about 1820, long after the harpsichord had lost favour. After about 1780 it began to inspire a literature of its own, exploiting dynamic and vibrato effects which had probably had little importance before about 1720.

C2 is a particularly good example of the type which was popular between 1650 and 1700 when the short octave and meantone tuning were in use. Clavichords sound weak and insipid unless the strings are struck and sounded in pairs. Some of these string pairs, however, are made to produce up to three consecutive notes by arranging the tangents to

Soundboard view of the two-manual harpsichord by Goermans (?), 1764. This was rebuilt by Pascal Taskin in 1783. (In the Russell Collection, Edinburgh.)

step out semitone distances at the rear of the keys. Naturally, the same pair of strings cannot produce more than one of its notes at a time and care is required when passing from one note to another on the same string pair, particularly in the downward direction. Trills between notes on the same string pair, on the other hand, are no trouble, and when the pair of strings has been tuned, up to three notes are automatically in tune.

For the music of Bach and his contemporaries the later clavichords, either fretted (C5, C6 and C11) or unfretted (C7–10) must be chosen. The later fretted instruments have separate strings for all natural keys, so that the sharing of notes on the same string pairs is hardly ever noticeable. These fretted clavichords still have an advantage for tuning and since they have about one third fewer strings than unfretted instruments of the same compass they are usually light and compact enough for one person to carry.

C7–10 are all large unfretted instruments and all but C10 have extra octave strings to add definition in the bass.

Early Pianos

The success of restorations of early pianos during the past 20 years has encouraged the building of copies of the rarer and musically most significant types. Since old 5-octave pianos with the admired Viennese action are rarer than old harpsichords, and their repertoire is of great importance, this kind of piano is most usually copied (P2 and P3). Its use for solo and chamber music of its period is becoming popular, because of the unnatural balance produced by using a modern piano.

The square piano developed from the clavichord and is now copied in small quantities, but so far only two drawings are available (P1 and P4) and these are both of untypical portable instruments.

The availability of drawings is due to the happy coincidence that their producers can gain financially, acquire a good reputation and at the same time save damage to instruments and trouble to themselves or their staff. Conservation and convenience usually lead in different directions, so the rare occasions when this is not so deserve to be celebrated. The list which follows was compiled in January and February 1980 from enquiries sent to all the sources known to me. It includes drawings which the sources gave as "in preparation" but the number of available drawings is increasing steadily and the present list will soon be incomplete. Nevertheless, it will remain useful for many years as a guide to the museums and private owners who are worth contacting for up-to-date lists. It is beyond my scope to offer advice on which are the most comprehensive or the best value for money, but the general discussion above will suggest the questions one should ask before buying a particular drawing. After the identification number (e.g. H14), the entries list the following features in order: maker, date, provenance, compass,

An unaltered transposing two-manual harpsichord by Joannes Ruckers,
1638. (In the Russell Collection, Edinburgh.)

pitch if abnormal, special features, approximate overall length of the instrument in
metres and the source of the drawing.

Sources of Drawings
Sources of drawings for the instruments listed below are shown by a single letter. If the
latter is in square brackets, the drawing was in preparation when the list was prepared.

A. The Vleeshuis Museum, Antwerp, Belgium.
B. John Barnes, 3 East Castle Road, Edinburgh, GB.
C. Christopher Clarke, 275 rue de Faubourg St Antoine, 75011 Paris, France.
E. Russell Collection, University of Edinburgh, St Cecilia's Hall, Cowgate, Edinburgh, GB.
G. Germanisches Nationalmuseum, 85 Nurnberg 11, Postfach 9580, Germany.

H.   Haags Gemeentemuseum, Stadhouderslaan 41, Postbus 72, Holland.
L.   R. K. Lee, 353 School Street, Watertown, Mass. 02172, USA.
N.   Metropolitan Museum, Box 255, Gracie Station, New York 10028, USA.
P.   Musée Instrumental, Conservatoire National Supérieur de Musique, 14 rue de Madrid, 75008
     Paris, France.
R.   Royal College of Music, Prince Consort Road, South Kensington, London SW7, GB.
S.   Smithsonian Institution, Washington DC 20560, USA.
V.   Victoria and Albert Museum, South Kensington, London SW7, GB.
Y.   Yale University, 15 Hillhouse Avenue, New Haven, Connecticut 06520, USA.

Virginals

V1	D. Pisaurensis?	1535?	Venice	GG/BB–c³		1·65 m	[B]
V2	A. Irena?	1564?	Rome	C/E–e³		1·57 m	[P]
V3	Anon.	c. 1580	Italy	GG/BB–c³ (Queen Elizabeth's)		1·52 m	V
V4	A. Ruckers	1620	Antwerp	C/E–c³	quint pitch	1·15 m	S
V5	J. Ruckers	1629	Antwerp	C/E–d³	quart pitch	1·30 m	E
V6	T. White	1642	London	C–c³		1·64 m	V
V7	J. Couchet	1650	Antwerp	C/E–c³	muselar	1·75 m	A
V8	S. Keene	1668	London	FF–d³ without FF♯		1·82 m	[E]
V9	J. de Perticis	1684	Florence	C/E–c³		1·49 m	L

Spinets

S1	Anon.	1708	England	GG/BB–d³ with C♯, E♭	1·68 m	R
S2	T. Hitchcock	c. 1730	London	GG–g³	1·89 m	S
S3	J.-C. Goujon	1753	Paris	FF–f³	1·74 m	[P]

Harpsichords

H1	Anon.	c. 1480	Germany	E–g²	1 man 8 upright, separate case	1·42 m high	R
H2	Jerome	1521	Rome	?	1 man 8 separate case	1·80 m	V
H3	A. Trasuntino	1531	Venice	C/E–f³?	1 man 84 (now 88) separate case	2·25 m	R
H4	G. Baffo	1574	Venice	C/E–f³	1 man 84 (now 88) separate case	2·16 m (now)	V
H5	Anon	c. 1575	Italy?	C/E–c³	1 man 8 (now 88) separate case	1·86 m	R
H6	D. Pisaurensis	c. 1600	Venice	GG–c³	1 man 88 separate case		[B]
H7	A. Ruckers	1637	Antwerp	C/E–c³	1 man 84	1·83 m	G
H8	J. Ruckers	1638	Antwerp	C/E–f³	2 man 84	2·24 m	E
H9	A. Ruckers	1640	Antwerp	C/E–c³	1 man 84	1·83 m	L
H10	A. Ruckers	1644	Antwerp	C/E–c³	1 man 84	1·82 m	A
H11	J. Couchet	1645	Antwerp	C/E–c³	1 man 84	1·82 m	[E]
H12	Anon.	c. 1670	Italy	C/E–c³	2 man 884 separate case	2·09 m	G
H13	Anon.	c. 1675	Italy	C/E–c³	1 man 44 separate case	0·93 m	G
H14	J. J. Couchet	1679	Antwerp		1 man 84	1·83 m	S
H15	J. A. Vaudry	1681	Paris	GG/BB–c³	2 man 884	2·16 m	V
H16	J. de Perticis	1681	Florence	C/E–f³	1 man 88 separate case	1·92 m	L
H17	G. B. Giusti	1681	Lucca	C/E–c³	1 man 88 integral case	1·96 m	G

H18	G. Ridolfi	1682	Italy	C/E–c³	1 man 88 separate case	1·90 m	[Y]
H19	Anon.	1693	Italy	GG–c³ without GG♯	1 man 88 separate case	2·33 m	S
H20	Grimaldi	1697	Messina	GG–c³	1 man 88 separate case	2·55 m	G
H21	T. Hitchcock	c. 1725	London	GG–g³	2 man 884	2·33 m	V
H22	A. Gregori	1726	Italy	C/E–e³ without e♭³	1 man 88 integral case	1·90 m	B
H23	C. Vater	1738	Hanover	GG/BB–e³	1 man 88	2·01 m	G
H24	J. D. Dulcken	1745	Antwerp	FF–f³	2 man 884	2·59 m	S
H25	J. D. Dulcken	1747	Antwerp	FF–f³	1 man 884	2·47 m	A
H26	J.-C. Goujon	1749?	Paris	FF–f³	2 man 884 with peau de buffle	2·33 m	[P]
H27	J. D. Dulcken	c. 1750	Antwerp	FF–e³	1 man 884	2·48 m	B
H28	A. Delin	c. 1750	Tournai	AA–f³	1 man 88 upright (height)	2·88 m	H
H29	H. Hemsch	1756	Paris	FF–e³	2 man 884	2·35 m	L
H30	B. Stehlin	1760	Paris	FF–f³	2 man 884	2·32 m	S
H31	J. van den Elsche	1763	Antwerp	FF–f³	2 man 884	2·67 m	A
H32	J. Goermans?	1764	Paris	FF–f³	2 man 884 with peau de buffle rebuilt P. Taskin 1783	2·28 m	[E]
H33	P. Taskin	1769	Paris	FF–f³	2 man 884	2·32 m	E
H34	R. & F. Cresci	1778	Livorno	FF–g³ without f♯³	1 man 88	2·55 m	G
H35	J. P. Bull	1778	Antwerp	FF–f³	2 man 884	2·54 m	L
H36	J. P. Bull	1779	Antwerp	FF–f³	1 man 884	2·49 m	A
H37	J. & A. Kirckman	1786	London	FF–f³	2 man 884	2·39 m	B

Clavichords

C1	Anon.	1652	Germany	C/E–c³	fretted in threes	0·98 m	Y
C2	Anon.	c. 1700	Germany	C/E–c³	fretted in threes	1·09 m	E
C3	Anon.	c. 1700	Germany	C/E–c³	fretted in threes	0·98 m	N
C4	Anon.	c. 1740	Germany	C–c³	fretted in threes, hexagonal	1·30 m	G
C5	Anon.	c. 1750	Vienna	C–d³	fretted in pairs	0·96 m	[P]
C6	Anon.	c. 1750	Germany	C–f³	fretted in pairs	1·35 m	S
C7	B. Fritz	1751	Brunswick	FF–a³	unfretted, 4' in bass	1·79 m	V
C8	J. A. Hass	1761	Hamburg	FF–f³	unfretted, 4' in bass	1·75 m	C
C9	J. A. Hass	1763	Hamburg	FF–f³	unfretted, 4' in bass	1·75 m	E
C10	J. H. Silbermann	c. 1770	Strassburg	FF–f³	unfretted, no 4'	1·77 m	G
C11	C. G. Hubert	1784	Ansbach	C–f³	fretted in pairs	1·29 m	B

Pianos

P1	A. Walter	c. 1790	Vienna	E–f³	portable square piano	0·92 m	P
P2	A. Walter	c. 1795	Vienna	FF–g³	grand, Viennese action	2·20 m	G
P3	J. L. Dulcken	c. 1795	Munich?	FF–g³	grand, Viennese action	2·18 m	S
P4	Anon.	c. 1800	Germany	E–g³	portable square piano	1·07 m	P

John Barnes has a small workshop at his home, 3 East Castle Road, Edinburgh; he is currently doing instrument restoration, making clavichords, and is also Scottish agent for Zuckermann kits.

[86]

CHAPTER 4

⁘

Malcolm Rose

Mayfield is one of the little Wealden showplace towns which seem to have hardly altered from the distant past. It can be seen from miles away, on the top of a hill, rooftops projecting through the dense Wealden tree cover. The main street is a mixture of half-timbered and Victorian houses while anything modern is discreetly tucked away. It was here that St Dunstan, who was not only a cleric of some importance, for he went on to become Archbishop of Canterbury, but also a practical ironsmith, is reputed to have tweaked the Devil's nose with his pincers in a confrontation over the anvil.

In a side road not far from the centre, Malcolm Rose has his workshop. It looks small from the outside but, in fact, is spacious for one man as it is well laid out on two floors, wood store and heavy machinery on the lower, the light and airy upper storey used for construction. The room is neat and tidy and tools are obviously put away after use. His work is precise, meticulous and done with careful and detailed attention. The Italian virginal he was making requires this kind of workmanship; it is of bare plain wood and the visual attraction lies in the perfect joints, and the mouldings and carving sharply and neatly cut.

MALCOLM ROSE:

Music, rather than making musical instruments, took first place at the outset of my career. Although musically a late starter, I managed to gain a place on the three-year graduate course at Trinity College of Music in London, a year after leaving school. This was thanks mainly to the help of my teacher, Richard Stangroom, who then became my organ professor for the years at college and beyond.

Woodwork had been my main interest since childhood and it became my relaxation during the college years to work on the clavichord which I had already started to make. The published design I used was poor; like so many instruments at that time, it had been set out by the designer with the piano in mind, a concept quite irrelevant to the earlier instruments. The tension was carried by heavy longitudinal members glued to the bottom board; the casework was added later and, far from being the vital shell of the instrument, was quite incidental. The specified stringing was far too heavy and I had to re-string it at a later date. But of course I learned a lot; the resulting instrument was at least adequate enough to make me realize the totally absorbing and fascinating quality of the clavichord. I chose the clavichord and its music as the subject of a thesis during my last year at College; not breaking any new ground, but in sufficient depth to show how great or small was the importance of the clavichord in each European country. I realized as well how much music was coming out of Germany before the eighteenth century and how much of Bach's music finds a source in earlier times. I also delved into the problems of differentiating the clavichord's music from that of the other keyboard instruments.

When College came to an end I set out to join the teaching profession, looking for a job with the primary age group under the mistaken impression that it was easier for an inexperienced teacher. When a job did turn up it took me from my home in Surrey to Tunbridge Wells. Whether the pupils learned more about music during the first year or so than I did about teaching, is doubtful, but the move did bring other benefits. Within a few days I found myself a member of the Gibbons Consort of Voices, the chamber choir based ten miles further south in Mayfield, under the direction of Kenneth Pont. The Consort specializes in English church music, an area of music I had had little contact with before. I soon afterwards became their organist, and the ten years so far spent with them, giving recitals the length and breadth of the country, has been an invaluable and fascinating experience.

I first came to know Ann Feldberg and the Feldberg workshops, not far away in Sevenoaks, when I hired a harpsichord from them for a concert in the school where I was teaching. This was my first chance of some extended practice on a harpsichord and it did not take me long to realize that this was the instrument I wanted to make. Largely by virtue of having made my first clavichord during my college years, I eventually per-

Malcolm Rose: two-manual harpsichord after Hemsch in pale green lacquer with gold leaf banding.

suaded Mrs Feldberg to take me on for a period of three weeks, during the school Easter holidays of 1972. Most of the time, apart from watching closely what everyone was doing, was spent preparing keyboards and making jacks and trying not to interrupt the flow of work. I must have managed this reasonably well for, at the end of the three weeks, Mrs Feldberg agreed that I should work full time from the beginning of that September.

Although the trial period had given me a taste of the work and confirmed my interest in it, I had to learn a great deal very quickly when September arrived. But it was an ideal time at which to join the workshop; they were making the last of the Feldberg Whale instruments before moving over entirely to copies. The FW instruments, designed by the manager Peter Whale, were lightly constructed, somewhat along Italian lines but using modern materials and they were responsive and versatile instruments. They were not quite so exacting to my inexperienced hands as the copies and they gave me a chance to gain some insight into the use of machinery for basic preparation, as well as a considerable amount of metalwork. Another aspect of the workshop which I appreciated enormously, was the system whereby each craftsman worked independently on his own instrument; I was thus able to gain first-hand experience of most aspects of harpsichord making relatively quickly. After a few months of making parts for other instruments, I was allowed to make an FW 1, the single-manual member of the range, under my own steam. This harpsichord belongs to a professional group and has travelled many thousands of miles with them on European tours.

By this time, the middle of 1973, I was often being despatched to tune and regulate the harpsichords that had been made in the Feldberg workshops during the previous fifteen years. My tuning until then had been self-taught and not very reliable, so Mrs Feldberg most generously allowed me to go on a day-release tuning course at the London College of Furniture. I gained some helpful guidance there and particularly some insight into the mathematics of tuning which has proved to be a useful background. But it is strange to think how hard we worked to be able to tune in equal temperament, whereas now most of us in the harpsichord making profession accept that the various unequal temperaments serve much better both the instrument and its music.

With three FW instruments behind me I was permitted to embark on a Goujon harpsichord. For some time past, Feldbergs had been making copies of this fine French double manual in the Paris Conservatoire collection and I had tried to lose no opportunity of watching the earlier examples being made. There were many new techniques to be learnt; apart from complex cabinet work and a good deal of mouldings to be made, I found myself making keyboards, slides and wooden jacks for the first time. I cannot overstate the value of the experience I gained in making my first copy, nor the sense of fulfilment which came from playing it when it was at last completed. The Feldberg Goujon is without doubt among the best of the French harpsichords now available. The last instrument which I made while at the Feldberg workshops was their copy of an anonymous German clavichord. In this unfretted yet compact little instrument, an oak case is first dovetailed together, then fitted with liner, wrest plank, hitch plank and keyframe; the resulting instrument is responsive and capable of a wide range of expression.

I left Feldbergs in the autumn of 1974 to take a one-year post-graduate teaching course. I had not yet decided exactly which way my career would turn, but I knew at least that I

Malcolm Rose: soundboard of harpsichord after Hemsch, decorated in tempera by Audrey Beer.

would continue to teach to a greater or lesser extent, as I enjoy the company of young people. The course was a valuable experience and changed my methods of teaching out of all recognition. Apart from the musical aspects, which included some conducting, I found how much easier teaching was to me at the secondary level and I would not now go back to the younger age range.

Towards the end of the course, in 1975, I began to investigate the possibility of finding a house with a workshop; I had had a tiny terraced cottage for some years and, with the idea of starting my own business at the back of my mind, it seemed the right time to consider exchanging this for something which would enable me at least to begin preliminary studies. The fact that an ideal house with workshops of 80 square yards turned up in Mayfield, combined with the fact that no suitable teaching posts presented themselves, decided the matter; I resolved to begin in business there and then.

The workshops, a builder's premises of the same age as the house, were in a poor state of repair. The lower workshop, of brick and stone and largely underground, was sound enough, but the upper part of timber construction needed a great deal of restoration. The first six months were devoted to laying a new floor, spraying preservatives, re-wiring, lining with insulation materials and installing heating to give a steady temperature. Equipping a new workshop is no small matter either; many hours were spent making benches and trestles, searching for old craftsmen's tools and restoring them.

By the summer of 1976 I was ready to begin work on two restorations which had been booked for some time. Both were Broadwood square pianos, one a very pretty Regency instrument of 1808, the other a particularly handsome example of 1823. They were suffering from the usual problems; apart from minor repairs to the casework, I had to devise a system of re-bushing the tuning pins to give them their original tightness when cleaned and returned, each to its original hole. I had to find a source of oil-tanned doeskin for hammer coverings and to match the other cloths and leathers which were not capable of further service. But the greatest technical difficulty lay in re-stringing; I was determined not to re-string in modern steel wire, and to match the original would clearly call for detailed research. By good fortune, the owner of one of these instruments is a metallurgist and he quickly became my colleague in a study which has expanded to include samples of wire from throughout the eighteenth and nineteenth centuries. The results of this study will be published elsewhere. For the restoration work in hand, we were able to have iron wire drawn to our specification, and subsequent tests showed a very close resemblance in its behaviour to original examples from the first quarter of the nineteenth century. The sound it gives in these instruments is rich and mellow.

From the start I had planned that a French two-manual harpsichord would be the first instrument I would offer as representative of my work. I did not wish to join the already sizeable number of makers copying the Taskin in Edinburgh, fine though this instrument is; I felt that a different instrument would contribute more to the general fund of experience. My choice fell eventually on the harpsichord of 1756 by Henri Hemsch, now in the Boston Museum of Fine Arts. Here was a classic instrument from the mature period of French harpsichord making, restored by Frank Hubbard and copied by his workshop, but not being made elsewhere in Europe. Four or five instruments by Hemsch survive, as well as some by his brother Guillaume; most are in private collections in France and one in particular has been used extensively for recordings.

Apart from the restoration work, much of the first year in the workshop was taken up with finding and selecting timber for the Hemsch harpsichords. The casework is poplar; I was fortunate in finding a tree of sufficient size and quality to give quarter-sawn planks of the right width. I had the whole tree quarter sawn and acquired the use of a farm building to stack it for seasoning. Similarly for lime; dry stock is readily available and I bought a whole tree at a later date to season for the future. Finding pear, holly, ebony, beech, oak and Swiss pine each presented their own problems, but by February 1977 the very considerable amount of work necessary on the drawing board was complete and all was ready to begin the first of the Hemsch instruments.

The workmanship of the original Hemsch is of an extremely high order. The Hemsch brothers came to Paris from near Cologne and there is perhaps something of a German influence in their methods of harpsichord making. The case joints are dovetailed, a demanding operation at the angles formed between each pair of adjacent sides; the internal bracing is somewhat heavier than that of Taskin. The belly rails and bottom braces slide up mortices which completely lock them into place. The ends of the upper braces are recessed firmly into the case sides, with substantial chocks against the liners. The resulting frame is extremely stable. The bentside, the same $\frac{11}{16}$ inch thickness as the rest of the casework, is soaked and bent in one piece around the former, which I had been constructing in the autumn of 1976. The wrest plank is a substantial piece of oak.

The soundboard, as in most harpsichords of northern Europe, is of Swiss pine. Growth rings on the original are fairly consistently between 15 and 20 per inch, but as close as 28 per inch in the treble, and I select pieces to follow this practice. Similarly with soundboard thickness; to put this in the more convenient millimetres, it is 2·4 mm for most of the way under both bridges, but rising to 3·2 mm along the spine and under the bass end of the 8ft bridge. The bridges are of beech and are both bent in one piece, rather than being scarf jointed towards the treble. The hitch pin rail, other edge mouldings and the nuts are also of beech.

The scaling is consistently longer than that of Taskin. The 8ft c^2 is $14\frac{7}{8}$ inches while the 4ft is 7 inches (37·9 and 17·9 cm respectively).

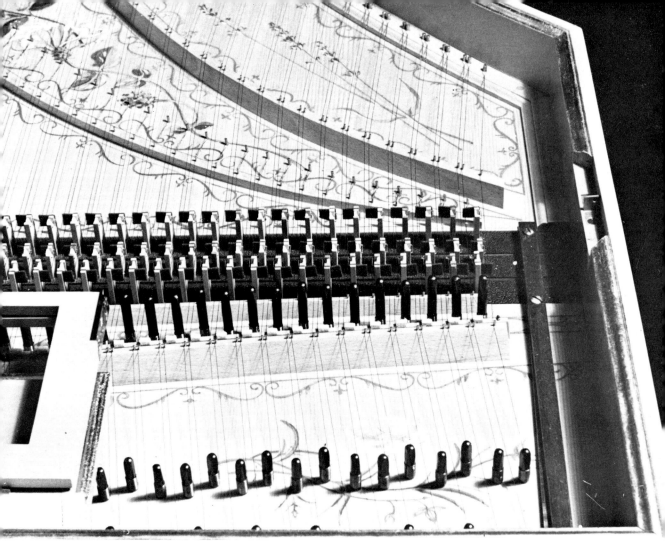

Malcolm Rose: harpsichord action detail.

Problems still abound concerning the stringing of harpsichords, and the related question of pitch. I hope that my own researches into the mechanical properties of iron and copper-alloy wires, along with other studies undertaken with my colleagues, will help to clear the air, and enable us to rediscover other aspects of the lost traditions of harpsichord making. For the Hemsch meanwhile I adopt the much used compromise of tuning the instrument at A=415 with the keyboards in the correct position, but the instrument will then transpose up a semitone to give A 440 when needed. The time will perhaps arrive when all early music ensembles are playing at A 415 or below and it will then be possible to dispense with this compromise.

Other detailing follows the French tradition; the rose, my own emblem of a Tudor rose and my initials, is cast in pewter from my original carving and then gilded. The jacks are of pear, the tongues of holly with boar-bristle springs. For quills I use Delrin where absolute reliability is the priority, but turkey quills have also proved successful. The Hemsch keyboards are typically French; the naturals are of ebony with arcaded fronts, the sharps of black-stained pearwood capped with ivory.

The painter Audrey Beer, who undertook the decoration in tempera of the first Hemsch soundboard, studied as many as possible of the surviving examples to assimilate the style and manner of this particular art. The Collesse harpsichord, which formed part of the touring exhibition of English and French instruments in 1974, is an especial inspiration. Its graceful flowing border pattern served as a model for this first Hemsch, as did the weight and distribution of the flowers. Other features are common both to Hemsch and to Taskin, notably the ring of dark and light blue round the rose which carries the maker's name and date in gold leaf.

Making a French cabriole stand in the manner of the Edinburgh Taskin was a particular challenge. I determined not to copy the stand exactly, but with Audrey Beer worked out a slightly more flowing line to the skirts and a simpler leg without acanthus leaves at the foot. The legs of this stand do in fact unscrew for transport in the same way as the more conventional turned and fluted legs.

The first Hemsch harpsichord, which is always available for visitors to play, is now much travelled. It was exhibited at the third London Exhibition of Early Musical Instruments, and has been used in many concerts, including a recital by Christopher Hogwood in the Mayfield Festival of 1978.

During the making of this harpsichord, and during the restoration work which followed it, I had been looking for another instrument to copy, but one of much greater simplicity. It needed to be in complete contrast of style to that of the harpsichord and more within the budget of people who want a compact instrument for domestic ensemble playing. I found the answer in an Italian virginal by Joannes de Perticis of 1684; this instrument, in private ownership in Boston, is of the true inner-outer type, though the outer case has not survived. The virginal itself is typical of the domestic instruments which were made virtually without change right through the seventeenth and into the eighteenth centuries. Other examples are in Fenton House, the Victoria and Albert Museum and in the Russell Collection, where the surviving outer case served as a model for that of the Perticis.

The soundboard and casework are of cypress, the latter being enriched with complex mouldings which can be cut so crisply in cypress. It was surely the delicacy and vulnerability of these mouldings which first moved the Italian makers to provide

Malcolm Rose: virginal after Joannes de Perticis.

protective outer cases. The bridges are of walnut, the natural keys of box and the sharps of ebony. The outer case is painted on the outside and lined with velvet within. One of the pleasures of these Italian instruments is to open the plain outer case and see the richly decorated virginal inside, its shape picked out by black inlay and ivory studs along the cap moulding. The stand, designed by Audrey Beer and made in sycamore, echoes Italian furniture of the seventeenth century.

The scaling of the single 8ft register gives a c^2 of $10\frac{3}{4}$ inches, and the scaling is pure right down into the middle of the tenor octave. It is well suited for stringing in yellow brass, provided the instrument is tuned to $A = 415$ and it will, of course, transpose up a semitone to modern pitch. The original Perticis virginal has a compass of C/E to c^3, bass short octave; I make copies either with this disposition, or enlarged slightly to give a chromatic compass down to C.

Since I made the first Perticis virginal, my contact with Italian work has grown in a way I had not expected. During 1980 I restored an early seventeenth-century virginal to playing order, and the research which this involved has been a great help in the restoration of another Italian instrument, this time a virginal by Honofrio Guarracino of 1678. The Guarracino has now become the third instrument of which I can offer copies; its clean immediate tone and its richness of mouldings have proved great attractions to people wanting something for domestic and continuo playing. Further plans include copies of a particularly fine Ruckers *ravalement* harpsichord. With new instruments, further restoration work, concert work and teaching, time is planned out many months ahead; but I hope to be able to offer the Ruckers copy during 1982.

Malcolm Rose has his workshop adjacent to his house at 1, The Mount, Rotherfield Lane, Mayfield, Sussex. He is currently making: a two-manual harpsichord after Henri Hemsch, 1756, an Italian polygonal virginal after de Perticis, 1684, and an Italian rectangular spinet after Guarracino of 1678.

CHAPTER 5

Robert Goble and Son

The Goble workshop is attached to the family house, a beautifully built red brick building centred round an old kiln. One's eye is caught by a vintage Aston Martin in British racing green. This is not an exhibition piece but the standard runabout of Andrea Goble, the head of the firm and the son of its founder, Robert Goble. The workshop itself

is spacious and well organized, with harpsichord cases on their sides in groups of up to half a dozen in various stages of completion. The firm have found that to be able to pay realistic wages and charge reasonable prices, the best method is to build instruments in batches. In this way the basic construction, including keyboards, is done on perhaps twelve clavichords or spinets (smaller numbers for harpsichords) and then they can be finished as required. A small number of workmen and apprentices are at work. The place is about the size of the old Ferrari machine shop at Modena, and has a similar air of planning and precision. Up a flight of stairs one moves into the old workshop, now used for finishing, voicing and tuning. Two lacquered harpsichords are almost complete, a Dulcken and a Taskin, and one finds Robert Goble still at work, incapable of relinquishing his profession of craftsmanship.

[98]

ROBERT GOBLE AND SON

ANDREA GOBLE:

The name Goble is probably derived from the Huguenot name Gobelin and our family ancestors may have come from Flanders in the seventeenth century and settled in Sussex. There seems to have been a tradition among them of working on the land or in rural crafts.

My great-grandfather was an estate manager in Earlham and his son John Goble moved to Thursley, Surrey in the first years of this century. There he set up his business as a wheelwright and blacksmith. Until the outbreak of the First World War trade flourished with the production of all kinds of farm wagons, bakers' carts and other specialized types of vehicles, using local timbers which were cut on the premises by travelling pit sawyers. Although of small but wiry build he could perform several feats of strength for the amusement of the young, rounding off by licking a length of red-hot iron! He was also in demand at village dances with his accordion.

My father Robert Goble, born in 1903, was brought up in an atmosphere of country craftsmanship where knowledge of timber and good workmanship were of prime impor-tance. His first connection with early music arose when Arnold Dolmetsch came to Thursley in 1917 and my family helped him find timber to be prepared for the clavichords and spinets with which he was experimenting at the time. Arnold Dolmetsch soon moved again, to nearby Haslemere, and my father, who had been inspired by the music and the precision of the woodwork at Dolmetsch's, joined them as an apprentice in 1925. He worked there until 1937 and specialized in helping to develop the early Dolmetsch recorders which he turned while Arnold voiced.

My mother Elizabeth had been a pupil of Arnold Dolmetsch since 1922, studying the harpsichord and viol. My parents married in 1930 and lived in Haslemere where I was born. I was named after Andrea Pallas, whose brother Marco was the founder of the English Consort of Viols, an enthusiastic champion of the early music revival generally, and who is also my godfather and a life-long friend of the family. In 1937 my parents set up their own workshop, in Haslemere, where a cabinet maker and an apprentice were employed. Any enterprise devoted to early music was inevitably a pioneering venture at that time. There was considerable resistance to this revival. The famous remark attributed to Sir Thomas Beecham about a harpsichord sounding like a birdcage being played with a toasting fork was symptomatic of the attitude taken by some of the musical fraternity. The problems of a new business were successfully overcome and my mother's musical and artistic gifts combining with my father's practical ability resulted in a very successful partnership. One of my recollections is of rafters being chopped away to allow the removal of our first harpsichord from the attic where it was built. Recorders were an im-portant part of our early production and prices ranged from £2 12s. 6d. for a descant to £15 for a bass!

[99]

Robert Goble and Son: two-manual harpsichord after the 1745 Dulcken,
in green lacquer with gold leaf banding.

My earliest musical experiences were of performances of the St John Passion in the
Haslemere Hall, when my mother played the harpsichord continuo and sometimes took
the alto part. Choral music has played and continues to play a large part in my life:
singing treble in the choir at St Edward's School, Oxford, has led to a participation in
various choirs. Fortunately Oxford provides many opportunities for this activity. Being
brought up in a family where the discussion was of music, harpsichords, timber and practical matters generally, led me from an early age to appreciate natural history. One of my

hobbies is planting trees, and another, starting with a natural-history outing when I captured my first swarm, has been a permanent interest in bee-keeping.

In 1948 I left school, and joined the family business a year after it had moved to its present location in Headington, Oxford. We were lucky to find a large rambling house built round a brick kiln in several acres of natural woodland under Shotover Hill. The garage which had accommodated six cars became our workshop. In 1967 a new building was erected for the cabinet making, and the garage was divided into finishing rooms for stringing, voicing and tuning.

During this early period at Oxford we received several interesting orders including one for a seven foot long harpsichord from Gustav Leonhardt. After some teething troubles, which my father and I flew to Holland to correct, this instrument performed well for some years, and we have recently heard that it is being restored in America. During the same period our instruments began to be in regular demand with numerous British and foreign musical institutions, including the BBC, and they have had to withstand hard use as teaching instruments in centrally heated conditions. We are very proud of the fact that George Malcolm has often used our eight foot long concert model over a number of years for his records and numerous solo engagements.

In 1954 I met Una, my future wife, at that time a history student at Oxford; we met as members of a madrigal group at Keble College. Our eldest son, Anthony, joined the business in 1975, specializing up to the present in the finishing side. He was fortunate in being taught to tune by Sybil Moscure during one of her visits to Oxford: at one time she had tuned for Wanda Landowska.

Our workforce has always been small, usually numbering between five and seven members. Visitors to Greatstones are most welcome: individuals and school parties can be shown the workshop and play the instruments in quiet surroundings.

The total of instruments which we have produced since 1937, including clavichords and spinets, is now 750. Probably our best known instrument is the eight foot long concert model, of which approximately eighty have been built. Its specification has always been 16ft, 2 × 8fts, 4ft, coupler, lute and two harps, all controlled by seven pedals. This seems to be a logical development of late eighteenth-century practice, when Taskin was introducing knee levers and leather plectra, and Kirckman and Shudi were designing new methods of changing registration. In our concert model the string scaling is long ($c^2 = 16$ inches) which, combined with the 16ft register adds considerably to the tension sustained by the frame and results in a marked sustaining tone. These instruments are basically of more robust construction than those of the eighteenth century. The aim we have set ourselves has always been to combine elegance, reliability, mechanical sophistication and a classical clarity of tone.

Robert Goble and Son: two-manual harpsichord after Christian Zell,
1728, in black lacquer with Chinese red and gold interior.

Of course this model has undergone various changes in construction and soundboard
layout since the first one was built in 1952. It gradually became apparent that the
longitudinal system of bracing which we used at first was inadequate to retain the case in
a stable condition. No bottom boards were fitted at that time; these are of course a basic
requirement for traditional methods of building. The modern Goble instruments have

Robert Goble and Son: single-manual harpsichord after the Spanish instrument in the Courtauld Institute, in dark blue lacquer with marquetry
and gold leaf decoration.

gradually evolved backwards to a traditional system of strutting. There were many stages
of this evolution which took twenty years, and our instruments can be dated by their
form of construction. Our approach to building has always been to use modern materials
and techniques where they do not affect tone adversely and can add to reliability. Well
designed light Delrin jacks, Delrin plectra, metal slides and modern glues can all save

time and reduce costs. However, for reproduction instruments traditional wooden jacks and slides can be incorporated when the customer desires.

In 1970, when we first entered the field of copying an original it was interesting to see that the North European form of construction confirmed our own ideas; it is I believe by far the most stable form with its simple three or four struts angling away from the spine and supporting the bentside. It gives a free and uncluttered resonating area between the bottom and the soundboard.

After the important case, the soundboard is the heart of any harpsichord and here adherence to the simple classical form is essential for "reproductions". However, on our modern range the soundboards all have an arrangement of bars passing right across and under the bridge. They transmit vibrations across the grain of the soundboard and so produce the many upper partials which are characteristic of the harpsichord. We use European white pine for all our soundboards. This and spruce were the traditional materials of the Northern makers.

In the last decade, following visits to collections abroad and in this country, my interest has been increasingly focused on the challenge of copying original instruments. Our first move into this field was a reproduction of the Taskin harpsichord in the Russell Collection in Edinburgh. After twenty years of building a successful range of modern instruments it has been an enjoyable experience to gain some insight into the economy and refinement of construction which characterizes the work of the early masters, based as it was on an unbroken tradition of several hundred years.

Our present range of reproduction harpsichords includes a copy of the 1745 two-manual Dulcken in the Smithsonian Institute, Washington, a spectacular late Flemish harpsichord of great sonority. Another double-manual model follows the Pascal Taskin of 1769, a typical example of the French school of harpsichord making. The depth of case, differing string lengths and plucking points result in a remarkable contrast between these two models. The Taskin embodies the particular expressive qualities so well exploited by Couperin and other French composers. The Dulcken on the other hand is ideally suited to the more intellectual and impersonal style of Bach, while at the same time it has all the incisive brilliance required for Scarlatti.

Our Spanish single-manual is a copy of the large and beautiful instrument in the Courtauld Institute, London, of Italian form, comprising an inner and outer case with two contrasting 8ft stops which divide in the bass. It is constructed of cypress and thought to be similar to one of the instruments mentioned in the inventory of Scarlatti's celebrated pupil, Maria Barbara, Queen of Spain.

Successful copies of the best surviving examples of the early Flemish and French makes can only be made by exact adherence to the original woods and scantlings of all constructional members. Soundboard thickness, string lengths, plucking points, etc., all play a vital part in recreating the original sound. The many intangibles of making a good copy all add to the fascination and frustration of the maker. The prospective purchaser should try as many types of instrument, French, Flemish, Italian and modern, as possible. Records are useful, and most record sleeves indicate what type of instrument is being used. Several museums have series of recitals on original instruments. The flourishing magazines *Early Music* and *The English Harpsichord* give comprehensive information in this field.

The decoration of soundboards was until recently always done by my mother; she specialized in wild flowers and grasses and usually incorporated butterflies and insects. The techniques she used were those she was shown by Mabel Dolmetsch when she was a pupil at Jesses.

We now have several artists who do painting for us and the choice is left to the customer. There is Susan Cave, a local art teacher who favours the detailed naturalistic approach, and Ann Mactaggart and Pauline Whitehouse, both of whom paint in the style of the period. The work of Ann Mactaggart is of especial interest as she is not only a fine

Robert Goble and Son: wing spinet in mahogany after the instrument by
John Harrison, 1749, from the Faculty of Music, Oxford.

artist but also a conservator who has done extensive research on the painting methods and pigments used for soundboard and furniture painting in the past.

The final, important stage of harpsichord making is the voicing, an art of its own which is vital to the amount of pleasure that will be obtained from the finished instrument. A fine balance must always be maintained between the weight of the touch, which should be light, and the quality of the tone. This department is now run by my son Anthony. Thus there are now three generations of Gobles working here. I have been privileged to belong to a family which has played a substantial rôle in the revival of early keyboard instruments; that I can see this continuing into the years ahead is something which gives me great satisfaction.

Robert and Andrea Goble have their workshops at their home, Greatstones, Kiln Lane, Headington, Oxford. The harpsichords currently made are: A Flemish two-manual after Dulcken (the one in the Smithsonian Institute); A French two-manual after Pascal Taskin and a Flemish single-manual after Andreas Ruckers (both in the Russell Collection, Edinburgh); a Spanish single-manual (after the Courtauld Institute instrument); their own design of a two-manual instrument in three sizes; a modern spinet and one after John Harrison 1749 (in the Oxford Faculty of Music). A new model is a two-manual harpsichord after Christian Zell (in the Museum für Künst und Gewerbe, Hamburg), and in addition there are two clavicords and a little 4ft virginal. The group photograph at the head of the chapter is of the Goble family, Robert and Elizabeth Goble, Andrea, and grandson Anthony.

CHAPTER 6

David Law

The Department of Musical Instrument Technology at the London College of Furniture has a long history, principally in the service of the piano industry, and in recent years has expanded to include virtually all instruments made of wood, bowed and fretted instruments, woodwind, and now early keyboard instruments. Since 1974 there has been a

full time course in the making of harpsichords, spinets, virginals, clavichords and early pianos and this is currently being expanded into a four-year higher diploma course. Until recently it was run by David Law, a harpsichord builder with a remarkable gift for spreading enthusiasm, and a sense of invention and adventure. Students under him work methodically: plans are drawn in full scale and mock-ups of actions are made comprising an octave or so. Historical instruments are copied, but not slavishly. Where possible, instruments are examined "live" rather than from plans and instruments owned by the section's founder, Michael Thomas, have played a valuable part in providing students with first hand experience.

There is great interest among students in the problems of tuning instruments to various historical scales and temperaments. John Spice, a part-time lecturer in ordinary piano tuning, accepted the challenge of devising and effecting practical teaching methods for historical temperaments. To this end he has had to undertake his own research, for it is by no means easy to ascertain exact details of historical tuning. His combination of research with practical teaching methods was very gratifying to encounter.

The shadow which hangs over the course is the question of the available employment which will await the graduates. My impression is of a contraction of employed journeymen, and this means that the graduates will face the problems of establishing their own businesses which will be far from easy. A very large amount of capital is required to acquire premises and somewhere to live, machinery, stocks of raw materials, instruments to show, and enough to live on for several years. The newcomer can only get his foot in the door by competing in the low price bracket, and this area is affected by the second-hand market, at present awash with second-hand kit-instruments. It is one of the axioms of trade that one is not in business to manufacture a product, but to make a profit; but in harpsichord making, of all businesses, the product must come first with the result that profits come rarely. Harpsichords are quite easy to make but making a living out of making them is extremely difficult. As always, those with the entrepreneurial edge will do best, but it must be admitted that so far few who have had this edge have advanced the art of harpsichord making.

DAVID LAW:

I have often wondered what it is that makes people wish to become makers of keyboard instruments. Relatively few people arrive at the profession via musicianship, and most makers have been trained in some other profession.

My own route was as unplanned as that of many others, I suspect. My schooling was very definitely channelled into science subjects for which I am grateful although I had a great deal of reservation both at the time and for the next few years. My hobbies usually revolved around making and repairing things of any nature. I liked music, and tried to mend or improve the instruments that local kids were playing. It was somehow never my serious intention to learn to play any instrument, although had I done so I should now be grateful. At the time I left school, or soon after, I began to run folk-music clubs – at first for no better reason than that I had no means of travelling to the nearest club in-dependently.

During my first four years of employment (in laboratories and later in silkscreen print-ing) my part-time activities grew to such an extent that the inevitable clash occurred and I found myself careerless. I must have been a terrible employee. I became involved with the local (Windsor) musical activities and somehow found rather unconventional employment in a junk shop. This was great fun although poorly paid – I still have some furniture which was obtained in lieu of wages. This shop collected, at first as a result of "house clearances", a number of old unwanted pianos. Much of the contents of the shop could be classified as "unwanted" since any nice pieces found their way directly across the river to the Eton antique shops. Feeling a bit sorry for these pianos, I began to repair what I could and soon we had enlisted the services of a local tuner. Piano tuners are rightly wary of passing on their knowledge, but I managed to convince our tuner that I might not always ruin the instruments, and with his aid I began regularly rebuilding actions, fitting felts, leathers, springs and strings, and re-regulating. To this end, I built a workshop within the shop, in which I also repaired other types of instruments "after hours". It surprised me that it was possible to improve new instruments: and that the older the instrument the better it played and sounded. So much for modern manufacturing industries. (I am still sometimes surprised that players are not more critical of the state of their instruments.)

Clive Dunkley: single-manual Flemish harpsichord made in 1977 after the 1640 Ruckers in the Yale Collection.

At this time (1969) square pianos were relatively plentiful and reasonably cheap. I remember, when first I took one apart, being impressed by the sheer standard of workmanship; I found I preferred their sound to that of the modern piano. I began to repair these square pianos, and received helpful advice from Clifford West who was then working for Michael Thomas. It was not long in fact before I joined him, and by this time I had rather fallen for the harpsichord.

During the next few years I worked on many instruments, both new and old, and made a few myself – I usually had my own workshop somewhere, and could work on my own projects. I had almost unlimited access to Michael Thomas's collection of antique instruments – not one of them is regarded as "pensioned off" and all are played on frequently. A few years of being surrounded by instruments, old and new together, must instil some sense of wonder at the total understanding that some of the old makers had of their craft. However, one's sense of values can in such circumstances be distorted. I hardly noticed a little 1777 Zumpe square piano, eclipsed as it was by more impressive instruments. Yet when I was recently offered a 1784 Garcka square I could not buy it fast enough.

Steven Spencer: rose made in 1974 of pearwood and vellum for a small Venetian harpsichord.

I think it was in 1972 that Mr Philip Shirtcliff, Head of the Musical Instrument Technology Department of the London College of Furniture, asked Michael Thomas to initiate some sort of harpsichord making class. This was intended as a part time study for students who were taking piano tuning and repairing, and fretted instrument making. Michael did this with some enthusiasm, believing as he does in the dissemination of skills and knowledge. However, business commitments meant that he could not attend on a regular basis, and I began to deputise for him. I found the challenge rather invigorating and the atmosphere pleasant, if frenetic. I soon found myself in charge, first for one day per week then two, of the progress of some ten to fifteen instruments and students. I certainly found that I had to learn as much and probably more than the students; I certainly had to learn faster. My experience up to this time had not involved a great deal of woodwork since I was involved mostly with finishing new instruments, and working on existing and occasionally antique instruments. I had of course to do a great amount of preparation work – at that time very few drawings were published, so I drew up instruments either from Michael Thomas's collection, or to serve a particular purpose, or more frequently simply taking an outline of a chosen instrument and "filling in" where necessary, using any available measurements. This all seemed to work quite well, and although inevitably not all of the projects were finished, some three or four single-manuals, one double, a spinet, a virginals and one clavichord were finished successfully. My attitude was that students should learn the spirit of the old makers if possible, rather than slavishly copying (which in any event would have been rather difficult in that situation), and that since we had limited machining and storage facilities at that time, the majority of the work should rely on hand techniques. All moulding sections were and indeed still are worked with scratch stocks. Our only machines were a bandsaw, a 10-inch planer/thicknesser and a drill press – which were shared with the other workshops making instruments, although they were housed in our workshop. You can imagine the noise, dust and activity.

Then something of a bombshell dropped: in 1974 full-time courses in Early Stringed Keyboard Instrument Making began – while I was teaching part-time, three days a week. We still ran part-time "elective" classes too, and fortunately Mark Stevenson, then working in Chelsea, agreed to do one day per week to help. I had to design a course of three years' study, using the additional facilities of the department and of the college, leading to a college certificate. By now, of course, I thought I knew what was wrong with harpsichord making in general and felt that we could run a course which would cure everything at a stroke. Naturally enough the vast inertia of the education system destroyed that idea – nothing within the system can happen either quickly or completely – even if the perpetrators have all the necessary skills, knowledge, energy and luck.

The initial concept of the course was that it was necessary to train the students to a reasonably professional level of competence in building instruments, to have a working knowledge of the different types of instruments, and to instill such historical awareness as was necessary in order that their future careers were coloured as much or more by the work of the old makers as by the work they saw around them from the hands of present-day makers of all persuasions. Academically, they should be taught acoustics, the mathematics of sound – a subject dubbed "Musical Engineering", timber technology (cell structure, timber identification, bugs and their elimination, seasoning principles . . .), wood finishing, history of music, some chemistry and physics, metal work, and machine woodwork . . . in short a course of additional learning to enable the student to have advantages over those few people in apprenticeships with instrument makers. This part of the course proved quite hard to run since the subjects were not always liked by students who could not see the future advantages. Anyway, it was some time before we found out the precise subject-matter needed.

In the workshop the original idea was that during three years each student should make one Italian harpsichord, one virginals or spinet, a double-manual, and possibly a clavichord. It did not seem too much to ask. Time has proved that such a task is virtually impossible in a college situation, and anyway it is not necessarily the best way to learn. Only one person, John Rawson, managed such an output, although two finished instruments and most of a third was achieved by rather more students. Nowadays, two instruments and a joint project by any one year of students seems much more realistic.

We had a large problem regarding voicing: it took so long for a student to make the first instrument that by the time it was nearly ready to play they were anxious to begin the next. In addition, since we had only one workshop it was a matter of room hunting to find anywhere quiet to teach voicing. This can really only be done individually. You show the student how to set up the action, do a bit to help, then leave them to suffer for a few hours, then go back and correct. We could not for the same reason teach tuning (and at first there was opposition from the piano tuning staff to this being taught). That problem is now, thankfully, solved due in the main to the superlative efforts of John Spice, who took it upon himself to study the required temperaments and work them into a "method" similar to those used in the teaching of equal temperament by the piano tuners. The college did not have instruments of its own – in fact we would have had nowhere to keep them. Neither did the department have models of actions, drawings or photographs. So naturally the formation of any method or policy took some time. I tried to find a method for doing every little job in the most logical and foolproof manner possible, be it constructing a case, simply stopping one piece of work sliding on another while glueing, marking out and making keyboards, or setting out string positions.

We soon found a policy where glue was concerned, when a frame of an Italian harpsichord (minus sides) was dropped on to a corner of the floor from a height of a few inches only: it had been glued with cascamite, and every joint between knees and liner cracked open . . . and of course repair was impossible. So now we use mostly Scotch or hide glues, and recently for some jobs the alphatic resin "Titebond" or "Woodworkers Glue". This dries hard, unlike white glue, and can be released by heat and moisture, yet sets quickly. I do not like using it on hardwoods, however, because I feel it does not penetrate sufficiently. I do hope nobody uses it on bridges or when glueing soundboards in: it is still something of an unknown quantity, and I remember having to assist in the removal of a soundboard from an antique harpsichord which had been "repaired" in the 1940s, using the then new white glue (PVA). I would not wish such a job on anybody.

These little methods of mine were intended to make up in some part for the lack of continuous tradition (such as violin makers have) or workshop practice; to look at the reasons why something is done, and relate it to the materials used, and the results required. They were certainly never intended to be a part of any book of instructions and I hope my teaching notes will never be viewed in that light. Teaching has the effect of making the teacher question everything down to the most minute details of technique. You have only to try to show somebody how to carve a piece of timber, sharpen a tool, or spin, in slow motion, a loop on the end of a recalcitrant piece of music wire to see what

Ian Tucker: Venetian harpsichord made in 1978, after an early sixteenth-century instrument formerly in the Michael Thomas Collection, in sycamore with ebony inlay.

I mean. Invariably the first demonstration is so bad that I now tell the student that it will be a lesson in "how not to do it".

Most of the students' instruments are made from drawings of old instruments sold by various museums. One or two have been measured and drawn at college (kindly lent by Michael Thomas for that purpose). "Workshop" drawings are always made from these, and often the compass is altered to suit particular requirements. For a first instrument the student pretends to be his or her own first customer. We have an increasing number of students who play quite well, and lessons in playing techniques are given by Dilys West, a long-standing friend. The college has a harpsichord made as a joint project by Ian Tucker and Roger Murray who both left in July 1979. This was envisaged as a 5-octave "general purpose" single-manual, and to achieve this a *grand ravalement* was done on paper to the 1640 Yale Ruckers, using R. K. Lee's published drawing. The result although known as the "College Ruckers" is in fact much more like a French harpsichord than Flemish, as one might expect. Other instruments were made from the same drawing at the same time. This sort of activity proves most instructive, since the results may be compared at leisure and in depth.

On rare occasions, students use commercially available jacks; but usually they make their own, since then at least they know what makes a good jack and how tricky it is to work with bad ones. Likewise all keyboards and registers are made. I use a jack design closely based on Shudi and Kirckman jacks, since I still find those old jacks and registers pleasant to work on – the workmanship was of a very high order. Most students use quill for the plectra. I feel that if you can voice quill, then Delrin will not be so difficult; and if you use the old side damping you see how much humidity changes affect a soundboard and the height of a string band. It is better to know the devil and his works (the old enemy humidity) than never to see the results of expansion and contraction of soundboards. Students usually keep their first instruments, so if they are largely traditional in concept they will be aware of the faults as well as the advantages of the old methods of construction and of action regulation, and so be able to evaluate any improvements and alterations they or others see fit to incorporate in their instruments.

At present (December 1979) we have nine full-time and two part-time students in the second and third years, of whom five are girls, and four are foreign students.

The instruments under construction are a 5-octave double, based somewhat loosely on the Vaudry in the Victoria and Albert Museum – using William Debenham's drawing, and another unaltered version; a 5-octave clavichord after Hoffmann, and a GG–d^3 aligned keyboard double, enlarged from the drawing of the Russell Collection transposing double-manual Ruckers; a bentside spinet after one in the same collection; and a version of the 1769 Taskin; two small Flemish harpsichords (and another one finished recently); a copy of Michael Thomas's 1747 Sebastian Garnier GG–d³ double-manual; an Italian harpsichord and a spinet after instruments in the Royal College of Music (Donaldson Collection), and two Italian instruments developed in college from "first principles". Tuition is given in playing techniques and tuning in a number of different temperaments from Pythagorean and meantone through Werckmeister, Rameau and Kirnberger to equal temperament (the latter seems rather unpopular with the students).

Miles Hellon: modern clavichord, made in 1976.

We have a system for calculating string gauges which seems satisfactory and is based upon supposedly original string diameters and lengths, combined to give graphs of tension against compass which seem to be markedly different for the various types of instruments. It is a bit longwinded but at least takes away some of the guesswork — the results seem acceptably good. We still find difficulty in finding strings made of materials comparable to the old flexible strings of wrought iron, but progress is being made and it should not be long before a good substitute is available. A flexible wire sounds so much better than spring steel in the tenor. The college has recently taken delivery of a modern string winding machine of German manufacture, so students should be able to make the open wound strings needed for late clavichords and square pianos.

Further Education in this country has been changing over the last few years — a national validating body has been set up (the Technicians' Education Council) to create a series of syllabuses in a particular form, for every subject from management studies to basket work. September 1979 saw the first intake of students embarking on this course in the Musical Instrument Technology Department, the staff having designed courses, re-designed courses and written syllabuses over the past two years. The course is split into two two-year blocks: first the TEC Diploma (for which students apply for discretionary grants from their Local Authority), followed by TEC Higher Diploma (for which the selected student is given a Mandatory Award). This system, with its carefully designed and controlled programme, is meant to produce musical instrument technologists, with a specific bias towards a particular family of instruments, as well as giving the relevant background general education.

Three years has always seemed far too short, anyway, and I can foresee the time when anyone who has satisfactorily completed the first two-year course being able to work for an established maker or firm without much additional training, and the students completing Higher Diploma being exceedingly well equipped to start a career making instruments. Hopefully such students would seek work with an established maker; it is the best way to gain experience – a few years in college should be regarded only as a beginning, as with any other subject.

For my own part, I feel that I need a change. My recent professional activities have been increasingly curtailed due to my teaching commitments and the increasing time it takes for British Rail to convey me to London. I never intended to teach for long, since I believe that a specialist subject should only be taught by a practising maker, and at some point one accepts as a compromise that it is better to change course and turn to the activities most necessary to moral survival.

There are a few types of instrument that I have become increasingly interested in: a small clavichord of my own design, and the very fine Hoffmann clavichord of 1784, owned by Michael Thomas, of which he has kindly allowed me to make drawings; small domestic harpsichords based on those of the Ruckers family, compass enlarged by use of a broken octave to GG/BB–d^3; and various virginals. Although I have a reasonable experience of large harpsichords, I feel happier making the smaller and more inexpensive instruments. They suit my present workshop better, although times may change that. Harpsichords certainly are rather expensive nowadays and should be, if they are well made. Still, I would rather see the time and money spent on quality than on quantity, and with only such frills of decoration as are required by the customer. A plain instrument can be just as tasteful as even the most superb, heavily or expensively decorated one. And reliability is usually inversely proportional to complexity and quantity, except perhaps when cost is no object. The history of the traditional instruments has lasted some three hundred years, and for only the last one hundred years of this time (and then for only a small percentage of customers) was the large double-manual common. I quite like small instruments provided they are designed well; and I have a feeling that in the production of large instruments a saturation point is fairly close if it is not reached already. Hopefully we have new generations of players coming along. Thanks to the good work of many performers recently, for example on the radio programmes of the late David Munrow, of Christopher Hogwood and their many colleagues, the musical education of young people has become rather more unbiased and open than at any other time in history – music is not quite so often divided into boring (classical) or fun (pop) as it was – the pop music of nearly a thousand years has been presented in appropriate styles, and many children now learn music on instruments which were merely historical names to their teachers when they were at school. This all helps to make an entertainment of music, which is what it should be, at whatever intellectual level. The makers of musical instruments have a duty (albeit self-appointed) to provide the tools for these future musicians, and I believe we should try to foresee what they may need, and provide the appropriate sensitive and reliable instruments. Makers, players and musicologists have in the past researched and rediscovered a tremendous amount of information; their job goes on, but we should build on their foundations to create simply and reliably, using sound and well-proven designs suited to the music to be played. Many makers who, even ten years ago, were designing plastic actions, trying to "improve" traditional jacks, registers and keyboards, have since found that the traditional jack and action normally works best and is simplest to maintain, either when used traditionally with quill and sidecut dampers, or when used with shorter delrin plectra and flat "hanging" dampers. I find that original Shudi and Kirckman actions are a pleasure to work on.

There seems to be a great interest in restored early square pianos at present. I wonder if this is mostly a matter of investment (since old harpsichords, etc., are in short supply, and expensive), or whether there is scope for makers to start producing new square pianos? Early pianos are rather special. Actions are light and sensitive and the sound is clean and clear, amazingly so in the bass.

I have a great admiration for those makers who can stick to offering only one style of instrument. They should be able to produce a better job than someone who offers dozens of different models, and no doubt they suffer less mental strain. I looked around the workshop in college the other day and counted some fourteen different models of harpsichords, clavichords, etc. . . . and suddenly realized why occasionally I become a bit confused. We know that the Ruckers family produced about eight different models, but probably not all at the same time (or even in the same generation), and they all had the same basic design. On the other hand it is very difficult not to be tempted by variety especially at a customer's request. It is clear that makers today have a different function in

[117]

some ways than in the past, and this is a pity. Imagine that, in some time past, a maker was asked to make an instrument in an alien tradition (rather like asking Henry Ford to make a Volkswagen). This is, in effect, what most makers are asked to do today. The labels Taskin, Hemsch, etc., seem to mean something to the customer, but two makers working from one drawing will quite easily make two totally dissimilar instruments. That a maker should one day be making a Ruckers and the next a clavichord by Hubert puts him in the class of modern makers of antique furniture even if he does not go quite so far as offering artificial worm holes.

Perhaps the problem is that we are not secure enough in our own knowledge and skills and experience to shelter behind no other name but our own. The labels "French", "Flemish", "Italian" have a meaning which, although vague, will indicate that the instrument will be acceptable for the music of the genre. These labels are of value, but we should be confident enough to become makers in our own right and not shelter behind names which have probably little to do with the instruments they appear to define.

The whole copying business has thankfully done what it was intended to do, that is to produce traditionally based instruments rather than plucking pianos. Now it is time for the lesser makers to know their craft well enough to stop messing about with many different models and concentrate on one or two *types* of instrument as makers used to do. In this way the standard of workmanship will show up.

The best respected names today have very little need for "props"; one buys a Dowd and then asks "which one?" rather than "I want a Transuntino, who shall I find to make one for me".

I regard my job as a necessary and fortunately rather pleasant continuation of old traditions, changing naturally with the times, producing something that serves its purpose well. I approach each instrument as a special project, and like to decide fine details of design and decoration with the customer – to be involved with him or her in the creation of that particular instrument. No maker can produce his best work without having the feeling that the result is really fit for its purpose, both musically and aesthetically.

I like working on antique instruments, too, but find the moral position incurred confusing. Some old instruments are quite unrestorable and probably should only be drawn. Others need only "running repairs" and could be kept in playing order. If any of my instruments are around in two or three hundred years, I would rather they were altered, repainted, rebuilt, than stuck in a glass case as a curio. But then, without that attitude there would be fewer surviving instruments for us to study today.

Perhaps this is above all what I find so enthralling about making keyboard instruments, that all the time I find new ways of doing things, questions that need answering, and unexpected results: nothing is ever quite the same the second or the twenty-second time.

David Law (address: 100 Amersham Road, High Wycombe, Bucks.) is currently accepting orders for single-manual and two-manual harpsichords, and virginals, based on certain extant Ruckers instruments; and clavichords based on Hoffmann 1784 (FF to f^3, fret free), the small fretted instrument in the Russell Collection, and the manuscript of Henri Arnault de Zwolle c. 1435. He also undertakes restoration work.

CHAPTER 7

✤

John Rawson

John Rawson rents a small workshop in Clerkenwell, in an old warehouse building which is now converted into craft units; he shares this with Miles Hellon, a restorer. Their room is packed with stocks of timber, and made more crowded by the modern machinery they need for working it. At John Rawson's end there hardly seems free space

to build a clavichord, let alone a harpsichord. In fact, he manages to find room to build a full-size harpsichord or a fortepiano there. On the wall is racked a beautiful collection of old moulding planes; in one corner there is a miniature harpsichord which he is preparing for his daughter. Once, such instruments were played by the princesses of Europe – now the daughters of harpsichord makers are their privileged owners. John Rawson is tall and looks young: in fact he is one of the few current makers to have worked with Thomas Goff. He is precise, both in his craftsmanship and in his words. He is extremely knowledgeable, both about harpsichords and their makers and knows exactly what he is doing and what he is going to do.

JOHN RAWSON:

I do not know whether I would ever have started to make harpsichords if I had not met Tom Goff. Our encounter came at a formative moment in my life, when I was in my late teens. However, this was many years after I first began to make things.

My career as a craftsman began when I was about four years old, sticking cardboard together with gummed paper tape, all that was available in wartime. We lived in the country, miles from anywhere, and I snipped away obsessively, making just about everything that could, or could not, be made of cardboard. My family were entirely literary, my mother being a translator, my father a dramatist, and my sister later an academic: they really did not understand me at all. My mother's interest seemed somewhat negative – she worried about the vast amount of gummed paper I licked, but I rejected her alternative, dampening it with a sponge, because this reduced the adhesive quality of the paper. The search for perfection began young. My father was always very interested in what I was making, but he could do little to help as he knew nothing about making things himself, indeed there were absolutely no tools in the house.

This situation was, however, improved when later I went to a school with a good workshop, University College School in London, where I was taught woodworking by George Stephenson (a descendant of the locomotive builder). I used to go to his workshop, after school had finished for the day, and work on projects of my own under his supervision. I built several pieces of inlaid furniture, a loom for weaving, a barrel organ and a grandfather clock. This last had an elaborate case and face and a movement made entirely by hand, all the cogwheels being cut out with a needle file. George laid the foundation of my skills, both in wood and metal, and encouraged me for many years. Recently he proposed me for membership of the Art Workers' Guild, to which I was admitted as a musical instrument maker, not as an architect, which I had become meanwhile.

By the time I was sixteen I had filled my parents' house to the eaves, not just with furniture but with other items as well, for in my spare time I did bookbinding, pottery and weaving. Indeed I was still unsure of the direction in which I wanted to go. It was then that a friend of my parents took me to see Tom Goff. He introduced me to his instruments, he explained how he made them, and pressed me to do the same.

When Tom Goff started to make harpsichords the present growth of interest in, and knowledge of, the traditional methods of designing and making keyboard instruments had scarcely begun. He started working almost by himself. He had left a career at the Bar, many years before I met him, to learn harpsichord making from Herbert Lambert, who had added amateur harpsichord making to his profession of photography. Tom was distantly related to the Royal Family and was obviously fairly well-off. He lived in a huge red-brick house in Pont Street, near Sloane Square in London, with his butler in the basement. The high gloomy rooms on the ground floor of the house were full of his harpsichords, which he rarely sold, though he hired them out for concerts. Above that, the middle floors were often let – Lord Waldegrave and his family lived there at one time.

John Rawson: fortepiano after Anton Walter, *c.* 1795, in walnut, inlaid and cross banded.

And then, right at the top, in two floors of attics, for the Pont Street houses are somewhat Dutch in design, he had his workshop scattered over several rooms. One room for himself, one for his cabinet maker, Cobby, one for passing helpers or students, one for polishing, one for storage.

Cobby – he was always called by his surname – was a genuine salaried highly-skilled craftsman of great experience, who was with Tom for many years. He did all the cabinet making, and his straightforward insistence on only the highest standards of work made a great impression on me. I remember that he could distinguish a true right-angle, 90°, from a corner of 89° or 91° at a touch of his finger and thumb. I made him prove this to me as it seemed so incredible. But it was typical of his approach. In consequence Tom did not have to do much of the work with which less skilled people are taken up; his instrument cases were always expertly made with great economy of time, effort and words.

Tom himself, though highly skilled as a cabinet-maker, generally concerned himself with the actions, stringing, tuning and voicing. He played very well, and filled his house with musicians, many of whom came regularly to practise. He was not an adventurous maker, he made only three sorts of instrument – a large double-manual harpsichord with a metal frame, a small double-strung chromatic clavichord, and a very small single-strung chromatic clavichord. The decoration varied but not the instruments. Indeed he sought to maintain a high unvarying standard. And to do this he used, for example, a lot of metal templates in the construction. The smallest clavichords had a thin tone and few were made. The larger clavichords were very successful, sounded well and were made in some quantity; they had a pressure plate over the strings and a fairly thick piano-style soundboard barred straight across underneath. The harpsichords, made with pedals, were very complicated, all registers being capable of half as well as full engagement, but they produced relatively little volume for such large instruments.

Tom had started his work on harpsichords many years earlier, long before all the recent research was begun, and I think he must have followed Herbert Lambert's ideas fairly closely, basing his instruments loosely on Kirckman's later work. He brought to it such modern knowledge and techniques as he felt to be appropriate, but did not do much research himself or make many experiments. However, as he did not discuss his approach with me I never found out why he did things that way. What I remember most was his and Cobby's dedication to fine workmanship, and his love of harpsichord music.

During the years that I knew Tom Goff I made a number of clavichords under his supervision. But it was not until I had committed myself to a training in architecture that he offered me a place in his workshop. By then it was too late and I went off to Cambridge.

I worked at architecture for years, but with the deterioration in the economic situation in the early seventies, I found life becoming increasingly frustrating and decided to go back to making instruments. At this moment I had a stroke of luck. The London College of Furniture was just starting its three-year course in harpsichord making, so I applied and was taken on a week before term began. This was my chance to catch up with the changes that had been taking place and to get back on the network of makers and suppliers.

I was thus enrolled for the first term of the first course. For the whole period that I was at the college Dave Law was the main workshop tutor, assisted by various other people part time. There were lectures on the physics of music, mathematics for instrument makers, timber technology, history of music and so on, and instruction in the practical skills of machine woodworking, tuning, metalwork, gilding, polishing, etc.

As my interests had been from the beginning concerned with keyboard instruments I naturally concentrated on this field. In my time at the college I made a single-manual harpsichord, a double-manual harpsichord, a virginal and a fortepiano. When I began I had listed the various technical processes that I wanted to work through and so my choice of models was influenced by my wish to explore the different techniques.

As soon as I began I ran into problems. As the course was newly established, there was no proper stock of seasoned timber, and using new limewood for keyboards and blockboard for lids and bases turned out to be disastrous. I slowly began to acquire my own stocks of timber and to dry them properly. During the time that I was there the course developed a lot and standards rose in the workshop. One student in particular, Clive Dunkley, an ex-jeweller who did exquisite work, did much to raise the level by his example.

Dave Law is a specialist in soundboards, stringing and voicing. With him we examined the problems of the production of the sound: how to string, quill and voice, and how to make a soundboard. The visiting lecturers were a bonus; Chris Nobbs in particular set high standards. We also studied related crafts relevant to case construction, including metalworking techniques, taught by Chris Browning, and woodcarving and gilding. Teaching in these fields was excellent.

I enjoyed my time at the college and learnt a lot. Indeed without it I could not be doing what I now am. However, my time with Tom Goff and with the college has led me to reflect upon the notion of college training in the crafts.

College courses were originally developed for education in the sciences and humanities. Although they have been used for a long time for craft education, they are less well adapted for this purpose. In an Arts course at a university one man can easily lecture to a large audience in subjects such as History or English Literature, whereas the crafts need a one-to-one relationship and this is well served by the apprenticeship system. The advantage of the apprenticeship is that it allows people to develop at their own rate over a long period through the successive stages of their craft. They do each process again

John Rawson: wing spinet in walnut with marquetry decoration, after
Stephen Keene.

and again until they are skilled at it; there is little limitation on the number of times it is
done and all this time advice is constantly available from a master working close by. This
is very different from a course of lectures with limited workshop time. I believe the
Mittenwald school of violin making achieves an apprenticeship system of education in
that the students study each part of the work separately and repeat it frequently before
moving on to the next part; they do not initially make complete instruments.

To be a good craftsman great patience and dexterity are essential, as is an enquiring and
retentive mind. Experience, as much as principles, is invaluable; experience of all likely
situations, good ways of doing things, disasters to avoid; all sorts of little bits and pieces of
information about all aspects of the craft, all gathered from people of greater experience.

Much of this vital information and experience in harpsichord making was lost during the nineteenth century when harpsichords were no longer made. Tom Goff, and indeed many of his contemporaries, suffered from this, and were in some cases tempted to go down what are now seen to be blind alleys, for example the use of metal frames for harpsichords. Returning to instrument making in recent years I was fortunate to have been able to benefit from the much increased interest and scholarship in early music.

When I left the college I looked around for a workshop, my search starting near my home. But it is not easy to find suitable accommodation in much of London as an instrument maker needs a very small industrial unit, which is unlikely to be permitted in a residential area, and unlikely to be found in an industrial one. A little advertisement in Smith's, the metal dealers, led me to Clerkenwell Workshops in Clerkenwell Close and soon I had a workshop large enough to share with a friend from the course, Miles Hellon. It is on the second floor, overlooking a churchyard, in a substantial Victorian warehouse-building that has been subdivided. We put in some second-hand machines, bought materials and started advertising. Nothing happened. This was not very surprising. But students tend to think that the world is waiting breathlessly for them to appear, when in fact it could not care less. However, attempting to be flexible in my approach to business, I made anything that anyone asked me to, furniture, toys or whatever, and began a small fretted clavichord. I sold it before it was finished and then I made several more. I made a chromatic clavichord for a friend and then some more. I made a couple for the Early Music Shop, and they ordered some more – so I fairly soon began to get established as a clavichord maker. From this base I began to work on larger instruments, both struck clavichords and fortepianos, and plucked spinets and harpsichords.

As I pressed on, with clavichords and spinets in particular, and as my orders increased in number, I began to feel overloaded. With a workshop of limited size I had nowhere to put an assistant, even if I had been able to find one, and I did not wish to double my output immediately. So I started to sub-contract some of the less complicated items, such as decorative hinges and sometimes keyboards, to other workshops. But I found it hard to get consistently high quality from sub-contractors, and this approach also introduced unwanted administrative problems in that I had to draw, specify, and probably provide a sample of each item that I required before I could negotiate a price for it. Then I had to chase progress, and when I finally got it I often had to rectify faulty workmanship. So after all it did little to reduce my workload and most of this work I again now do for myself.

Although I normally follow original designs closely because they embody a wealth of long-tried experience, I have had occasionally to design my own instruments. I have for example recently made a miniature harpsichord for my daughter. In doing this I have come across an interesting problem, which seems to me to raise an important general point. It is that the design of an instrument proceeds in the reverse order to the sequence of operations required for construction. A harpsichord is designed on a drawing-board by choosing the lengths, the thicknesses and the materials for the strings and by relating them in a suitable way to the keyboard and action. When these essentially musical decisions have been made, a case can be arranged around it. In building a harpsichord, the process follows the reverse order, first the case, then the keyboard and action are made, and finally the instrument is strung. If improvements are needed once the instrument is completed, the only change that can be made is to the strings, and even there only small variations can be made to their diameter. Anything greater, such as change of the length or material of the string, will actually invalidate the whole design and may in fact be impossible to do without partial rebuilding, as the strings were determined first and are the

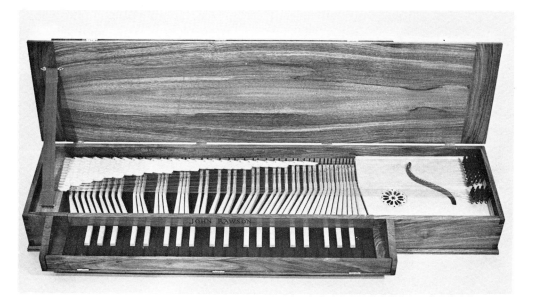

John Rawson: fretted, portable clavichord in solid walnut, after the anonymous instrument in the Mirrey Collection.

basis of the design. This is one of the major problems in making keyboard instruments; it is a circular process begun and ended with the strings. The only solution is to evaluate the completed instrument with great care, and to decide on small changes that must be incorporated in the next instrument. If such changes are to be effective the standard of craftsmanship must be high. Poor work will introduce random uncontrolled variations between instruments that may have greater effect than the intended changes. I have found it important to make a sequence of similar instruments so that accumulated experience can be incorporated. Making instruments is a three-stage process – design, production, evaluation.

Working from designs of instruments by the best makers from the past does at least help with the first stage. On the whole such a maker used designs without obvious faults. It is not easy to be sure of this if the instrument under consideration is not in playing order, but if it is one of a known series it is possible to make certain deductions as to its quality.

Unfortunately copying an old design of known worth does not automatically produce a good instrument; production too has its problems. There are several areas where it is not at all easy to follow original methods. It is not always possible to obtain exactly the same materials. Clearly the makers often used just what they had to hand, but where they selected particular materials for special reasons then I believe that it is important to make great efforts to use the same things. Changes in methods of work have also had an important effect. Although simple jigs were probably used, the original instruments were made entirely by hand. Now, machines are used for accurate repetitive work, producing a different result that may not be so good. Lastly, the preconceived ideas of the public as to the desired standard of finish creates problems. Workmanship of the seventeenth century, beneath its venerable patina, often looks a little crude in these modern days, as we are used to smoothly-finished machine-made products. Copies made to the standards of the old instruments may look unacceptably rough, whereas if they are finished to a higher standard they may not match the original in all respects.

Evaluation is the key stage in the process. When an instrument is finished and voiced and adjusted, the maker and others will have some opinion of it for its musical properties. But only the maker is likely to be able to decide what changes can and should be made in the next instrument to effect the desired improvements.

My different experiences with spinets and clavichords have provoked some thoughts on the different quality of the sound and the way it is produced. Plucking a string is technically an efficient way of making a sound – a small effort applied to a small string can make a loud sound. Instruments of this type are comparatively easy to construct; a large number of makers scattered all over Europe made workable instruments for three hundred years. The use of jacks and quills for plucking allows sufficient latitude for the maker to be able to reduce the strength of the pluck at any part of the compass that may be too prominent in order to get an even or desirable balance to the keyboard, and to set it at its most acceptable level of volume and tonal quality. Instruments that are struck work rather differently. The energy is not efficiently transferred to the string either by the light sharp blade of the clavichord tangent or by the soft piano-hammer that damps the vibrations as it makes them. Struck instruments are inclined therefore to lack volume and, because there is little tolerance for adjustment once they are completed, precision of workmanship and skill in design are very important.

Clavichords were not made as widely as harpsichords. They had, however, a particular appeal in Germany, and it is from this base that the fortepiano seems to have developed. The construction of the soundboard of the clavichord for example is more like that of the piano than that of the harpsichord. It has occurred to me that it was Tom Goff's experience of the piano tradition that led him to make good clavichords but less successful harpsichords. I have gone on from clavichords to build fortepianos, and believe that these are probably the most beautiful keyboard instruments of all. They represent a considerable challenge: not only is the soundboard not easy to make, but the action, which can be likened to a row of 63 identical wooden clocks in closely graded sizes, needs the very best workmanship and the most careful adjustment.

The problems of plucked instruments are not in fact less – they are different. It is comparatively easy to overcome such technical problems as to make them reliable, but it is not easy to make them produce a musical result. There are few first-class old harpsichords in good enough condition to work and sound as they should, but the best to do more than just play – they fill the room with a magical sound of glory which is so marvellous and so unattainable that it is almost enough to make a modern maker throw his tools away in despair. The only modern instrument I have heard that approached this exquisite sound was made by Derek Adlam. Other makers may have achieved this result but I have not heard it either on the concert platform or on records.

The decline of the harpsichord in the face of the growing importance of the fortepiano was part of a radical change in the composition of western music, which has progressively moved towards larger and more complicated harmonic structures. Orchestras have grown in size and now play more complicated music. The component parts of those structures, the sounds of the instruments themselves, have been developed to be, though still recognizably distinctive, purer and therefore more suitable for mixing. This has happened in all the instrumental families, though perhaps it is most obvious in keyboards, where the sound of the harpsichord, with its many overtones, necessitating the spreading of chords, has given way to the purer sound of the piano where more abstruse chords are played unspread. If a sound is pure, with fewer overtones, it is more suitable for mixing with other closely related sounds, as there is less chance of the overtones forming discords. This process has resulted in a gradual change in the tone of instruments.

In addition, three developments have taken place in the construction of instruments. Firstly they have become louder; they now have to hold their own in big orchestras in

John Rawson: keyboard detail of wing spinet after Thomas Hitchcock,
c. 1710.

large halls. The modern world is also a noisier place, and no longer is the clavichord a common practice instrument. Secondly, they are easier to play. They will have to play ever more difficult music so anything that could cause problems to the player must if possible be eliminated. Thirdly, they have become cheaper to make. Such developments may be the outcome of the normal commercial pressures of competition, with mass production causing a simplification of construction or a lowering of standards, or they may have come about because the first two trends caused such a significant increase in complication to the instrument that something had to be done to stop the price rising too much.

It is worth noting that these factors have a converse: a copy of an early instrument may be both difficult to make and difficult to play.

In considering not only instruments but all artefacts from the past and present, it appears that in many, if not all, a classic design has at some stage been achieved; a design which encompasses all aspects such as function, production methods and resources. Classic is here used in the sense of unsurpassed, highly developed and economic or with an inner simplicity. A design that may have endured for a period without alteration, as did the bicycle. It may, however, disappear quite suddenly as a result of some change in its required function or in the supply of its materials. For instance, the clinker-built boat, used for a thousand years almost world-wide, was ousted by the introduction of a new material, glass fibre; the mechanical watch, used for a hundred years, is now giving way to electronic ones. So it was with harpsichords, which were played throughout Europe for three hundred years, but disappeared in thirty when music's needs were better met by the piano.

It seems to me important that, when instruments of the past are revived, all the surviving examples are considered, both as instruments in isolation, and for their part in the music of their own time as we understand it. Although some of the earliest instruments have a fine tonal quality, they have such restricted keyboards that they can be used only to play music of their own time and no other, thus severely limiting the number of people who wish to use them now. Some of the slightly later instruments have a good tone and a reasonable compass, which make them more acceptable to modern users, and indeed such instruments were popular in their own day, as the survival of similar examples from different workshops makes evident. Into this category I would put Keene spinets and Hubert clavichords, and these I would suggest had the attributes of the classic design. I think standardization is probably the first clue to the usefulness of the instrument – if large numbers of instruments of similar design were constructed they must have worked well. The second clue, tonal quality, is more elusive if the originals do not work properly now, but a combination of fine workmanship, without excessive decoration, and with a controlled development between successive examples from the same maker may indicate a high point in the design.

Harpsichords, being made in different ways in different places, provide several competitors for the title of a classic design, but in my opinion I would have to award the title to Flemish instruments by Ruckers and Dulcken.

Makers of pianos have produced two classic designs, differentiated by their mechanisms. The first is the Viennese fortepiano, perfected at the end of the eighteenth century by Walter, Stein and others, an instrument of beautiful tone and lightness of touch, but lacking volume. The second is the English Action Grand of the middle of the nineteenth century, which had volume but not lightness, and which has endured to the present day.

In making instruments now, it is necessary at times to deviate a little from an ideal classic design, and to compromise for practical reasons. People often want to be able to play instruments at modern pitch, they certainly want to keep them in heated houses, and they may want to carry them around in cars. They may be prepared to compromise a little on materials – Delrin instead of quills for cheapness and convenience, bone or plastic instead of ivory, because of sympathy for the elephants. But not much further; the public has been educated and will not longer accept plywood soundboards, chipboard cases or plastic jacks.

As a maker I have had to tread a middle way between what I would like to make and what other people wish to buy and use; between what I can obtain and stock materials for, and what I can afford to do. These are choices that I never contemplated when I first entered the attics of Tom Goff's workshop, but they are the guidelines of my work today.

John Rawson has his workshop at 27, Clerkenwell Close, London, and is currently making: a wing spinet after Stephen Keene and a similar instrument after Thomas Hitchcock; a fretted clavichord after C. G. Hubert, in the John Barnes collection; a chromatic clavichord and a portable fretted clavichord, both after anonymous instruments in the private collection of Dr Roger Mirrey; an Italian pentagonal virginal after the Marcus Siculus in the Benton Fletcher collection; a fortepiano after Anton Walter, c. 1795 and a harpsichord after Vater, 1738, an interesting German instrument with a short scale and brass stringing, both in the Germanisches Nationalmuseum, Nürnberg.

CHAPTER 8

Mark Stevenson

Mark Stevenson works in a large brick workshop at the far end of the street of terraced Cambridge cottages where he lives and this provides him with ample working space and room for seasoning timber. He has the vital machinery for reducing bulk timber but uses it only for this purpose; in essence his instruments are hand made. At the time of visiting

him two old instruments were being restored: a single-manual Kirckman for a private owner in Somerset and a "French Ruckers" from the Villa Medici in Rome, which seemed characterized by the holes of a species of woodworm of tropical size — a special mutation, perhaps, sent to try an instrument repairer's ingenuity. Mark makes a strong impression with his shaggy beard and vigorous way of speaking and explains the points he wants to make with the very clear certainty that he is right. A scientifically-minded craftsman who has a strong sense of what is important and also practically feasible in the reconstruction of historical instruments.

In his home, he demonstrated a harpsichord some four years old, which he regarded as now playing maturely. One of the odd, interesting things about instrument making is the time it takes for instruments to settle down. They start raw, begin to show some quality after six or eight weeks and then mature gradually. It is a well-held belief of many makers, including Mark Stevenson, that they have to be played regularly in order that they will reach this desirable state. The harpsichordist for whom he made this one had painted it herself in blue with a *trompe l'oeil* decoration of her own design. It is always gratifying to see an instrument which is decorated with a sense of freedom and not as an exercise in imitation.

MARK STEVENSON:

My childhood in Cambridge was not a musical one. Neither of my parents played or listened to music although, to be fair, my mother sang incessantly while cooking, and piano lessons were mandatory. Technical progress, however, was measured in dexterity rather than musical attainment, which was not altogether surprising considering the pieces one was given to play, which embraced the entire kaleidoscope of music from Clementi to Kuhlau. The family never went to concerts and the only other musical stimulations were hymns in church on Sundays and my sister's ballet 78's, the latter of which only succeeded in engendering a lifelong distaste for that particular repertoire.

Most of my time as a child was spent making things out of whatever household refuse I could lay my hands on, ranging from detergent packets and cotton reels to my elder brother's Meccano. More often than not these took the form of slot-machines, with mechanisms heavily loaded in my favour; and the cash, gained from my unwitting (or indulgent) family, went to supplement my finances, which always seemed to be in a parlous state. There was always some project in hand which required financing, whether it was huts or rafts, clocks or radios. I wanted everything to work as in real life and despised models as time wasting. Alas, the grown-ups rarely seemed to understand this passion and one memory springs to mind when at the age of eight I rigged a mast and lugsail (all painstakingly hemmed on my mother's sewing machine) on the front fork of my bicycle. I set sail down the road with the benefit of a stiff breeze on a broad reach, but turning left into the main road, I was obliged by contrary winds to start tacking and was promptly arrested by my father, who was on his way back from the University library for lunch. It seemed most unfair at the time after all that work.

After King's Choir School, where I failed to get into the choir, I was sent away to public school, an experience about which I still have mixed feelings. At the time the particular school would have made Tom Brown's schooldays seem like a continuous vicarage tea-party. The only escape from the gratuitous mental and, occasionally, physical torture was the art room and here my musical education was taken in hand in earnest. While the piano was taught badly (more Clementi) the art master bombarded us with music as we painted. While his tastes were mostly late romantic, and preferably conducted by Beecham whose work he followed with evangelical zeal, it is to him that I owe my basic musical education. I ended up at school sitting A-levels in science and maths, but my main interest at the time was painting and I yearned to go to art school.

Mark Stevenson: two-manual harpsichord after the original by Nicolas Blanchet, *c.* 1720, in the possession of Hugette Dreyfus, in black and white with gilded bands and mouldings. (Collection: Kunio Imai, Japan.)

However, my parents, by the subtle ruse of allowing me to go to the British school at Rome and then to Chelsea Art School for a term between school and university, persuaded me to take my place at St John's, Cambridge.

Rome was a fantastic experience for a shy seventeen-year-old and the time was spent talking, painting and going to concerts. The British school was sent courtesy tickets for every concert and, as the archaeologists and Rome Scholars seemed to have no interest in music, I set about educating myself on complimentary tickets. I still vividly recall my first musical experience there. This was a rare public recital by the Sistine Chapel Choir singing music by Palestrina. I was overwhelmed, not simply because Italian choirs produce a gritty nasal timbre, charged with excitement and emotion, but by the (to me) amazing discovery that music had existed before Bach. While my personal taste in music began to go steadily back in time, I set about gorging myself on a diet ranging from the pre-Renaissance to the avant garde.

After five concerts a week for five months, I knew most of the classical repertoire and a lot more besides and returned to England to go to Chelsea Art School. One term was quite enough. No one there seemed to do much work and the intellectual climate was depressing. I was happy enough to take up my place at Cambridge and went up in the autumn of 1962.

At Cambridge I read for a degree in Archaeology and Anthropology and then, for the last two of the three years, the History of Art. I spent most of my spare time working for the then thriving undergraduate tabloid *Varsity* where I was critics' editor for a time, and with three essays a week to write life was incredibly busy. I talked, listened to music, discovered the opposite sex and irritated my professors by arguing with them and sometimes being right.

In my first long vacation, I saw a factory-built clavichord in a music shop and decided that I could do better. I had no idea that there were merchants from whom one could buy bridge pins and the odd bits of chandlery in an instrument, so these I made myself out of ground down nails. The instrument worked and went into my rooms in college; I started practising the keyboard again. This first clavichord was followed by a virginals made during the next vacation. I was not so happy with this and on graduating destroyed it and set about making a harpsichord proper. I also had to set about earning my keep and managed to get some part-time teaching in a couple of London art schools. By the end of the first year I was teaching three days a week and could afford to find a flat in deepest Battersea which doubled as residence and workshop. I was able to use my salary for tools and timber and soon a combination woodworking machine was squeezed into the tiny flat. The bed went up on stilts to accommodate a bandsaw underneath and the floor seemed permanently knee deep in shavings, out of which one climbed to sleep. Another flat in the house was occupied by a music critic and, by accompanying him on assignments, I was fortunate enough to go to all the best concerts without depleting my limited budget.

It soon became clear that I needed more space. To buy a property one needed a mortgage and to get a mortgage one needed a full-time job. I decided to accept a lectureship at Kingston Polytechnic, where I had already been doing two days a week in the History of Art department, and began looking for suitable property. Alas, it was the time of the property boom and, while my salary went up each year, property went up faster. I was further than ever from owning my own workshop.

During this period my day started around 6 a.m. and I could get in a couple of hours' work before college. By six in the evening I was back home and could work again until midnight. As full-time lecturing entailed only four days a week, I had three days which I could devote entirely to the workshop, and then of course there were vacations. In 1968 I managed to obtain the lease on an old sculptor's studio on the Chelsea–Fulham borders

Mark Stevenson: virginals after the Couchet in the Vleeshuis Museum, Antwerp, 1650, with block printed paper decoration. (Collection: Melvyn Tan, London.)

and shortly afterwards gave up teaching apart from one day a week at the newly formed course at the London College of Furniture.

In 1976, again pressed for space, I moved to the present workshop in Cambridge and gave up my last formal teaching commitment. It was certainly not the easiest way to become an instrument maker, but most of the experience gained has stood me in good stead. I exhibited at the First London Exhibition of Musical Instruments in 1973 by which date I had been building instruments based closely on originals for some time.

Perhaps the most important thing for a young maker is to have his instruments played in public and by the best professionals. Musica Reservata commissioned an archicembalo which was one of the four instruments I took to the Bruges exhibition in 1974, along with a Taskin and a spinet after Hitchcock. The gifted young French harpsichordist and composer Claire Schapira ordered one of my double-manuals. This was an important break as she had concert and broadcasting commitments in Paris. At a visit to the Festival Estival de Paris in 1976 Blandine Verlet asked to use one of my Blanchets for her broadcast recital and I returned home with a year's work in hand.

The City Literary Institute in London also had a Blanchet of mine at this time and, as they were willing to hire it out for recitals, it began to appear at the Purcell Room and the Wigmore Hall. This was also important as at the time I could not afford to keep a single display harpsichord, and potential clients had to be taken on a trip round London to see various instruments.

These first solo recitals were nail biting experiences, praying that nothing would stick and that the tuning would hold. With no major disasters as yet, I still find the occasions a little harrowing even though my instruments have been used in concerts and recordings by Kenneth Gilbert, Gustav Leonhardt, Blandine Verlet, William Christie and many others.

One of the main problems in harpsichord making today is that the original tradition was lost at the end of the eighteenth century and that the craftsmen working in this field today have had to rediscover skills which are no longer part of an oral tradition passed down from master to apprentice. As such, harpsichord makers of my own generation have had to be, by necessity, self taught. Much of the original information remains, but it has become diffused throughout many other disciplines and much time has to be spent piecing together information and ideas from cabinet makers, turners, decorative painters and, indeed, makers of other musical instruments that did not go out of fashion and whose knowledge, once common to the harpsichord makers, is still passed from generation to generation. There is a perennial problem in copying antique instruments. Should one attempt to make an instrument which sounds like the original does now, or make an instrument which one believes sounded like the original did when new? Because of the

[139]

Opposite: Mark Stevenson: single-manual harpsichord after the J. D. Dulcken of 1747 in the Vleeshuis Museum, Antwerp. Painted in black and white with gilded bands and mouldings.

gradual increase of compass over the three centuries of harpsichord building, old instruments tended to be superseded by more modern ones. There is certainly evidence that
viol players preferred an aged instrument, but apart from the French penchant for
rebuilding Ruckers instruments to take a five octave compass, it is unlikely that many
musicians had other than newish instruments. In any case surviving examples do not
suggest that the extended doubles sounded much like the original instruments. Further-
more the number of contemporary eighteenth-century French instruments which were
built new and then antiqued and sold as Ruckers suggest that it was a fad rather than the
search for a well aged instrument. It is quite easy to make a new instrument which sounds
like an antique, but it will be an instrument unlikely to have any lasting quality. These
techniques are well known to violin makers who sensibly frown upon them. However,
many modern makers attempt the suave sonority of an instrument two hundred years old,
thereby condemning their instruments to a short life. It is, moreover, the supreme
anachronism to go to the lengths of playing music on the correct instrument for its
epoque and then to provide an instrument which has a sonority which the composer
could never have lived to hear.

In violin making, a front can be thinned to produce an instantly pleasing effect but over
the years the sound is known to become dull and lifeless. Some contemporary harpsichord makers thin their soundboards excessively, even backing the bass area with silk to
keep it together. Side draft and down bearing (the angles in two planes where a string
crosses the bridge) can also be reduced with the same intention and with similar results.

Another way of achieving an instant effect need not lie in deception, but in laziness or
inexperience. Some makers – and inevitably new or young makers – have no stocks of
the seasoned traditional timbers which were used in harpsichord making. Yellow pine
and Canadian red cedar, which are commercially available from every local builder's
yard, are often used by those who have not taken the trouble (or had the time) to husband
their stocks of poplar, lime, oak, spruce, pear, cherry, walnut and service wood. Some
commercially available timbers when kiln dried have a consistency very like aged (not
simply dry) poplar, the most common timber traditionally used for French and Flemish
cases. Use of these timbers is effective in producing a rich full sonority reminiscent of an
antique instrument but, in instruments built this way, the sound does not last and many
have simply broken up after some years.

The state of the revival is a peculiar one. The instruments built in the first half of the
century indeed attempted to extend an oral tradition of craftsmanship but, alas, the
revival became intrinsically involved with the nineteenth-century concept of perfec-
tibility. There were few lessons to be learned from the piano, any more than one can
graft a new trunk on to the topmost branch of a tree. The instruments produced were

cumbersome, heavy and so different in sonority from the originals that it is strange to imagine that the player thought he was returning to a timbre which would have been appreciated by the composers. These instruments were not even more reliable in action, nor were they more stable in tuning. Instead of the lightness of touch and responsive action of an original, their keyboards have the solidity and responsiveness of a lorry. At a time when there were antiques capable of being put in playing order, it still seems incredible that the twentieth-century makers got it so wrong. However, even twenty years ago the demand for harpsichords was so high that virtually anything which plucked a string mechanically by means of a keyboard could be sold.

Very few makers at this time paid any attention to traditional values, and they were content to produce a keyboard instrument which plucked rather than struck strings. The idea became current that the tonality of an instrument could be designed with engineering principles and that the tone produced was simply a question of manipulating string lengths, plucking points, string gauges and soundboard thickness. The case itself, which is probably the largest element in tone production after the soundboard, was all but forgotten and was built of plywood or blockboard, or any kiln dried timber the maker could lay his hand on.

At the same time, instruments described as "copies" began to be current and the new makers of these began to make inroads into the markets of the makers of "modern" harpsichords with their heavy, open bottomed cases and their pedals. As harpsichord making had become an academic discipline requiring the knowledge of many apprenticeships, a flood of graduate makers (including myself) began to appear. There was no chance of acquiring experience by working for another maker, as virtually none were building copies, so we all had to return to the museums and to start looking at and measuring old instruments and also to start seeking the remnants of the lost tradition when and where we could find them. It was no longer possible to follow an oral tradition and in any case constructional techniques and materials differ so radically in different European countries during different epochs that one would have needed the knowledge of fifteen or twenty apprenticeships. At the same time another watershed occurred, between those who wished to rediscover the lost skills of the old makers and those who thought that musical instruments could only be faithfully reproduced with a micrometer.

The term "copy" is in itself misleading. Anyone who has been to the International Harpsichord Week at Bruges, which takes place as part of the Festival of Flanders every three years, can play half a dozen or more "exact copies" of the Russell Collection Taskin (a popular instrument even though it comes right at the end of the harpsichord tradition). He will find that each instrument is entirely different. In the early days of the revival, there was much talk by writers such as Hubbard and Russell of "plucking points", as if the sonority of an instrument could be manipulated by the variation of this one small element. This naïveté contributed to some of the aberrations of the modern movement, engendering as it does the concept of designing an instrument to produce a specific tone. What Russell in particular seemed to fail to appreciate was that an instrument is an extremely complex interlocking system, the mechanics of which are far more important to tone production than the point along which a string is plucked. If one compares the scaling and plucking points of the Smithsonian Institute Dulcken and the Russell Collection Taskin, one would expect the Dulcken's long scaling and short plucking point to produce an astringent timbre, even on the richer 8ft. This is not, however, the case. The fact is, that the two instruments are constructed on completely different lines. The harmonics of the string which the case and soundboard wish to amplify are far more important than the actual harmonics set up in the string by plucking it at a specific point along it.

In Dulcken's construction he supports the soundboard on a separate interior bentside, and the exterior bentside is braced from the spine by bars cut through this interior panel. The hitch-pin rail covers this gap, but the tension of the strings is not imparted to the portion of the soundboard between the 8ft bridge and the bentside. The soundboard in this area thus stays flat and the shallow dip characteristic of more typical harpsichord construction is not present. Many makers copy Dulcken's instruments in form only and omit his interior bentside which is both awkward and time consuming to make, but this seems to me simply to be producing a working harpsichord without trying to learn the subtleties of Dulcken's thinking.

It is arguable that an exact copy cannot be made. The change in ratio between the lengths of summer and winter mean that there is no way that soundboard wood of quality consistent with that used by the original makers can be obtained. Those who think that copying measure for measure is anything to do with instrument making deceive themselves. The original makers made small changes from instrument to instrument and you will not find even two instruments of the same model by the same builder in which the treatment of the soundboard in terms of measure is identical. It seems obvious that they were attempting a mechanical consistency and not a dimensional one. Two pieces of wood are simply never the same, they vary in density and most important of all in elasticity. In making a copy one needs to divine the maker's original intention and then to treat the wood in order to achieve the same result.

The only real way to learn is to go on repeating the same instrument over and over again making small changes each time. Thus, by controlling the experiment, one can learn as the original masters did, by experience. It is for this reason that it has been important to me to employ apprentices and more latterly skilled helpers. This has allowed me to

Mark Stevenson: wing spinet
after Thomas Hitchcock,
c. 1735, in solid walnut with
the interior decorated with
cross banded walnut, and
mahogany herring-bone
inlays. (Collection: Lawrence
Boulay, Paris.)

increase output while maintaining overall control of the finished product. Now, with
more than one hundred keyboard instruments to my credit I am content to run a
somewhat smaller workshop with two or three assistants.

There has been a confusion in the twentieth century between craftsmanship and
obsessive neatness. The original makers paid little attention to neatness where it was not
visible, as anyone who has examined the interior of an instrument will know. Even
painted finishes were freer than anything which would be acceptable today and the
Flemish makers certainly found that sticking block-printed papers over their instruments
was quicker and cheaper than rubbing down the wood. The best modern makers are now
so skilful in working wood that it is possible for us to render instruments sterile as visual
objects, as if no hand had touched them. Look at the mouldings of an antique instrument.
They were never cut or scraped completely evenly and their slight variations impart a
shimmering life to the work. In contrast, many modern instruments seem to have been

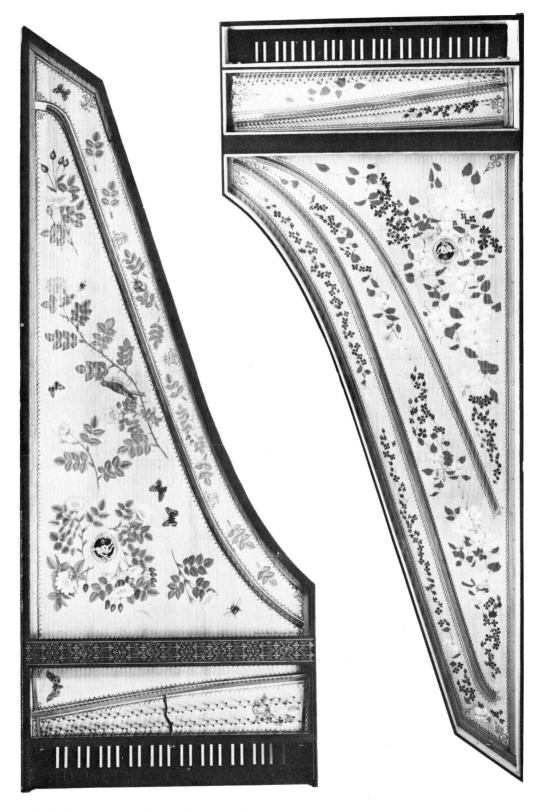

Mark Stevenson: two harpsichord soundboard views. Single manual after the original in the Villa Medici, Rome, *c.* 1700, painted by Rosalind Bliss (*left*) and single manual after the J. D. Dulcken in the Vleeshuis Museum, Antwerp, decorated by Kris Ellam (*right*).

drawn with a pencil and ruler and their makers have failed miserably to enter into the spirit of the originals. A harpsichord is not only something to delight the ear, it is a substantial piece of furniture and needs also to please the eye.

One of the main advantages of buying a reproduction harpsichord is that it remains as valid as the original and is not subject to changes of taste. Those who bought factory-made modern harpsichords in the fifties and sixties (and even later) have not invested well, and find difficulty in selling them when they wish to acquire one closer to an original. A harpsichord is a considerable investment for most musicians who should be entitled to an instrument of which the original makers and composers would have approved, and made with the correct materials. Some makers use commercially available timbers because they have no stocks of what was originally used. The originals have lasted well and a reproduction should be built to last at least as well.

Another consideration is the action. The crudest way to make a key return, and one often used by contemporary makers, is to put a lump of lead in it. Original keyboards were built extremely lightly and the return of the key was effected by carving the underside so that each had not only a similar weight of back fall (or none at all) but also a similar mass. In order to keep the mass and therefore the inertia of the action to a minimum, the key was, in most cases, carved at both ends. With this low inertia, the action is not only light, but fast. While I prefer traditional wood jacks, there is no musical reason why plastic should not be used, as long as they are no heavier than wooden jacks. Keyboards should also be guided from the back rather than the front, as in original instruments. In the modern piano, and in many contemporary harpsichords, the keys are guided at the balance point and the front. This means that any play in the guides allows the back of the key under the jacks to waggle slightly, wasting energy at a critical point and imparting an imprecise feel to the action. Even the construction of the frame supporting the keys is an important consideration. One celebrated modern piano firm claims that its instruments sound better when the key frames are made of pine. It is not so much that they sound better, they feel better, because the player senses the vibration through his fingers as well as his ears. This sort of subtlety is even more important in the harpsichord, where one is dealing with far less energy and where one is in direct contact with the string. A good instrument can be sensed through one's fingers, one's ears and, on a good sprung floor, through the seat of one's pants.

Since 1973, I have tackled an increasing number of restorations both for British and foreign clients and these are an invaluable source of inspiration. A genuine instrument in pieces in the workshop gives one more insight into original constructional methods than any museum drawing can ever give. There is always something new to be learnt: in a seventeenth-century French or Flemish double, recently restored for the French Government, the bottom braces had been inserted with unglued dovetails, radically increasing the looseness of the carcass construction. This may have been common practice – bottoms were often simply trennailed on and, where these joints are found, glued – it may well be the work of later restorers. The quality of tone when two instruments are built with only such a difference is significant. In this and other instruments which I have examined, what one does find is evidence of sure and quick work. It is clear that the carcasses were put together in a matter of hours rather than days, a practice that radically alters the tensions built into an instrument which, as in the Dulcken mentioned earlier, is one of the most important elements in tone production. Like a good omelette, a harpsichord needs to be made quickly. As a case ages, the tensions built into it tend to iron out, significantly maturing the tone. Even very small changes in tension make a vast difference, as when an antique violin has to have the front removed in restoration. The owner must wait months for the instrument to regain its true sound.

It seems clear that the original makers (and those who truly follow them) were seeking a looseness of construction which can only be achieved by very swift work. If even small portions of the interior bracing are fitted twenty-four hours after the case sides, the resonating properties of the mechanical linkage are completely altered. Anyone who has glued a piece of veneer on to one side of a panel will be aware of the tensions created by sticking one damp, though thin piece of wood on to another – the thicker panel will bend under the stress created by the drying and contracting veneer. A case put together in one afternoon is reduced to the same level of humidity and the whole dries together without inbuilt tensions, rather like aspic setting. Evidence of speed and fluidity of construction can be found in almost all French and Flemish instruments and many more besides. In a single manual Francois Blanchet recently unearthed (literally) in France, it is obvious that the upper braces were any old bits of scrap lying around the workshop floor. They vary in dimension and material, have been roughly cut to fit, and nailed in. Some of them still have their bark attached. However, they do their job and certainly went in at the same time as the rest of the frame, without tension or compression. This instrument would be a nightmare for the conscientious copyist armed with calipers and facing the problem of how to find a piece of wood with just the right amount of bark on it.

Harpsichord making is in many respects like Haute Cuisine. Given the basic recipe the chef then relies on his common sense, skill and most of all his experience. The amateur cook who relies on weighing every ingredient and timing each manoeuvre rarely produces good results, except by the occasional happy accident. Just as the same cut of meat varies from piece to piece, a plank of wood is never the same from tree to tree, even from adjacent planks in the same tree. Just as the chef makes adjustments as he goes along, in order to achieve consistent excellence, so must the harpsichord maker weigh up his materials and treat them individually in the light of his experience, both conscious and unconscious. I do not countenance the goulash harpsichord with its case bought from one maker and its keyboard from another. This will satisfy those who like to eat in restaurants serving instant mash and canned vegetables, and the culinary analogy holds true – a kit is for those who think they eat like a Maharajah when they buy a box of do-it-yourself curry dinner: it may be fun but it is certainly not an experience!

Mark Stevenson has his workshops in Upper Gwydir Street, Cambridge. He is currently making the following instruments: two-manual harpsichord after Blanchet, 1720 (collection Hugette Dreyfus); two-manual after Dulcken, 1745 (Smithsonian Institute); two-manual after Thomas Hitchcock, c. 1720 (Victoria and Albert Museum); two-manual after the Franco/Flemish instrument in the Villa Medici; single-manual harpsichord after Dulcken, 1747 (Vleeshuis, Antwerp); single-manual after the instrument in the Villa Medici; virginals after Couchet, 1650 (Vleeshuis, Antwerp); wing spinet after Thomas Hitchcock, c. 1735; clavichords after Hass, 1763 (Russell Collection), after Hubert, 1784, and after a sixteenth-century instrument in the private collection of Dr Roger Mirrey.

CHAPTER 9

Dennis Woolley

I knew Dennis Woolley in the days when he lived at Haslemere but, as I prepare this chapter, he is recently removed to Cumbria and still coping with the problems of altering and rebuilding his new home-cum-workshop. This is an old stone barn, weathered and attractive, looking out along the length of the dale of Dent and which has now been con-

verted into a typical dale cottage with substantial workshops attached. He is a member of the older school of harpsichord makers, those who have passed through the period of modern design and innovation to return to first principles, quiet, capable and immensely knowledgeable. When I visited him he was working with his assistant Nigel Hourahine on a copy of the John Barnes single-manual Dulcken, an instrument I remember as of fabulous tonal quality. Completed, was a single-manual after Hans Moermans, 1584, and also a muselar after Couchet. He is a close but not a precisely exact copyist, often extending a short bottom octave to be fully chromatic, something which many players find useful and which does not detract from the value of a copy.

Dennis Woolley has many of his instruments decorated by Ann Mactaggart, an artist remarkable for her ability to work in the style of all of the important periods of sound-board painting of the past.

DENNIS WOOLLEY:

I had a desire to study piano playing from my early teens but the war and National Service brought interruptions which hampered this ambition. I had been a part-time student at the Guildhall School of Music but it was not until I had finished my service in the Navy that the opportunity arose for full-time study. This was followed by further part-time studies at Trinity College, London, where I graduated in music teaching. My career began as a teacher of piano, at first privately and then as music master at Ealing Grammar School.

It is difficult now to remember the time when the harpsichord had not entered my life, but I first encountered it, I suppose, when a student at Trinity College. Lectures on sixteenth- and seventeenth-century music were held at the house in Cheyne Walk where the Benton Fletcher Collection of keyboard instruments was kept. A remark by George Oldroyd, then professor of music, pertaining to the rôle of the harpsichord in instrumental ensembles has remained in my mind ever since: he likened it to a shimmering thread of silver embroidered into the midst of the musical texture. This image of the shimmering, silvery quality of the harpsichord fascinated me then and, thirty years later, still does.

Dennis Woolley: two-manual harpsichord after Pascal Taskin, 1769, in eggshell lacquer, with gold leaf banding.

Dennis Woolley: two-manual harpsichord after Kirckman, 1772, veneered and cross banded in mahogany.

Teaching was not something I revelled in and the introduction to the instruments at Cheyne Walk made me recognize the pleasure I would find in actual making. Irvin Hinchcliffe (then in charge of the Benton Fletcher Collection) gave me the opportunity to measure some of the instruments and I started on a clavichord, following on soon afterwards with a spinet in the Hitchcock tradition from the same collection.

One of the problems in those early days was that hardwoods were obtainable only on licence, so that I was compelled to scrounge from whatever source I came across. My first soundboards were constructed from wood salvaged from old pianos. My experience of woodwork had been acquired from the laborious putting together of small items such as bookcases and stools and I had to transfer this slowly achieved ability to the process of instrument making. The time spent on those first two instruments stretched into years, although it was of course only a part-time activity.

In those days, unlike the present, there was very little information available on instrument construction and searches in various directions resulted only in vague descriptions of the obvious. So I began the move towards designing instruments which at that time satisfied my own ideas of what they should sound like. It seemed to me, as it did then to other makers, that it was logical to apply to the harpsichord those methods of construction which would ensure mechanical reliability and tuning stability and to strive for a brilliance to match the instrumental forces with which they were then compelled to compete. This concept of the modern harpsichord was very successful, the aims of its designers being fully realized but, taken to extremes, resulted in the self-defeating complexities of mechanical trappings.

Being caught up in this phase of harpsichord making, I too began producing instruments owing but little to their eighteenth-century counterparts except the principle of plucked strings. There was the rigid framed structure which would accommodate the relatively high tension of the long string scaling, the open bottom, the barred soundboard vibrating as one area, all features reminiscent of piano construction. The casework too was often reminiscent of the piano, the projecting keyboard with its sloping cheeks, the long piano-hinges at the lid folds. Power and brilliance were the somewhat elusive goals to be sought after. But at what cost! The touch of such instruments was often heavy, occasioned by the force required to drive the highly tensed strings into activity and the sought-for power was drained away by the heavy masses of bridge and casework.

At the same time, it must be remembered, these instruments served well the many players who were essentially pianists and organists, relatively insensitive to the nuances of touch which the lightly voiced and more resonant instruments make possible. So, undoubtedly, these hybrid instruments did have a useful rôle to perform in establishing the wider use of the harpsichord which is now taken for granted, and in providing a transitional instrument for the majority of players.

Experiments with the structural aspects of the casework, designing framed structures to match the demands of the high tension, trying different string scalings, setting up jigs for jack making, designing pedal mechanisms and making tools and punches all required a great deal of development time. Several years passed during which I was making three or four instruments a year but the demand, always outpacing my rate of production, increased to the point where it appeared possible to relinquish my teaching and devote my time entirely to building.

During those early years I had, of necessity, to get together the minimum of workshop space and equipment to enable me to work single-handed and I had already involved the aid of two cabinet makers. They began by making up just the framed structures for me, then progressed to making complete cases, veneered and polished. Thus, when I eventually gave up teaching I had evolved all the necessary procedures and facilities and had the trained assistance to enable me to expand the business. I was fortunate enough to find a cottage at Liss in Hampshire which had a large wooden hut in the garden. Lovely as was the cottage itself, it was this necessary working space which decided me to buy it.

About twelve years ago, having by now taken on a full-time assistant, Nigel Hourahine, I began to build instruments based upon the classical models of the seventeenth and eighteenth centuries, notably the 1769 Taskin which at that time seemed to epitomize the typical, fully developed, eighteenth-century harpsichord, suitable for playing most of the repertoire. Soon afterwards, these instruments were followed by the production of copies of the double-manual Kirckman, two of which had passed through my workshop for restoration. Although not yet generally in demand, these later English instruments provide a means of realizing much of the music of eighteenth-century England, though equally well suited to earlier English composers. They may very well deserve a revival of popularity. There is certainly a call from outside Britain for this standard English harpsichord, and we continue to build these handsome instruments in their cross-banded veneered cases, occasionally even the lavishly marquetried version.

Close on the heels of these French and English harpsichords were Italian and Flemish instruments, derived from original models which included Sodi, Dulcken, Ruckers, Couchet and Moermans. These instruments are all so different in many ways that one is at a loss to decide exactly what it is that determines their qualities. The Sodi is a late, wide-compass, Italian instrument, having aspects that are extraordinary. It derives from seventeenth-century Italian construction in having a short scale, brass stringing, the simple 8 + 8 with no 4ft, and a cypress soundboard. The body structure, though, is heavy: quite solidly built, rather like a late Flemish harpsichord. The soundboard barring derives from neither tradition, being heavily cross-barred. This remarkable combination gives an extraordinarily rich, full and sustaining quality, especially in the bass, while there is a distinct contrast between the two registers. The Sodi is late to the point of being well into the piano period and yet did not acquire any of the unnecessary stops of the late northern instruments. Sodi was not an innovator or an improver like his contemporaries, he was a man setting out in a completely new direction, and this makes the instrument unique.

The Dulcken is another remarkable example of a harpsichord maker striking out in a new direction, with his double curved side. Both the single and two-manual Dulckens provide a sharpness of clarity throughout their compass which is particularly useful when one needs the quality of transparency for part playing, yet they retain in the lower register a fulsome roundness of tone.

I have used the expression "derived from" deliberately, since, although one can set out to copy an instrument, it is unlikely that such a reconstruction will result in anything more than a close representation of the original. This is not to say that such a representation will be inferior to the creation which inspired it. It may well be a superior instrument, especially if its reconstruction is backed by some considerable experience of instrument making. In any case, the reconstruction will bear the stamp of its maker and reflect

Dennis Woolley: wing spinet after Thomas Hitchcock, in solid walnut
with marquetry decoration.

his philosophy of the craft. Mechanical copying, without an understanding of the
physical properties of the materials used or of their acoustic functioning, may by chance
produce a serviceable musical instrument. It requires a wide spectrum of experience to
ensure consistent results.

In this respect, it may be pertinent to cite as an example the care to be taken with one of
the crucial aspects of instrument making: that of the soundboard. The selecting of grain
structure to suit the various vibrating areas, with the consequent balancing of density and
stiffness (something to which the fingers become sensitive with experience, almost intuitively selecting the most suitable timber to be used in any particular location of the instrument), can influence the quality and quantity of the tone produced. There are many
details in instrument making which require similar careful consideration if something
other than mere copying is desired.

At the present time, the fashionable demand is for instruments based on particular
models of the past. The builder of today must try to absorb the spirit and philosophy of

the makers contained in the surviving instruments, and select the fundamental essentials of each, if he is to produce instruments of similar character. Failing to do this, he will be floundering in a welter of insignificant detail contributing nothing to the success of the exercise. But from this careful study it is possible there will arise a new generation of harpsichords having the characteristics of the original instruments but being closer to the personal expressions of their makers.

Dennis Woolley, workshop address: Tubhole Barn, Dent, Sedbergh, Cumbria, is currently making the following instruments: single-manual harpsichords after Moermans 1584, and Dulcken c. 1750; Italians after an anonymous original of c.1600 and after the Sodi of 1782; two-manual harpsichords after the Dulcken of 1745, the Taskin of 1769, a Kirckman of 1772; spinets after Stephen Keene and Hitchcock; a muselar after Couchet 1650, an original clavichord and another after Hoffmann.

Dennis Woolley:
single-manual
harpsichord after
Moermans, 1584,
with block printed
paper decoration.

MVSICA
MAGNORVM
LEVAMEN LABORVM

CHAPTER 10

Trevor Beckerleg

Trevor Beckerleg lives in the same road as Mark Stevenson, in a corner house at the terrace end, which he has extended backwards into his garden to provide a small but very well-appointed workshop. He has been making harpsichords for some sixteen years and is an experienced experimenter who is still searching for perfection. His system is to decide on a particular instrument, of which he makes a number of cases, and then as he works on each one he introduces variations until he feels that he has mastered that type. When I visited him he was working on a series of spinets. He apologized for the decoration but I found it entirely to my taste – strikingly original in its inlaying and in a quite unexpected style which seemed to spring from the twenties and the Sitwells. The sound was remarkable, as rich as I have ever heard from an instrument of that size.

TREVOR BECKERLEG:

I was born in Morpeth, Northumberland, in 1941, my Cornish father a teacher of geography at the grammar school, my mother the daughter of a furrier, a self-made man, the youngest of a family of twelve, who had left home in New Zealand at the age of eighteen to seek his fortune, and found his first job in the ladies' underwear department of Liberty's. Music is not, as far as I know, in the family. I align myself most strongly with a photograph of my father standing on his hands and drinking lemonade through a straw. (He also wrote a story for *Boy's Own Paper* about where elephants go to die.) He was killed in Belgium when I was three. In 1948 we moved to Hertfordshire where I went to school. First I wanted to be a chef, since I had been reared in the female arts (or some of them), and then a potter, spending all my spare time in the school pottery. I threw a dreadful pot in some uncontrollable clay for Bernard Leach, which he very kindly said he would keep to show his wife. He offered me a five-year apprenticeship at £2 a week. I do not know if those were his usual terms, but I read English at Trinity Hall, Cambridge, instead. Later I came across an essay by Leach, published in 1947, about the function and direction of the studio craftsman in the post-war epoch. His approach was rigorous and disciplined, almost mystical, and demanded total commitment, hard to sustain I imagine among the almost inevitable mugs and ashtrays, the perpetual packaging, marketing and paperwork. I had envisaged myself alone in a studio on the Cornish coast: I even drew the building, bleakly functional, a terrifying premonition. I think I already wanted to be a harpsichord maker. The first harpsichord I saw was brought to the school by Carl Dolmetsch for a concert; a friend tried to make one in the holidays, and I could tell it wasn't going to work.

After a brief spell of teaching in South London, I returned to Cambridge in 1964 intending to find a workshop and planning to finance myself while I was setting up by teaching English to foreign students. In my last year at college I had had lessons with the harpsichordist Mary Potts, and Mary now took me on as a lodger. She was the most marvellous landlady. She played a good deal on the radio, and recording sessions in her sitting-room on the $5\frac{1}{2}$-octave Shudi were frequently interrupted by birdsong. I always turned the pages. Once at the Wigmore Hall a young man approached her with shy enthusiasm:

"Are you Mary Potts?"

"Yes" – Mary (demurely enjoying the recognition).

"Not *the* Mary Potts! – Barry Needham's landlady?"

The winter after my arrival she suggested we might clear the junk room in the basement, so I had my first workshop there until she moved from Bateman Street in 1971.

The house was full of all kinds of people, particularly musicians. Christopher Hogwood and David Spence Lyons were residents. Among the many visitors I remember David Munrow and his future wife Gill (later the Early Music Consort met there sometimes for rehearsals), Thurston Dart, Charles Cudworth, Wilfred Brown, Peter Williams, Robin Orr who bought my first spinet for his daughter Jeannie, Colin Tilney, Rafael Puyana (who named our kittens Ricercar, Tiento and Canzona – Canzona was adopted by Mark Stevenson who has his workshop down the road from me; it is

Trevor Beckerleg: two-
manual harpsichord of typical
French eighteenth-century
construction in ivory, grey
and maroon lacquer.

another black cat that sleeps now on the soundboard of the clavichord in his window)
and Michael Thomas. I had already met Michael at his home in Hurley. He was enormously helpful, answering all my naïve questions, overflowing with information and
encouragement. He took harpsichords to Bruges for me in 1968 and 1971, the second
returning full of sand from a night camping on Calais beach. He told me many things that
it has taken me years to rediscover for myself, and goes a long way to counteract a
common notion that harpsichord makers are secretive, and chary of discussing their
methods and ideas.

My years at college had given me time to collect information and work the thing out in
my head, but I had and still have no formal training in carpentry and cabinet work and,

[157]

Trevor Beckerleg: wing spinet, made freely after one of 1690 signed by
Tisserant and Slade, in walnut banded with mahogany and lined inside
with figured sycamore.

apart from a two-week trial period with Dolmetsch when I was eighteen, no apprenticeship. Because of this I suffered for a long time from the feeling that I did not do things
the right way, until I realized that there is no right or wrong way, only ways that work
and ways that do not. It was an idea slow to dawn, but of very broad and useful application.

   After you have worked for a time at a craft you can take on more or less anything
without fear of failure, and my lack of training may have had a latent advantage in that I
am continually changing and improving my techniques. Mary Potts' house provided an
ideal environment for a first workshop, but although I have always been in touch with
fellow craftsmen and musicians, my lack of formal training and solitary working
temperament are factors in my experimental approach to harpsichord making. Such an
approach is also by choice. However, after the break in tradition in the nineteenth
century and the increasing irrelevance of the re-invention of the harpsichord in the first

half of this century, I recognize that such an approach has its dangers. It is lamentable that the revival of the harpsichord in the twentieth century has not been accompanied by a significant reappraisal of the instrument by modern composers, but perhaps this is still to come. The equivalent of Leach's attempt to define the function and direction of the post-war studio potter has been for the harpsichord maker the rediscovery and reproduction of the harpsichords of master builders of the past, but Leach had already absorbed the old traditions and was seeking to point a future for his craft that would be both relevant and vital. Without such a new direction the excitement of the rediscovery of the last twenty years could be dispersed in mere reproduction, for much of the appeal of the old instruments is in the individuality of their voices and the inventiveness of their makers within an ever changing tradition of music and craftsmanship. Our modern culture is wayward, fragmented and insecure, but certainly not exclusive, and harpsichord makers are remarkably fortunate in having such clear guide lines laid down for them. If there is no right way, then it is what goes on.

Harpsichord makers in the past used the best materials that were to hand. Since I am not making exact copies of particular old instruments, I feel free to use unauthentic materials, but I do so within what understanding I have of the old spirit of making and of the music. I make my own keyboards because this allows maximum flexibility, and for the same reason I do not use plastic jacks. Also, if you are mainly concerned with learning to exploit the acoustical, structural and visual qualities of wood to the best advantage, plastic becomes uncongenial because it is so alien. Delrin, which has been generally used as a plectrum material by makers of exact copies of old harpsichords is also, to my ear, unsympathetic. It produces a percussive and sibilant initiation to the note which overrides the tone colour of the instrument and conceals its true identity. The importance of the initiation of the note can readily be discovered by playing a tape recording backwards, and a harpsichord is most powerfully recognized as such because it is plucked, and plucked by quill. Since quill is a natural material, it can be selected and voiced to suit different instruments, and when regularly rubbed with a soft pencil at the point of impact is sufficiently reliable and durable. It is much easier than Delrin to cut and fit. Birds of prey seem to furnish the best quill, and quill from water birds is unsuitable, possibly because it is too oily. Such quill becomes increasingly rigid as the oil dries, until it is brittle. The question of whether iron or brass wire was used on short-scale harpsichords has been much discussed, but remains unresolved with a preponderance of historical evidence indicating a general use of iron. As with quill, iron produces a less specific colour, allowing the instrument to speak for itself and, while brass can make a poor harpsichord sound more plausible, iron to my ear is less cluttered.

Stringing and quilling merely interpret an instrument. I have had long discussions with fellow makers on even more incidental matters: is it not vital that the stick supporting the lid should be made of the same material as the lid itself? Does the extent to which the bridge is double-pinned affect the aggressiveness of the harpsichord? Had someone really discovered that to pull all the bridge pins out a further sixteenth of an inch was the secret of the dark Ruckers tone? These are not the fundamental considerations: if they are the sort of matters that preoccupied makers of the past, then we are really in the dark. While research and restoration have shown largely what the old makers did, the questions of why they did it and to what extent they achieved their objectives are far from being understood. Some would have been working within a tradition, others with a more experimental approach may have failed, as can happen today. The scope for failure is important. Undoubtedly some harpsichords regarded as comparative failures by their makers have been impeccably copied in our time. While it is right to be wary of experimental harpsichords, the customer who requires simply a "Ruckers" is being very naïve. In abdicating from the responsibility of using his ears he obliges the maker, who is inevitably involved in an inconclusive guessing game, to masquerade. I have seen the faces of customers flood with horror when I talked about the uncertainty of what I was doing, because they wanted the supposed security of an exact copy; but there is no "Which" guide to harpsichords. Most modern makers, even when copying, produce a distinctive sound, and the word "Ruckers" covers a hundred years of development. While it is very convenient to receive an order, I myself would not buy a harpsichord until I had played it. On the other hand, most harpsichord makers are unusual perfectionists and totally and idealistically involved in their craft. They benefit from open discussion with their colleagues and frank and informed response from players and audience.

Makers in the past often worked their entire lives with a small number of acoustical woods, in the case of Italian cypress harpsichords with only one or two. I have myself used five different soundboard woods, five case woods, five bridge woods and four barring woods. Four of these woods were never, as far as I know, used in the past, and at the risk of being compared to a sandwich bar I will admit that there are still combinations that I want to try. There are also some I would not use again. I met an American builder whose interest was in the harpsichord before the middle of the seventeenth century; he was working in a native timber. There is historical precedent for such approaches. English seventeenth-century builders, while incorporating many Italian features, used native timbers and made instruments for an eclectic music. An English spinet of about 1690 that I restored recently is of walnut banded on the inside with cypress and with a cypress key surround. The soundboard is barred under the bridge in an Italian manner and is of a heavy, dark-striped wood unlike any other soundboard I have seen in an old

Trevor Beckerleg: single-manual harpsichord of typical English
seventeenth-century construction, with rosewood cross banding,
olivewood interior, and stringing of ivory and lignum vitae.

instrument. It has an exceptionally rich, dark tone and speaks particularly well for Purcell and Louis Couperin. My rather free copies (the spinet had had its compass extended in the bass by two notes) had overall a lighter quality which I attribute mainly to the use of Swiss pine for the soundboard. It can take courage to make an exact copy.

The restoration of the Victoria and Albert Museum's Vaudry by Derek Adlam has called into question assumptions about the standardization of French barring and opened up a new area for research and experiment. If I were to copy the Vaudry I would want to make access to the underside of the soundboard after the instrument was finished in order to move the barring around to see what it did. This apparently direct and conclusive kind of experiment can be misleading. Harpsichords can take months and even years to develop their true character, particularly in the treble, and usually internal barring and bracing combine a structural and tonal function. Moreover no two pieces of wood are the same, and a barring system that works with one timber will produce a completely different result with another.

Nevertheless, such experiments lead slowly to a clearer understanding and more certain use of materials. It is often necessary to test ideas in order to establish whether they are wrong and this can only be done very slowly because one cannot afford to make a truly bad instrument. The thickness of the soundboard in relation to the vibrating area, barring and bridge dimensions in different parts of the compass, are of great importance. If a soundboard is planed too thin in the bass it cannot be made thicker, but one can learn to compensate by changing the dimensions, or altering the position, of the barring. I have altered barring in harpsichords made ten years ago because it was too slack and the tone had weakened as the initial stresses of the soundboard relaxed. Some harpsichords have to have a rather rasping quality when new if they are to develop well, and it is necessary to take that into account. The work of the Italian makers is confident and serene in speech and appearance, changing little over three hundred years. The modern harpsichord maker cannot hope to work always with so sure a touch. It is better to resist the temptation to make a wide range of harpsichords and instead to persevere with a few models until you know them. It has taken me some years to learn how little latitude to allow myself, and in retrospect I think I might have done better to have begun by copying. In fact it is absurd to design one's first harpsichord, as I did, oblivious of the quicksands, although by luck it was quite successful. I find restoration work extremely valuable: to have a harpsichord in the workshop for some months and slowly come to know it. The 1690 spinet was full of implications and suggestions and I shall make at least fifteen variations on it because the man who made it was so obviously playing with the rich possibilities of combining Italian and English features and doing so with a great sense of freedom. The sixteenth-century Italian virginals that I have in the workshop at present, perfect thoroughbred that it is, could only be copied.

No player can hope to develop a true familiarity with the harpsichord repertoire without the experience of playing upon appropriate contemporary instruments. They are by far the most important interpretative reference. However, there is as much difference between an Italian harpsichord and a Shudi as there is between a Shudi and a modern piano, and few can hope to own a complete range of instruments to span that gap. While the harpsichords of the past are often seen as conforming to various more or less standardized schools of building, this is only really true of the Italian harpsichords. Players and composers saw significant changes in the instrument and the music within a lifetime, and in this context it is the transitional harpsichords which are the most interesting, since composers often wrote not for a standardized harpsichord of their day, but from familiarity with an eclectic and changing tradition moving slowly towards a new definition. We cannot afford to ignore the ground of Italian influence in English seventeenth-century harpsichord making and the prevalence of imported Italian harpsichords – for example in the music of Purcell, who did not in fact write for an established school of English building. This was not to emerge until the following century. It is

Trevor Beckerleg: wing spinet in course of construction, in English walnut with burr-walnut front panels and stringing of ebony, ivory and boxwood.

[163]

tempting in concert performance to aggrandize the music by using the latest form of the harpsichord that might have been known to the composer, but the virginals and wing spinets of the seventeenth century are probably more informative about the music of a period when public performance was a novelty and the musical tradition was still largely domestic. The significance and excellence of the English seventeenth-century wing spinets has yet to be recognized, and such instruments are seldom seen on the concert plat-form. The large number that survive from this period, their variety and transitional nature, and the particularly fine cabinet work of many, evince their musical importance, not only in the music of seventeenth-century English composers but as a key to the experience of these composers of their musical heritage from Italy and from the virginalists. Our assumptions are based too often on a convenient myth of classification.

If we fail to see the thing for what it is, this is often because of the dichotomies of our culture: the essential privateness of much early music compared to the music of the concert platform, itself now accessible in private through the gramophone.

If the objectives of the modern harpsichord maker are not clear cut, those of the record-ing engineer are even less so. The sound of a harpsichord changes according to where it is placed in a room, where you are sitting if you are not the player, the nature of the surface on which it is standing; it is subject to the tuning system, the moment and your mood. A harpsichord can even change its resonance with the humidity. However, there is a prevalent notion that this sound can be captured and reproduced by a gramophone or even idealized by a synthesizer. Attempts to analyse by scientific means the sound of the harpsichord beg a thousand questions, especially when assuming the possibility of perfec-tion or uniformity in a musical instrument. While a harpsichord will have good and less good qualities, it is essentially a thing of parts susceptible of an endless variety of relationships. A note sounded separately may be more or less appealing, but it only really comes to life in relation to other notes and will shine out with extraordinary beauty at some points of the music and be quite discreet at others. A "good" note does not imply the possibility of a perfect harpsichord where the qualities of that note can be reproduced throughout the compass. Such an effect can be reproduced with a synthesizer but it does not have intrinsic life, only plausibility.

When the first string is put on a harpsichord there is some indication of resonance, sustaining power and tonal qualities, but none of its total character, and response to notated music, will be recognized until the whole thing is strung, voiced, damped, tuned and the music played. Treble strings in particular, pick up from the rest of the instrument as on an Aeolian harp and can sound distressingly dull on their own, and this is par-ticularly true of old short-scale harpsichords, where meantone tuning is heard to best effect. It is in this respect that brass wire, with its stronger harmonics, is so overriding when used in the treble. Any discussion of the tonal qualities of wire divorced from such considerations is not directly relevant to the harpsichord maker. The harpsichord in its Italian form is a vivid epitome of Platonic philosophy. The mathematical arrangement of the strings in a perfect curve is emulated in the essentially imperfect tuning system and layout of the keyboard. The voices have each their own character and importance, but form an harmonious whole to imitate the music of the spheres. Emphasis is on the serenity of just relations, most sublime in the interval of the perfect third, so that each note exists as part of the whole. The gamut is thus that of the great chain of being, and the music is the music of Milton's "On the Morning of Christ's Nativity" – "full consort to th'Angelike symphony", not the abandoned and moody fluctuations of Dowland and Froberger. In its development the harpsichord is coloured by a fiery assertiveness and the differentiation and dark implications of the Christian eschatology. As a microcosm of earthly imperfection, its beauty is in the ephemeral blending and contrasting of its parts, the concords and discords of its tuning systems and the falling away of the note.

The dilemma of the modern maker is often between the intrinsic beauty of the old instruments and the needs of the customer, who all too often requires one harpsichord on which to play the whole repertoire. It is commonly supposed that a recital cannot hold the interest of the audience unless it runs the gamut of four hundred years of music but, in fact, it is much more likely to sustain interest if the music is represented to advantage. One alternative is a Lisztian type of entertainment in equal temperament. If this is appreciated, the harpsichord maker may be freed at last from the obligation of making endless five-octave double-manuals of the eighteenth-century style which are not ideally suited to the music of any of the major composers in the repertoire, and so do not help the player or the audience to any close understanding of the music. Many musical institutions have now equipped themselves with such harpsichords, so it is to be hoped there will be a less burdensome demand for them in the future. Few people would choose now to play the harpsichords of earlier twentieth-century makers who were the victims of unreasonable expectations of variety of tonal coloration, and tuning stability.

Trevor Beckerleg has his workshop at his home, 135 Gwydir Street, Cambridge. He is currently making a series of English bentside spinets (as referred to above) and two-manual harpsichords, in walnut, that are also of a transitional English seventeenth-century character. He is planning copies of the early Italian virginals belonging to the Faculty Board of Music of the University of Cambridge and also some single-manual Italian harpsichords in cypress. He also makes instruments on commission.

CHAPTER 11

Donald Garrod

Donald Garrod lives in a seventeenth-century cottage in Suffolk which he bought during the war when he was teaching in a residential school and needed somewhere to live during the holidays. It has served him as a base ever since, through a varied and hardworking career, which has taken him to Jamaica and the USA, as he himself describes.

Apart from teaching posts in London and Suffolk, he has worked in a progressive school in the West Country (a "do it yourself school" in every sense of the word), ran the first assessment centre for deprived children in London, for which he was awarded an MBE in 1961, and set up the first training course for house-masters in Approved Schools (now Community Homes).

His cottage, surrounded by farmland, is known as the "Wheelwright's house". The old smithy has long since been incorporated into the cottage as living accommodation, but the wheelwright's workshop, a separate timbered building, has been adapted as a harpsichord workshop. Some of the old tools still survive there, including a "beck iron" he uses for making wrest pins, an adze for roughly shaping timber before machining and an old five-foot cooper's plane — a museum piece for visitors!

Only one of his instruments was available on my visit, a version of the "Jerome" harpsichord in the Victoria and Albert Museum, which he keeps for his own use.

A craftsman in wood of wide ability, Donald Garrod has many practical interests. He has partly rebuilt and furnished his own home, and is involved in nature conservation and the breeding of wild fowl.

DONALD GARROD:

My interest in early keyboard instruments dates from the war years. I had been reading *The Fountain* by Charles Morgan, and was much taken by his description of a clavichord being played in an attic room somewhere. There may have been a personal romantic accompaniment to my fascination at the time, and my continuous interest since might not have been justified by either the instrument itself or the acoustics of the attic – if it had ever existed outside Charles Morgan's imagination.

Donald Garrod: single-manual harpsichord (second version) after the Jerome in the Victoria and Albert Museum, played by the owner, Mrs Mavis Morgan.

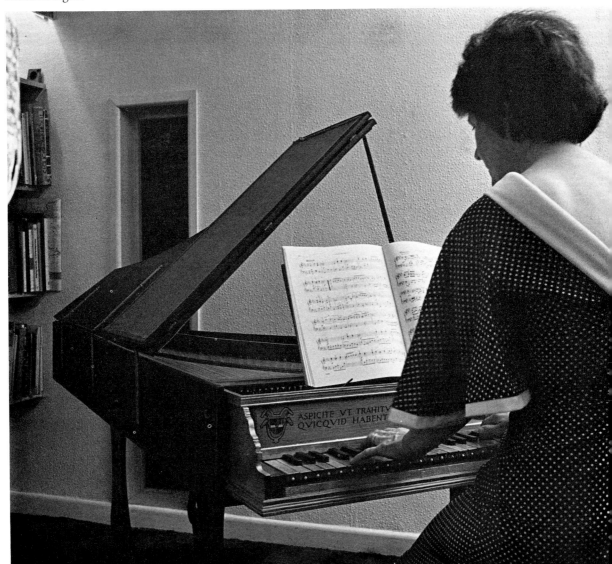

Donald Garrod: detail of Italian virginal of separate case construction, based on the instrument known as "Queen Elizabeth's Virginals" in the Victoria and Albert Museum.

Very soon after, I went to work in Jamaica, taking a virginal made for me by Alec Hodsdon who was one of the few early keyboard instrument makers in the country at the time and who still lives nearby; not now making harpsichords but flying around the streets of the mediaeval village of Lavenham in his steam car.

The first time I ever saw the "works" of an early keyboard instrument was on the quayside at Kingston, Jamaica, when the customs officials had become suspicious of the large oblong box of one-inch elm which housed the virginal. In spite of my protests that I was not a smuggler, that I was coming to take up a bona-fide teaching post in a well known Island school, they insisted that everything movable should be removed, including the front board, keys and jacks. It was a difficult exercise for a novice but I succeeded in putting the virginal together again, and with William Byrd's "Queen's Command" convinced my inquisitors that it really was a musical instrument I was bringing in. Perhaps it was this experience which has influenced the way I have constructed harpsichords since – any particular part easily replaced, altered, adjusted?

Some time later I produced *Lady Precious Stream* for the Jamaica Little Theatre Movement, and John Bull and the virginals supplied the exits and entrances of the various characters in the Chinese dramatic tradition. Perhaps this was the only appearance of an early keyboard instrument in Jamaica. I never discovered another on the Island, though there were references to some being shipped out there in the distant past. Perhaps the termites devoured them before the simple precaution was practised of standing the legs of susceptible furniture in little bowls of kerosene. I am reminded that every time I practiced, a lizard would appear from the verandah, climb on to the bottom rail of the virginal stand and puff himself out either in protest or acclaim! Could it be that Jamaican lizards had heard that sound somewhere before?

The intention of making a harpsichord in Jamaica – which I had before I left England – evaporated in the sweat of making a few articles of essential furniture out of the native mahoe wood. Its deep greens and yellows would make a beautiful looking instrument but its grain running all ways might not enhance the sound and it was certainly a reason for postponing the project until I reached a cooler climate.

This happened to be in Greenwich, Connecticut, where I eventually arrived via the then poverty-stricken islands of Haiti and Cuba. From Greenwich, I used to travel to New York to visit the Metropolitan Museum which housed many historical keyboard instruments. I made the acquaintance of the Englishman who was then in charge of the musical instrument department and examined and measured several. There were more instruments waiting for repair in the basement than there were on show, all damaged by the central heating and lack of air-conditioning – a situation long since remedied, I don't doubt.

On show was a harpsichord by Arnold Dolmetsch, made presumably when he was working for Chickerings of New York. The registers, as I remember, were a long way from the front and, I concluded afterwards, it was probably an experimental instrument with both bridges on the soundboard and plucking points near the middle of the strings. I marvelled, at the time, at what must have been extraordinarily long keys.

Back at school, I made a start with one of the instruments after I had gained the confidence of the head of the Crafts Centre. Although he was primarily interested in becoming a recognized sculptor with a statue on Broadway, and I sometimes had to work in an atmosphere of flying stone chips, he was a first-rate cabinet maker, having been apprenticed to that trade. He gave me invaluable help in solving some of the problems in making a keyboard, because up to this time I had had no formal training in woodworking except the rudimentary, but thorough, instruction given to elementary school boys before the war. Later experiences with a friend's father who was a wheelwright had not contributed to my liking for woodwork; running round with kettles to cool the sizzling rims of cart-wheels when they were shod with their iron tyres, or taking a turn at the bottom of the saw pit were to be avoided.

After my return to England with a partly finished harpsichord – I suppose one would now say "in kit form" – I saw Alec Hodsdon again and was given further advice on

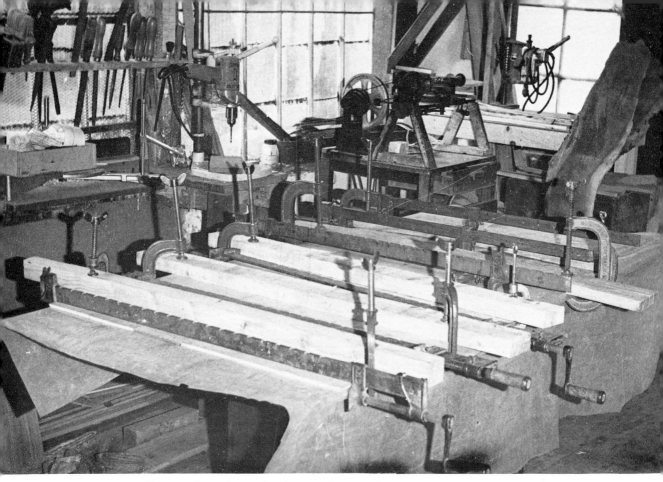

Donald Garrod: a harpsichord maker's workshop; a soundboard cramped up for jointing.

harpsichord making. His final suggestion was: "You should be prepared to throw your first instrument away." Good advice, which I nearly carried out!

In between my first efforts at wood bending by soaking (in the pond or in the bath), jack making and, in those days, the endless search for suitable materials, I made the acquaintance of the curator of the Benton Fletcher Collection of Musical Instruments, then housed in a large house in Cheyne Walk, Chelsea. For sixpence a visit (old pence), I spent many afternoons shut up with the Shudi single-manual harpsichord, playing, examining, and finally measuring it. My first completed harpsichord, with the bits and pieces I had brought with me from America, was based on it.

This was the instrument I nearly threw away. I left it in a garage where it deteriorated for several years before opportunity and interest aroused by Frank Hubbard's book, which came out in 1965, jogged me into activity again. Instead of burning it (there was a good precedent for this in the French Revolution when they burned harpsichords when fuel was scarce) I took my harpsichord apart as if it were an antique worthy of restoration, hollowed out the wrest plank and replaced the front bridge on an extension of the sound-board.

Reading what Hubbard says about this (page 24 in *Three Centuries of Harpsichord Making*) I am in no doubt this construction materially alters the tone, as he conjectures. It is also an authentic feature of early Italian keyboard instruments, and their makers must have had a good reason for introducing this form of construction. I have a personal pre-ference for the kind of sound which is produced which was confirmed for me by copying the Jerome instrument in the Victoria and Albert Museum. This beautifully simple instru-ment has the front bridge on an extension of the soundboard on a hollowed out wrest plank. The instrument in the Museum is unplayable. Andrew Douglas, who partially restored it some years ago, left notes to the effect that it could not be brought up to playing pitch without risking serious damage. In fact, half of the jacks are missing and any extra tension would seem likely to pull the wrest plank away from the sides of the case.

Although this simple harpsichord is believed to be the oldest domestic instrument sur-viving anywhere, I am sure that the sound it produced would have justified the mediaeval Latin verses on the front board:

> Aspicite ut trahitur suavi modulamine vocis
> Quicquid habent aer sidera terra fretum.

> (Consider how musical rhythms summon
> and draw out sweet delights
>   In these are held in trust the air,
> The stars and the earth).

I have made three harpsichords based on this instrument with slight variations of design, though all with the same basic scaling. It is fascinating to speculate on the original maker's intentions, though alterations of the instrument over the years have obscured these; there was probably only one set of strings for example, and the outer case is later by a hundred years than the instrument itself.

The three instruments I have made based on this harpsichord have a distinctly virginal-like tone which can only be due to the soundboard construction with the front bridge on an extension of the soundboard; but the reasons for positioning the soundboard bridge far out from the bentside, and the barely discernible angle of the registers to the front, continue to baffle me.

Herein lies the fascination of harpsichord making. However much you try, you can never produce two identical-sounding instruments. Two may look alike; they may have identical measurements, but they will have different sounds. The reasons must be in the nature of the timber as well as in that of the maker himself.

At the time I picked up and rebuilt my first harpsichord I was living and working in Birmingham, earning my living as a teacher of social work and teaching pottery to my students as a diversion. An abiding interest in my life has been the therapeutic effects of arts (music, painting, drama) and crafts on human development, and particularly as these helped children who were separated from their families or maladjusted. Music was the exception. I used this only for my own private, unshared recreation – and therapy.

With the idea of going on and making more instruments I converted the cellar of the large Victorian semi-detached house in which I lived into a workshop, but before I had used it for long, events decided me to make a complete break. From out of the blue a telephone call from the Nationwide studios in Birmingham asking if I would participate in a "Midlands Craftsmen" series was the beginning of a series of decisions which brought me to the end of my teaching career and the beginning of another; a spell in hospital concluded the matter. I jocularly told my students that I was "going into trade". As a number had already come from it, as craftsmen or otherwise, and were sickened or weary of it, it seemed a strange decision for me to make. I imagine there are other musical instrument makers who find the "trade" side less acceptable than the making, unless they hope to employ others to do the work, or to make money. They are unlikely to do this unless they establish a production line for a standard sort of instrument. I remember a fellow exhibitor (not an instrument maker) pointing deprecatingly to some furniture he was showing: "It sells well. It is not the sort of work I set out to do – but I have a family to keep."

The decision to be a full-time maker of musical instruments was easier to take because I already had premises in Suffolk which could be used. They had been for hundreds of years the premises where the village carpenter and wheelwright had worked; the last "Old spit on the point to save the grease" as he was described to me by one of his former apprentices, had long since retired if not deceased. I had only used the workshop intermittently in the intervening years, when making items of furniture which had no critical working parts to be affected by stone floors, draughts and lack of consistent heating. For these the old wheelwright's shop with its earth floor was adequate if time was allowed for parts of the furniture to settle down in the house before being finally put together and glued.

To avoid the earth floor, I decided to use an upstairs paint shop. In Suffolk the wheelwrights always seemed to paint their carts upstairs, taking them up and down on wooden ramps. This workshop, plastered over weatherboarding on the outside, I insulated with glass fibre and insulating board and heated with a night storage heater. There are windows all round and although there is never any excessive moisture, last winter showed me that there was still need for a supplementary electric heater. The downstairs workshop, where there used to be three benches, I use for machining. There is also a separate adjoining store for timber.

It is a far cry from making carts and barrels to making harpsichords and I sometimes regret having dismantled the sawpits which were built over the ditch in the front of the workshop. I used the timber from this to repair the house when wood was hard to find. But sawpits would today only be museum pieces.

There are some days when the work goes well and the distractions are few, though I count myself fortunate to work in a remote country workshop used continuously for the past two hundred years, with no near neighbours and few extraneous sounds. When the noise of aircraft becomes obtrusive, then concentration can wander; something has to be done again and I am sure it is not done as well because it is not an enjoyed activity.

Donald Garrod: single-manual Italian harpsichord of separate case construction (first version) after the Jerome in the Victoria and Albert Museum.

I make only two or three instruments a year, although working from 8 a.m. to 6 p.m. This is because I have never made two instruments alike from a set plan, because I prefer to make every part of the instrument myself, and because I tend to work out problems, as I go, with the materials I have available.

So far, I have maintained a few constants: my soundboards have always been extended and made of Sitka spruce. Scaling has always been between 10 and 12 inches, registers have always been made of beech and jacks of pearwood with hogs' bristle springs. I have used various materials for plectra — leather, quill and Delrin. Who can distinguish between the sound produced by the last two? Delrin is far easier to replace by a harpsichord owner. It is interesting to note that the leather plectra in Alec Hodsdon's virginal lasted thirty years! They had become hard and brittle but few had broken.

One of my pleasures is converting timber which has grown on the premises here — apple, laburnum, quince and walnut — and although the quantity is not large, there is great satisfaction in working in this way, much as a potter finds in digging his own clay.

It would seem to be limiting to continue to make one type of instrument as I have done with the early Italians, especially as this often necessitates making an outer case. This presents problems of construction in making a stable spine-side and takes up as much time, if one includes the stand, as the instrument itself. It has, though, always been my primary concern to be able to play the music that these instruments were designed for, even if I am not taken with some of the ornate cases and stands which would be out of place except in an old Italian palace. Moreover I do not like painted furniture and the necessity to cover good and bad craftsmanship with paint and paper.

Although the Italians persevered with the same construction for two hundred years, this does not mean that they were self-satisfied, or had come to the end of the road in the development of their harpsichords. The Baffo harpsichord of 1574 in the Victoria and Albert Museum is still playable and is a vindication of its design and craftsmanship. How many modern harpsichords will survive that long? If we survive the nuclear age, the appetite of woodworm for plywood will ensure that their demise is not long delayed.

There are still experiments to be made even though there seems to be nothing new under the sun. Recently, I made a small 5ft harpsichord without a belly rail and with a gap in the soundboard for the register. Michael Thomas, who has examined more Italian instruments than anybody, assures me that there are several early harpsichords without a belly rail! So I was unwittingly on already trodden ground.

It is interesting to speculate on points of construction like this, as well as on the tonal differences between instruments. It could well be that the first harpsichord makers proceeded by rule of thumb: "I have no suitable piece of timber to hand for a belly rail . . . why should there be a piece of wood shutting off the keyboard from the rest of the instrument?" So they adapted the design accordingly.

Many of the early makers had begun their working lives as run-of-the-mill woodworkers without any musical knowledge and constructed their instruments within the limitations set by their materials and techniques. For instance, there is a sound musical reason for bridges to be higher in the bass than in the treble. However, I doubt whether the early makers had much understanding of this. If you steam- or heat-bend a bridge after it has been moulded, it tends to skew at the bend with the outer edge cocked up. If you now plane this edge down so that the bridge lies flat for its entire length, the treble end becomes lower than the bass end. Perhaps this is how the old makers proceeded and what modern musical scientists square with physics.

Although I shall continue to make this kind of harpsichord, I am aware of the disadvantages as well as the advantages of the design. However close the tolerances between jacks and their slots, however well-made the keyboard, the action will be noisier than in a French instrument. Apart from the shorter distance of the balance point of the keys to the front and the resultant heavier fall of the jacks and the shallower touch, the extended soundboard means greater resonance for the sound of the action as well as the strings. This may have been the reason for Burney's comments on noisy Italian harpsichords in the eighteenth century. The absence of a belly rail would accentuate this still further.

The perfect sound still eludes me but I shall continue to seek it!

Donald Garrod has his workshop at his home, Luckey's Corner, Hitcham, Ipswich, and is currently making copies of the Jerome of 1521 in the Victoria and Albert Museum, the anonymous Italian harpsichord in the Russell Collection, and a small Italian harpsichord, 5ft long, to his own design. He also undertakes commissions to make Italian instruments.

CHAPTER 12

Martin Huggett

Martin Huggett lives on the Suffolk/Essex border and with his brother and father run their respective businesses from shared workshops which are on the Essex side of the Stour estuary. His father is a computer specialist, his brother is in precision engineering. The three help one another in their converted grain store. Its title "Maltings" is perhaps

misleading, for although it was actually used for the process of producing malt, it is much smaller than most maltings in East Anglia. Harpsichord making, requiring more room than the making of precision components, occupies rather more than half of the accommodation. Martin Huggett's equipment is of the same order of refinement and precision as his brother's.

His time spent making the de Blaise harpsichords has given him a practical background to instrument making. Although he does not always agree with dogmatic purists, one feels that when his new production is properly on its way, his instruments could be relied upon to be what he claimed for them – reconstructions, not precise reproductions – and that any deviation from the strictly classical idea would be made by men who understood the principles of acoustics as well as the craft of instrument making.

MARTIN HUGGETT:

My interest in early music started while I was still at school. During the year prior to my leaving Bedales, I built a clavichord to a design published in *The Woodworker*. In retrospect it was not a design that I would now choose to follow, and after I had been in business for about two years I had acquired enough knowledge to be able to redesign it. This was a most useful exercise which was to throw light on both the advantages and disadvantages of semi-classical construction and design. Although it is possible to learn a lot from reading books and articles on the theory of musical instrument design, and by studying the instruments themselves, there is nothing that can replace practical experience as a teacher. Only when the maker or student-maker has had practical experience can he get a real insight into the nature of the work.

Martin Huggett: wing spinet in cross banded walnut, an original design.

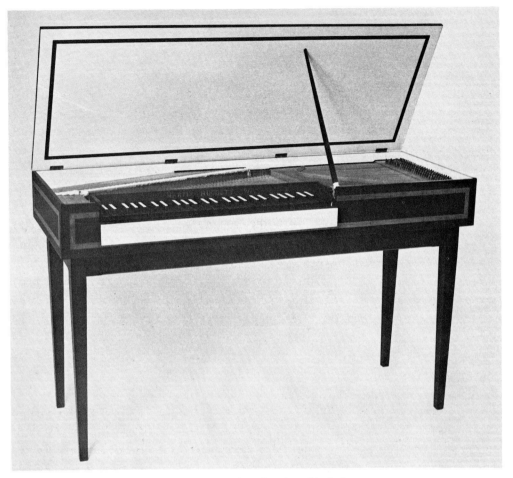

Martin Huggett: double-strung, fret-free clavichord in black lacquer
with gold leaf banding.

   Some of my redesigning studies were carried out while I was doing a course in musical
instrument technology at the London College of Furniture. The course, of two years,
was centred round the piano – its tuning and maintenance. Initially, it gave me nothing in
the way of training for the early music business but it increased my knowledge of physics
and acoustics, subjects I had not been good at when at school. It also stimulated my
interest in trying to rethink an old idea. Having taken the second-year examinations at the
end of the first year, I was left with three terms to fill. The idea of designing and building
a harpsichord was conceived, the emphasis being on trying to incorporate aspects of
modern technology into an old set of rules. In the event the instrument was not finished
until two years after I left the college, and a number of things were changed in the design
as I increased my knowledge. It turned out to be quite a success and achieved all its aims in
showing that practically every aspect of the instrument had the possibility to be

redesigned. My intention was to maintain all the main principles of the original idea while making the instrument in a modern way. There is no such thing as a perfect harpsichord, clavichord or spinet, contrary to the belief of some! There are so many differing ideas as to what combination of factors makes a good instrument that, in the end, it is the people who buy them who will dictate what sort of instruments will be made. There are, though, generally accepted standards of tone and craftsmanship that have been set up by many fine makers of a very diverse range of instruments, and these standards must be met.

On completing the two years at the London College of Furniture, I was lucky enough to be able to work at Glyndebourne. 1970 was the year that Cavalli's opera, *La Calisto*, was realized by Raymond Leppard. It called for two harpsichords and my job was to look after these and also the pianos in the practice rooms. Surrounded by famous people, working in such a place and seeing at first hand the standards achieved, not only in singing, gave me an experience I shall long cherish. Quite apart from the enjoyment I had from this work, I was fired with enthusiasm to get into the early music business in some capacity or other. I achieved this when I joined William de Blaise, at the London based company of Whelpdale, Maxwell and Codd later the same year.

William de Blaise gave me quite a new outlook on musical instruments from that to which I had been exposed up till this time. My own instruments reflect his ideas inasmuch as, if possible, I try not to copy. There is a satisfaction, I know not shared by all, that comes from having created a new and individual instrument. Famous instruments are known to have been changed and rebuilt by other well-known makers, to suit the change in thinking at the time.

To build a harpsichord, clavichord, or spinet one of course has to abide by certain rules, but there are many areas that offer a potential for change. Modern living certainly does not match with living conditions of two hundred or more years ago, and I feel it is therefore unwise to apply to strictly classically built instruments the expectations imposed by these living conditions. I always look around for materials that may do the job better and often wonder what the old makers would have done with the technology we have today.

In the summer of 1979 I left Whelpdale, Maxwell and Codd to form my own company with members of my family. Musical instruments comprise about half the business of the company, the other half being devoted to precision engineering. We were fortunate to be able to acquire a near derelict building of 1839, once an old maltings, and convert this into our workshops. After a large amount of major structural work, which included new floors and part re-roofing, we were able to go in and start work in October 1979. From necessity the engineering occupies the ground floor as many machines have to be levelled and on concrete, while the musical instrument section occupies the first and second floors.

William de Blaise: two-manual triangular harpsichord in walnut.

Although it may appear that engineering and musical instrument making have very little in common, there is more connection than meets the eye. As I have said, I believe there will always be the need to improve and develop production methods, and to incorporate new materials where they will enhance both the principles and the product. Although the instruments we make are classical in appearance and sound they are produced to try to incorporate as many of these points as I think are necessary. With an engineering side to the business we have the capacity to develop techniques as and when necessary.

It is difficult to predict what types of instrument, keyboard or otherwise, will be in demand in the years to come. Whether there will be a continuation of the present historical trend or whether there will be a drift to something less classical, is impossible to say; I believe that historical puritanism will fade.

Nevertheless, I hope that the instruments we make will conform to the directive laid down by the Renaissance writer Sabba di Castiglione that an instrument must "charm the ear as much as it must animate the spirit and ravish the eye".

WILLIAM DE BLAISE, *an appreciation by Martin Huggett:*
William de Blaise was born in Latvia at the beginning of this century. His early life in the turbulent Baltic States was both eventful and colourful and had a great effect on him later. He was a fascinating man to talk to and it would be impossible to do justice or to pay a full tribute to him in the confines of this passage. Not only had he a great practical ability but he also possessed a thorough theoretical knowledge of his subject and was a true harpsichord maker and designer.

As a young man he travelled widely, and as a result became a natural linguist. He spoke the majority of European languages fluently and, in addition, Hebrew and Chinese. His associates have witnessed him on occasions conducting a business conversation in three or four languages, jumping from one to the other with the greatest of ease.

As a practical musician he was an accomplished flautist and for some years played with one of the leading orchestras in Jerusalem, where he lived for some time during the Second World War. It was during this period that he turned his attention to the idea of designing a small harpsichord. Living at that time in a flat where space was limited he was obliged to restrict the size of the instrument. Its design was a cross between a harpsichord and a spinet with one 8ft and one 4ft register; the interesting point being that it was strung diagonally and thus enabled him to obtain the maximum string length with the obvious benefit of enhanced tonal quality.

In the early 1950s he and his wife moved to London where he continued to develop his ideas in both harpsichord design and production. It is interesting to note that, although modified, his early design with diagonal stringing was to form the basis of a very successful range of instruments. He was impressed by the sophistication of the later harpsichord makers, in particular the English. In later years, as his range of instruments increased, the design of his most popular two-manual harpsichord was strongly influenced by a Kirckman in the collection at Fenton House, London. By 1958 he had reached the position of having difficulty in meeting the demand for his instruments. He formed a unique working partnership with the firm of Whelpdale, Maxwell and Codd Ltd, a company long established in the craft of piano making. This association was to last until his retirement in 1976 and indeed the company today is still actively producing instruments to the original designs of William de Blaise, and has sole production rights. To date, over a thousand harpsichords have been produced and exported throughout the world.

William de Blaise was very conscious of the fact that although, of course, most of the music for the harpsichord was written in the seventeenth and eighteenth centuries, a considerable amount is being written by contemporary composers. In a sense the harpsichord has also become a modern instrument used by both modern musicians and pop groups. He supported the view that a true harpsichord maker should have a full knowledge and understanding of every aspect of design, including string design and scaling, and he was intolerant of those who meticulously copy the older instruments without thought or question. Only with a full understanding of design is it possible to analyse the old and, with the aid of modern materials and technology, produce instruments which are a true reflection of the age in which we live. The William de Blaise range of harpsichords was developed to provide instruments for performers who appreciate all periods of harpsichord music. The instruments are of robust construction, well sounding and with a good length of tone, and suit a wide variety of both performer and playing environment. The historical purist may not be attracted towards them, but those who can accept the concept of a modern harpsichord, based on historical instruments but incorporating modern developments, will find his harpsichords both rewarding, reliable and enlivening.

Upon his retirement in 1976 William de Blaise moved to the Bordeaux area of France, where he continued to develop his ideas until his death in 1978. The production of his harpsichords continues with Whelpdale, Maxwell and Codd, under my own supervision.

Martin Huggett has his workshops at The Old Maltings, Stour Street, Manningtree, Essex, where he is currently making: a range of single- and two-manual harpsichords of varying specifications loosely based on those of the late eighteenth century and which include the $4\frac{1}{2}$-octave clavichord and the bentside spinet illustrated.

CHAPTER 13

Morley Galleries

John Morley runs a workshop in Lewisham. It is large enough to qualify as a small factory. His family firm has made pianos for many years and his father was an outstanding piano designer, but for 20 years the firm has made only harpsichords, spinets, virginals, clavichords and harps. Pianos (and concert harps) are now bought from other makers for sale and also, occasionally, the firm buys and restores old keyboard instruments, both plucked instruments and early pianos. John Morley likes to be able to organize his work so that there are always sufficient instruments for sale from stock, but is willing to take special orders for decorated instruments. Unlike most harpsichord makers, who tend to be casually dressed (to put it kindly), he is always dressed formally and looks like a well-organized businessman, but the eye of the craftsman shines through when he talks about instruments or supervises the details of his workshop.

JOHN MORLEY:

I became aware of musical instruments when taken as a toddler to the family factory to watch the craftsmen at work making pianos. The assumption was there that I would enter the family business and I was given every encouragement to make things from an early age. When I was five my (paternal) grandfather gave me a wooden hut, complete with bench, as a Christmas present; it had been made for me by the piano craftsmen. On Christmas morning this was complemented by a set of woodworking tools, including saws, planes and chisels, which arrived from my maternal grandfather, a Nottingham builder who had specialized in ecclesiastical joinery.

My grandmother was far from sure that I was safe that Christmas as I sawed and chiselled away at pieces of wood on the rug in front of her drawing-room fire, occasionally using the brass fender as a stop against which to saw; in fact she was quite glad when I was taken home. The hut was a great success during the following summer, and I had considerable enjoyment in making boats and aeroplanes from the factory off-cuts which arrived at our home as firewood.

As might be expected, I was encouraged to play the piano, unfortunately with very modest success; I did, however, have quite a good voice and nearly found myself at choir school. The outbreak of war intervened and instead I was dispatched to my grandparents in Nottingham, returning home several years later to attend Eltham College.

My first introduction to early keyboard instruments took place in 1945 when my father took me to visit our cousin John Sebastian Morley, the harp and spinet maker at Old Brompton Road in South Kensington. (Both my father and I call him cousin; in fact the relationship is a more distant one going back several generations.) Among the multitude of harps and early keyboard instruments and rows of square pianos, for which he was well known, were two new clavichords. In 1938 my father and John Sebastian had decided that the time had come to start making early keyboard instruments on a joint basis. A suitable antique instrument was chosen to be copied and two cases were made, one in the factory and one in the harp workshops where, subsequently, both were strung and completed. These were not the first Morley early keyboard instruments – clavichords and spinets had been made in the harp workshops on an occasional basis for many years. In fact the family interest started much earlier with Joseph George Morley, the father of John Sebastian who, as a young man, had left *his* father's workshop to gain experience at the Erard factory for harps and pianos in Paris. He had arrived in 1870, shortly after the fall of the Commune, and was to see the first modern harpsichords constructed by Erard and Pleyel some years later.

Subsequently Joseph George returned to England to develop his father's workshop where he started to make concert harps to his own design and also purchased the stock, machinery and work in progress of the Erard–London harp factory. He established showrooms in Old Brompton Road and in Paris (until 1914) from which to sell pianos and harps, together with all kinds of antique stringed keyboard instruments.

It was therefore perhaps predictable that by 1953, when I started to help my cousin in the harp workshops, plans to make early keyboard instruments should have been revived.

John Morley: wing spinet in curl mahogany, inlaid and cross banded,
after the original by Joseph Mahoon, 1742.

This was the year I finished my training: a three-year full-time course at the Northern
Polytechnic followed by attendance at the Meisterschule für Piano und Orgel Bau in
Ludwigsburg. Until that time it had been more or less possible for John Sebastian to
match demand for early keyboard instruments with the antique spinets and harpsichords
which he would buy, restore and resell. Antique harpsichords still cost little more than
new instruments and possessed tonal characteristics which he admired far more than the
modern instruments, developed principally in Germany and influenced by the work of
Pleyel, which were beginning to flood the market.

It is difficult to imagine, now, some 25 years later, what might be considered a "Dark
Age of Harpsichord Making". Musicians were provided with, and were keen to
purchase, instruments of heavy construction with foreshortened bass scales to reduce
overall size, lengthened treble scales to add brilliance, thick soundboards with piano-type
bridges and bars, overspun strings, occasionally iron frames and frequently 16ft stops
with no historical precedence. The list of modern innovations is almost endless and must

also include pedal registration and piano keyboard spacing, weighted jacks, unresponsive touch and tone which bears little resemblance to that of the original instruments known to Bach, Handel and Mozart.

The aims, therefore, in making John Morley instruments was to produce a range closely based on historic examples of known musical worth and suitable for use in conditions existing today, at a reasonable price for the enthusiastic amateur and professional musicians who could no longer find or afford an original instrument.

The first choice was obvious; clavichords had always been scarce in England while the demand for these instruments was strong. I had examined a Scheidmayer 1782 in Stuttgart which appealed to me and now my cousin found a suitable light South German example of just over four octaves which was very similar. I drew up the plans and had the soundboard and case made at the Bromley piano factory (for which I was now responsible) and subsequently my cousin and I made the keyboard and tangents, strung and completed it. This plan of work was used for the first several dozen clavichords, after which all the clavichord making was transferred to the piano factory under my direction.

A similar course was adopted for a spinet based on the 1748 Joseph Mahoon: the soundboard and case were made at Bromley, and my cousin and I made the jacks from pearwood, holly and hogs' bristle and finished the instrument at Kensington. Demand for these instruments proved brisk and it was decided to embark on a double-manual; my cousin had an extremely fine 1775 J. and A. Kirckman two-manual harpsichord which we copied. Although a number were made, the times were not right for them; they were considered too large, and musical taste at that time was predominantly in favour of a double-manual of about 6 feet in length, preferably with a 16ft, seven pedals, sloping cheeks and grand piano-type lyre and legs.

It was fortunate that I came by a very nice Longman and Broderip made by Culliford which was unusual in having a foreshortened bass scale and an overall length of 6 feet 6 inches. This was just about an acceptable length then for a modern single-manual. This instrument provided the basis for most of the single and double-manuals which we made until the taste of the musical public became sufficiently developed to permit a return to the scaling of Kirckman and Shudi.

I have an affection for that Longman and Broderip. It was sold to George Demus in 1959 for £450 and when bought back in 1974 for considerably more, provided a further opportunity for enjoyment. Unfortunately it was sold again, the Morley family are makers and dealers, not collectors. They may enjoy ownership of many splendid instruments for a short time – to keep some permanently would deprive them of the opportunity to seek out many other old instruments; opportunities will surely come, though less frequently as time goes by.

John Morley: two-manual
harpsichord after Kirckman
in walnut with box stringing
and banding and with burr
walnut key well.

During the next few years I designed instruments based on a number of interesting
originals, two of which are still in continuous production – an Italian virginal after an
instrument in Berlin, and a five-octave clavichord after one by Silbermann. Some
instruments are also made on an occasional basis, including pedal clavichords, pedal harpsichords and fortepianos. Since my cousin and I made the first John Morley clavichord
there have been changes; he is now eighty-four and retired to Suffolk where he lives in a
mill house set in unspoiled countryside. My father, who designed many highly original
pianos during the inter-war years, also retired a number of years ago. I am now helped by
my brother Clive as Sales Director of Morley Galleries, where we now offer the largest
selection of fine pianos and harps in the country. We are still agents for many internationally famous makes of pianos including Bechstein, Broadwood and Blüthner,
which my great-grandfather started to sell nearly a hundred years ago when he opened

his music store at Lewisham in 1881, the family having previously been instrument makers and music sellers in the City of London since Regency times.

The Old Brompton Road workshops were transferred into a substantially larger industrial building at Lewisham during 1979. The advantage of a location within walking distance of the Galleries was too good to miss, and with twice as much workshop space it has been possible to separate the piano activities from harp and early keyboard instrument making and restoration. Another advantage is the substantial improvement in productivity which can be gained by the more effective use of craft time. There is the reduced handling of timber and instruments, a logical sequence of constructional activities and ability to ensure that all voicing can be carried out in quiet conditions unaffected by extraneous machine noise, while all lacquering and polishing can take place in a dust-free environment. It may be useful to remember that the principles of division of labour were known to English eighteenth-century harpsichord makers who used a degree of specialization within their shops, together with standardized designs to ensure good consistent quality. Craftsmen made the soundboards and casework, other craftsmen strung the instruments, fitted the mechanism and carried out tuning and voicing operations. Keymaking and jackmaking were specialist activities as were the making of brass and iron fittings, the writing of nameboards and the cutting of fret panels.

Our workshop activities are arranged in a similar manner: a cabinet maker who is also a safe and skilled wood machinist will select timber and machine a set of parts required for the basic framework of a particular type of instrument. These he will subsequently assemble and then go on to make and fit the soundboard; this will be of Bavarian pine with bridges of English sycamore. Having completed these operations he will case up the instrument individually, veneering, inlaying and cross banding to provide the casework finish required.

The completed case will then pass to a polisher who will prepare the surface and polish or lacquer the wood. There are numerous finishes to choose from, and which may be specified by customers, though demand is predominantly for mahogany or walnut polished and waxed to a medium antique shade and patina. Subsequently the instrument will pass to the voicing department, where the strings, keyboard, jack racks and jacks will be fitted by another craftsman who will also carry out the actual tuning and voicing work. It may therefore be appreciated that this traditional system allows the sort of specialization which leads to a high degree of job satisfaction and considerable personal interest in the construction of an instrument by the team of craftsmen who work upon it. This enables the individual craftsmen to specialize in those activities at which they are most talented and avoids the lack of involvement which is encouraged by de-skilled assembly systems commonly known as "mass production" on one hand and a "Jack of all trades" approach on the other.

[188]

As one might expect with an established concern, some craftsmen have reached a considerable age during their time in the workshops. The current record, which is unlikely to be equalled, is held by the chief piano technician, Mr Kenneth Rolfe, now aged eighty, a direct descendant of the Rolfe family, piano makers during the first half of the nineteenth century. Mr Rolfe was originally apprenticed in 1918, after the engineering works in which he was employed was destroyed when the Silvertown explosion devastated a large area of East London. Another craftsman is Mr P. E. Bishop, now in his seventy-seventh year, a jig and tool maker by trade, who also makes up decorative harpsichord hinges from castings and prepares jack rails and jacks.

Craftsmen of this kind of durability are now unfortunately few and far apart and their contribution is unique; however, since the harpsichord revival has quickened, the craft has become a calling for much younger men. Roger Blackbourn joined the workshops as an apprentice in 1964 because of a keen interest in music and a desire to work with his hands; having progressed through the piano departments he transferred his interest to the harpsichord and is now, at the age of thirty-two, chief voicer and harpsichord shop manager. He and other younger craftsmen are more typical of our staff today.

A planned and progressive programme of craft training for new young entrants is essential to establish and continue any craft workshop. Just as the interest in playing harpsichords is keen, so is the enthusiasm of young people to make instruments. Last year I had some fifty applicants when we needed four more craft trainees; the standard was very encouraging, so many were highly motivated and potentially capable of developing into competent craftsmen that it was not an easy choice. Craft training at the Morley workshops has, both from design and necessity, become an organized activity. The usual pattern is for craft apprentices to enter the workshop on leaving school, work under a senior craftsman and attend the Department of Musical Instrument Technology at the London College of Furniture for ten weeks, spread through every year, over a period of from three to ten years. In this way they learn both the theoretical and technical aspects of some of the many crafts needed to make a musical instrument. The choices, which depend on individual abilities, include harpsichord making, tuning, polishing and wood finishing, cabinet making, jig and tool design, wood machining, antique restoration and management studies. The concept of substantial Further Education linked to a planned scheme of in-workshop practical training was encouraged initially by the Piano Manufacturers Association and the Furniture and Timber Training Board, whose senior training adviser, Fritz Muller (now retired), was and still is a keen amateur musician; it was subsequently developed by the Institute of Musical Instrument Technology.

Like any other good training scheme the continuous monitoring of progress linked to an examination structure, organized in this case by the City and Guilds of London, has proved invaluable in developing craft ability, providing a broad spread of knowledge

John Morley: detail of Italian pentagonal spinet in Cedar of Lebanon, after an anonymous instrument in the Berlin Collection.

and encouraging the development of outward looking and enquiring craftsmen. I participated in the development of the musical instrument making component of these courses and am actively involved through work with the Institute of Musical Instrument Technology, the City and Guilds, and as Governor of the London College of Furniture. The staff of Morley Workshops have been impressed by the proved value of courses of craft training introduced by the London College of Furniture, both in the Furniture School and in the Department of Musical Instrument Technology under the guidance of Philip Shirtcliff. His enthusiasm for stringed and wind instruments as well as the harpsichord has added new and unexpected dimensions to an establishment which was previously piano orientated.

One of the difficulties of harpsichord making shops and of any other small-scale specialized craft workshop is that it can very easily become isolated and inward looking. I hold the view that it is essential to know what is happening in the wider musical world outside one's own workshop, become involved in larger issues, and help where possible. I am therefore involved with a number of organizations: the Galpin Society and the Harp Society as a member; as a Fellow of the Fellowship of Restorers and Makers of Historic Instruments; and as a Past President of the Piano Makers' Association, the Institute of Musical Instrument Technology and the Early Musical Instrument Makers' Association. Over a twenty-five year period more than 3,000 John Morley early keyboard instruments have been made; although most remain in this country a significant number have been exported, some to quite unexpected places, as diverse in climate as Alaska, Singapore, Iceland, Hong Kong, Nigeria and Kuwait. A maker may have complete control over the environment in which his instruments are made only until such time as they are delivered to their owners. From then onward the maker has no control and it is therefore essential that owners be well advised of the limitations that design and construction will place upon the tolerance of an instrument to climatic change.

It is not unusual in these days of high population mobility to learn that an instrument owner who appeared quite happy to live in Hampstead, has departed to Washington and may expect after a few years to live in Sweden. A maker should ensure that all steps he feels he can reasonably take to produce stability in varying climates have indeed been taken. Stability in an instrument is dependent on many interrelating factors, all of which are critical. Design will need to follow the principles of antique instruments with due regard to the known defects which have become apparent through the years; materials will have to be chosen for musical suitability and be of a standard that will still perform well when subjected to climatic variation.

It can therefore safely be deduced that I think the modern instrument maker should not be a facsimile copier (making slavishly correct replicas of earlier masters), but should be prepared to learn from the past and evolve instruments enjoying the tonal qualities of earlier times while taking advantage of new knowledge and opportunities. It is possible to list in some detail many of the common structural faults found during restoration of antique keyboard instruments. These can include undue distortion and corrugation of the soundboard, split soundboards, failed glue lines, hitch pins which have pulled, bending movement of the case at the treble end, and corrosion of iron wrest pins in oak wrest planks.

The list can be extended; however it would appear desirable that, where practicable,

John Morley: wing spinet in black lacquer with gold leaf banding and chinoiserie decoration.

design should be modified to avoid problems which known defects will certainly bring. New instruments should be designed and built with the intention that they will survive longer and in better condition than their antique predecessors.

Just as there are modifications which are desirable for reasons of stability, there are equally valid reasons to look with care at the specification offered by the larger antique harpsichords; for instance there are significant drawbacks to both the typical English and French double-manual arrangements. It may be thought that the 8 + 8 + 4 arrangement on English harpsichords provides too little variation in tonal colour between the principal

8ft and the upper manual 8ft, and that the French arrangement of 8 + 4 + 8 is preferable. It could equally well be suggested that the English dogleg arrangement which prevents separation of the lower manual 8ft and the upper manual 8ft places an unwelcome restriction on the performer who would wish to enjoy contrapuntal music. The most obvious drawback to French instruments must be the need to couple manuals, which tends to reduce the lightness and sensitivity of touch provided by an otherwise straightforward and elegant machine. It is for each maker to resolve, should he wish, such questions to his own satisfaction. My own standard practice is to separate the 8fts by the 4ft to provide 8 + 4 + 8 as on French instruments, to retain the English dog-leg jack on the front 8ft, and make the lower keyboard slide so as to disengage the dogleg from the lower manual when required. This effectively provides the advantages of the manual coupler without the disadvantages.

In my opinion these are matters to which modern instrument makers can reasonably apply themselves. The harpsichord is now in greater demand than at any time in history, and interest, not only in all music but early keyboard music in particular, is growing at an unprecedented rate. The need is to make good reliable musical instruments for use in the conditions we enjoy today and therefore the practices of the original makers can reasonably be re-examined.

It is questionable whether exact duplication of the work of old-master harpsichord makers will necessarily prove any more likely to provide an exact tonal duplication than the exact reproduction of Stradivarius violins can recapture the sound of the master makers of Cremona. What is certain is that the makers of the eighteenth century worked with the best materials which were available to them at that time, and it is unlikely that, had the techniques and materials which are known to us been available to them, the potential of these would not have been explored. Some years earlier we came to the reluctant conclusion that most owners were unable to maintain wood jacks and to voice leather or quill plectra. Before Samuel Pepys played his spinet he would have expected to replace any faulty plectra in exactly the same way as he would expect to shape a quill with his pen-knife before writing. The ability to manipulate a pen-knife on quill may be regarded as a lost art which it is unreasonable for makers to expect most owners to acquire; maintenance needs to be easy.

The ideal material for a harpsichord jack would be suitable for both injection moulding and working with conventional machine and hand tools, and possess the same density as pearwood as well as superior mechanical properties which are unaffected by temperature and humidity changes. The only modern material fulfilling our requirements is a glass-reinforced nylon, and jacks of this material are used in conjunction with moulded Delrin plectra developed with the help of accelerated wear tests and tonal analysis testing carried out at University College, Cardiff. Since we offered these new jacks and plectra, maintenance has ceased to be a problem and many owners have confirmed the advantages of instruments equipped with jacks made from this unique and expensive material. There are many other examples of modern techniques and materials to be found in our early keyboard instruments; the main object, however, is still to make instruments which faithfully reproduce the sounds of earlier times and retain the elegance of the original designs at a reasonable price.

Since 1958 we have exhibited at the Design Centre and our clavichords are included in the Design Index. I was awarded a Silver Medal at the Milan Triennale for a clavichord, and we exhibit our instruments regularly at the Early Music Exhibition in London, the Harpsichord Festival at Bruges, and occasionally at the Crafts Centre in London. I feel that it is most important for the maker to show at exhibitions in this way. It enables contact to be maintained with other makers and provides invaluable opportunities to meet informed members of the public and so to obtain that necessary feedback without which it is impossible to tell if one is making the right instruments in the right way.

John Morley has his showrooms at 4 Belmont Hill, Lewisham, London, and is currently making: a wing spinet of typical early English design; an Italian virginal and an Italian harpsichord; single- and double-manual harpsichords to his own design after a Longman and Broderip; a classical two-manual after Kirckman and a small and large clavichord.

CHAPTER 14

Robert Davies

Robert Davies is a trim, sailor-like man (and he does in fact sail a beautiful yawl in his spare time) with a Captain Kettle beard. His house and workshop look like a small bungalow, which cunningly disguises not only a floor at attic level but also (because of the steep, Lakeside slope on which it is built) a basement giving ample workshop space.

In his sitting room there is a harpsichord which he has never sold – his fiftieth, dated 1975, a two-manual after Taskin. In another room is his first, a Thomas Goff inspired instrument in a rich walnut-veneered cabinet; he kept it because the fashion changed as soon as he had made it. His hundredth has just been safely delivered to Trinity College of Music, while the next after this is complete in the workshop, awaiting final voicing. Two cases, just started, occupy the remainder of the workshop space, which is tidy and well organized. His assistant, Frances Dawbarn, helps him run it – the task when I arrived was the completion of the soundboards for the two new instruments.

The house is well stocked with fastidiously chosen furniture and a number of paintings by talented friends hang on the walls. The views from the windows are superb: the crests of the Lakeland hills still (near the end of March) covered in snow. One felt that he had chosen the perfect setting for his craft. He certainly appreciated his good fortune in being able to practise it there. So did I for my visit to himself and his wife – a lively and entertaining couple who fed me with invigorating stories and wonderful cakes until, alas, it was time for my return.

ROBERT DAVIES:

None of us over the age of fifty could ever have seriously contemplated harpsichord making as a sole career either on leaving school or even, I suspect, for a few years after the war. It follows, therefore, that I did a good many other things before deciding to make harpsichords as a business. I may have been fortunate in this in so far as a good many attributes (I hesitate to say skills) go towards making both a good harpsichord and a good harpsichord maker. Fortunate also was I in having a long tradition of artists and craftsmen on both sides of my family, and also having had an early training in music, both instrumental and vocal.

It is often said that a child brought up either by parents or contemporaries who excel at an art or craft is fortunate. Somehow, I suppose, the abilities are meant to "rub off" on to the child. My parents had abilities equally distributed between them in ballet and painting and in playing the violin and piano. Certainly in these circumstances it frequently happens that no barriers are put up against the young person attempting the adults' pursuits even if no really active encouragement is forthcoming. But children are perverse and often want to be different from their parents. Moreover if the parents' art comes easily to them, they in turn tend to be impatient of childish imperfections and, however they may try to hide disappointment, the child detects it. As to inherited ability, if such a thing exists, I am certain that it will take its own good time in making itself apparent and that it resents being prodded into activity.

All this preamble is clearly my excuse for starting late and trying a thousand pursuits before arriving at the harpsichord. Make no mistake though, I thoroughly enjoyed my childhood and I suppose that several generations of artists and craftsmen must have some effect upon one even if it is only a sort of distorted pride! Naturally I was encouraged in my early attempts at model making by such phrases as, "If a thing is worth doing it's worth doing well", and when at the age of about six I found a certain difficulty in drawing a Sopwith Camel's wings in correct perspective I learned that, "If it was easy it wouldn't be worth doing – everyone would be a Rembrandt!" And so on. I think our school in Leicester in the late thirties was more liberal than most. Whilst prowess on the Rugby field was more than welcome, you were not considered a cissy if you played the piano or liked painting. Anyway it has produced more than one household name from among my contemporaries. The piano and something of the organ I learned both from school and outside teachers, but my passion for trying everything from chess to girls precluded any lengthy practising and whilst I suppose I was a fair performer (and have remained a good sight-reader) it was rather later that music as a way of life dawned.

Two years after the beginning of the war it was necessary to decide my career. My form at school were just too young for call-up then, but a few acquaintances had been

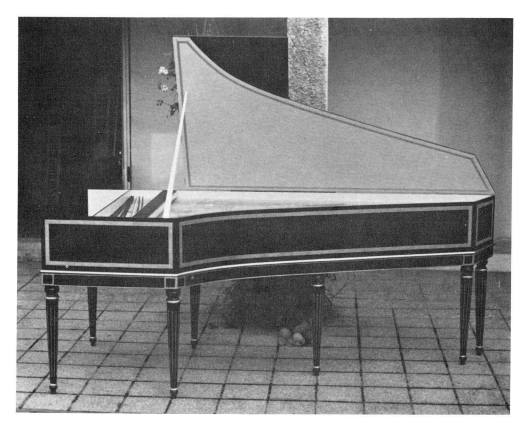

Robert Davies: two-manual harpsichord after Pascal Taskin, 1769, in
dark maroon lacquer with gold leaf banding.

drawn from the short-lived "Bevin-boy" hat and had gone to the coal mines in lieu of the
army. I had discovered the outdoor life and, with three farmer uncles who looked as
though they were going to want all the help they could get if the war went on long, it
was decided that I should go to Agricultural College. If our yearly exam results were
above 65 per cent, we stayed. If they were lower, it was the army. I was lucky until 1945
but then the war was over and everything one had been doing seemed in need of change.
I persevered with the Ministry for a few years, married the girl I had met at college and
then went into partnership with two friends in a photographic processing laboratory
where we worked eighteen hours a day in summer and about as many minutes in winter.

During this time (1948–50) I first heard Wanda Landowska and, just as when I first
heard Bach as a small boy, I needed no explanation or further knowledge, I simply liked
it. A bit more knowledge has come since, of course, but I still remember the emotional
impact of my first Toccata and Fugue and first harpsichord (albeit a Pleyel) more than
almost anything since. Also during this time I had more attempts at serious model
making, principally marine, and this "hobby" has remained with me – I have in fact (in

1980) just received a commission to make a scale model of a new sailing cruiser from a boat builder. Essays into photography followed but apart from occasional bouts of record photography, this art has palled: though I am sure that it is an art when approached correctly.

For a time I managed a photographic business, our earlier partnership having closed, and taught a little. I joined a firm of light engineers after moving to the North West and tried to learn more skills. I must say that the intractability of metal has never sparked my enthusiasm as has homely timber, and accordingly I started to make full-size sailing dinghies (before the advent of the immense kit business), to sail them, with some success, and to paint again with oils. Soon after this period, I think it was in 1960, I used to have lunch in a coffee bar in Kendal where I met Robin Bagot. He would talk about his concerts at Levens Hall and the harpsichord he had built in 1956, after studying the late Thomas Goff's methods. He heard about my sailing dinghies and I remember him saying, "I think you should make something really useful, like a harpsichord!" I shall always be more than grateful that he gave me the opportunity to work with him in his workshop on two large harpsichords of his own design, which were subsequently played and broadcast by more than a few well-known performers. Just as they were finished, Robin went to America where he met the late Frank Hubbard and Bill Dowd. The Hubbard *Three Centuries* was about to be published.

On his return he had to break the news that after two years' work, we were clearly on the wrong track! This could have been the end of the road, since the effort seemed so great, but for the encouragement I received from Robin Bagot and Geraint Jones – who ordered one of the "new" French harpsichords and persuaded others to do the same. Clients do not wait for ever and it became clear that full-time work it had to be. It has been full time ever since. Robin Bagot made a Hubbard two-manual in 1970, but since then he has applied himself constantly to fine art, in particular his much sought-after watercolours are a monument to his search for perfection in everything he undertakes.

For two years I tried to work alone with help from Margaret ("Mudge"), my wife, and apart from the Hubbard kits we built I always tried to make everything here. Of course it has since become apparent that a specialist keyboard maker makes a far better keyboard than most of us instrument makers and I have lately had my keyboards made from my drawings by such specialists, apart from the odd clavichord and virginals keyboard "to keep our eye in".

I am much happier working at the instruments than administering a business, or perhaps I should say that I am not happy when I am not working at an instrument and have very strong feelings of frustration or even guilt! Because of this I started to employ what I fervently hoped was a secretarial assistant, Mrs Tyson. Since our administrative

Robert Davies: two-manual
harpsichord in the Flemish
style, with marbled panelling
and gold leaf banding, and
interior decoration of block
printed paper.

Robert Davies: virginal after
Ruckers with marbled pan-
elling, gold leaf bands, and
interior decoration of block
printed papers and flower
painted soundboard.

and secretarial work by no means occupied her wholly, she soon turned to the little fidgety jobs we have, filing hitch pins, assembling jacks, inserting dampers. This progressed to rubbing down, filling, painting, covering keyboards, morticing registers and so on. Her willingness to attempt virtually anything has been handed down to other and later young ladies – Rozanna Harris, Jane Stables and Frances Woolley, all of whom left in due course to get married. Frances Woolley married fellow harpsichord maker Dennis Woolley, and they live 20 miles from here at Dent. We now have another Frances, Frances Dawbarn, still here having started three years ago. She attended the Purcell School, and then spent some years in America, where she continued her interest in music. I am of the opinion that for more than a few operations women take a lot of beating. In particular if they persevere with painting techniques, by which I mean cases and lids, not decoration, I believe they are better than men. Of the latter we have also had one or two, including a student who worked with Frank Hubbard and who went back to the States after a month or two in disbelief that we had a view of the Cumbrian mountains, since it had been one of our glorious misty summers! He sent me a very good off-set ratchet screwdriver which we still call "Douglas" after him. Robert Deegan worked here for six years or more and became skilled in all aspects and then started his own workshop in Lancaster. During his time here he earned his Churchill Fellowship by visiting virtually all the makers in the USA and from them has gleaned more than a few tricks.

Over the years our instruments have become a bit lighter in weight and, I suppose, closer to their original prototypes. Is there another trade or profession, I wonder, which evolves steadily by regressing so assiduously? We all experiment, I suppose, but since it is the performers who pay pipers and call tunes, it is they alone who can answer. For myself, I try to give a client the instrument he or she seems to need. If a professional has a need for several harpsichords, he can choose precise, or very close, facsimiles. If an amateur feels justified in owning only one but still wants to play everything from Bull to Mozart, something has to be compromised. To this end we do extend compasses below and above that of the smaller old instruments where necessary. Of course we delude ourselves if we think we faithfully copy anything in wood and wire, quite apart from an original's original sound!

Imagine being presented with a delicious chocolate cake and told, "Have a nibble, but no more, and then go to your kitchen/laboratory and make one exactly like it." After many attempts, some more successful than others, which involve chemicals, food colouring and a considerable amount of guesswork and indigestion, you are suddenly given the recipe. You can choose to do one of two things, either receive the recipe with cries of joy and discard all previous attempts and make yourself a cake as nearly like the original as the memory of that small first nibble will permit, or reject the recipe out of hand and continue blindly on the assumption that you will get it right eventually and might even improve on it.

The original "chocolate cakes" are, of course, the old instruments seen but hardly played, in the museums of thirty years ago. The "recipe" was only given to us after dissection and restoration of originals by those who were able to do it in the 1950s. I myself saw no reason, having tried the experimental method, not to adopt the recipe when it was presented.

Valuable though the early modern attempts at harpsichord making were, inasmuch as they introduced to the listening public the "new" sounds of the harpsichord, I feel sure that it was essentially to the harpsichord *as an instrument* that they were listening and not to the actual music. After all there is still virtually a whole generation of quite erudite listeners who have yet to overcome almost a lifetime of listening to all keyboard music on the piano. The acquisition of a taste for an authentic instrument is no doubt a fairly slow one for most, and this coupled with our inherent conservatism is, I think, responsible for the continued acceptance of non-harpsichord sounds.

As regards modern composers for the harpsichord, they are quite entitled to compose for whatever type of instrument they wish, but I think that, given the several basic differences between harpsichords of different schools, they might be advised to indicate the type that they have in mind as being best suited to their compositions.

The construction of our instruments and the materials from which they are made follows very closely that of their prototypes. However, it is my opinion that for casework the species of timber used is of somewhat secondary importance provided that the mass of the sides is similar to the original's and, of course, given that the material is very stable. The cross bracing for each type should certainly not exceed in weight or dimensions that of the prototype. For soundboards, however, there seems little doubt that the traditional Swiss Pine has no counterpart. I don't know that we have ever deviated from traditional bridge materials and so cannot say whether alternatives are suitable.

We make instruments with traditional jacks of wood, or of Delrin, and on at least two occasions we have been asked to substitute the latter for the former when a client's exasperation seems to have overtaken his desire for authenticity. Of one thing I am convinced, and that is that however traditionally correct the instrument, the last stages of voicing and adjustment can mar a potentially good instrument if not carried out with the utmost care. Unfortunately the reverse is not true and a poor instrument is not to be coerced into being a bright one by any amount of subtle voicing. This is not to say that most new instruments produce of their best in the first months of their life, and if they are not played at all regularly it can be up to four or five years before they reveal their true selves. Even after a short period of intensive playing every day, however, a light scraping

Robert Davies: two-manual harpsichord after Pascal Taskin, 1769, nearing completion in the workshop. Finished in lacquer, dark blue exterior with gold leaf bands and pale blue interior.

of the undersides of all the plectra can produce quite a startling difference to an ordinary sounding instrument.

When it comes to decoration we are, to some extent, allowed a freer hand, although I would certainly draw the line at anything downright outlandish. We like to decorate our own soundboards, lids and sometimes outer cases, although this work has occasionally been given to an outside artist. Harry Kellard, for many years stage designer at Glyndebourne, came to Kendal to retire and while here did some painting for me which has always been greatly admired.

Although I like to *think* that I am "self-taught" (some would say obviously so!) surely this only means that one lacks formal attendance at an art school? My father taught me, and his painting now at the age of eighty-three is better than ever; I look at paintings with close attention, particularly natural flower and bird paintings and I have learned techniques from all and sundry – marbling from one, Chinese detail from another. Is this not the way we learn virtually everything? Wherefore all this "self-teaching" then? Probably there is no such process: it is a conceit.

Original soundboards that I have examined seem usually to have had two or three thin wash coats of shellac, or occasionally thinned spirit-varnish, prior to being painted in egg tempera. Absence of oil in either coating or paint was certainly of prime importance, and is sensible on several counts. Personally I prefer a slightly darker ground on the sound-board when it is to be decorated, but this has no traditional basis.

We have painted soundboard flowers in tempera, but have now gone on to use acrylic colours which are, of course, water soluble and are just as capable of producing transparent tone as is tempera. The fast drying attributes of acrylic can be put to good use, although clearly for shading of large areas it is a bit of a pest. The proprietary matt mediums are a help with this, but brushes need constant washing out. To achieve the more free-flowing styles of French decoration, too careful a drawing is probably a mistake. I allocate flowers to their positions on the soundboard by rough outlines and indicate by letter their final colours to make sure that all the pinks or all the blues are not together. Much of original flower painting certainly seems to be simply one brush stroke per petal, but work like this today would be regarded as crude.

Flemish and earlier decoration is much stiffer and more carefully drawn, and on some instruments there is clear evidence of the painting having been worked to a fair extent. With any soundboard decoration one tends to over strengthen colour, in the sure and certain knowledge that soundboards with strings covering them are very rarely dusted. Lid paintings of any sort (unless one is very sure of oneself) are probably best done on a separate board and then applied to the lid with a small edge rebate added last. The types of lid decoration available to us are too numerous and well known for me to make any comment.

The number of instruments we have made is just over a hundred in the last ten years, which points to a clear average of ten a year. Of course this has included smaller in-struments, clavichords, virginals, etc., and when we had four or five people working here we were able to work on two or three instruments at a time. This average must now drop, not least because it seems the longer we work the more elaborate we are asked to become. In particular, the Flemish muselars and other small instruments which now seem to be required completely decorated, with marbling in some cases, take us so much longer, and certainly approach the time needed to make single-manual harpsichords, that I have wondered for some time why it is that most of us make a very clear price gap between a harpsichord and a virginal. There are not as many jacks of course, and the compass is usually shorter, but I suppose one can only ask so much for the smaller instruments.

Until the pound sterling began to improve last year, probably up to 70 per cent of our instruments went abroad – from Australia to Canada, from Israel to Sweden. Of late, however, we seem to have made a higher percentage for the United Kingdom. Apart from the Bruges Festival I have never attempted to sell abroad, but no doubt *Early Music* magazine reaches far and wide.

Looking at the future, I see no signs of abatement of interest in early music. That material costs are going to rise goes without saying and it is likely that in the short term there may not be as much cash about. However, those of us whose sole work is instrument making and of whose output a goodly percentage is for export can feel reasonably secure, I think.

The instruments currently being made by Robert Davies are: two-manual harpsichord after Pascal Taskin, 1769, a single-manual version of the same instrument, a two-manual and two single-manual Flemish harpsichords and a Flemish virginal, after either Ruckers or Couchet. He also makes a number of other instruments to order, including early French and late English copies and a copy of the 1745 Dulcken. His workshop address is: Holly Gate, Levens, near Kendal, Cumbria.

CHAPTER 15

The John Feldberg Workshops

I always regretted not meeting John Feldberg; I passed his workshop in 1960 when delivering a harpsichord to London, stopped with the intention of calling but, short of time, went on again. There was not another chance as I heard a few weeks later that he had died. The decision and will of Ann Feldberg to keep the workshop going and the

ability of Peter Whale actually to do so, was, seen in retrospect, remarkable. They have now completed twenty years in combining to run the workshop, Ann Feldberg running the organization and Peter Whale the construction. The combination works, I think, because they have talents which do not overlap.

Like most harpsichord makers, and this is an interesting trait of the profession, they show great friendliness and willingness to help. I have several times

taken work up there to be machined and their own work promptly stopped while it was done for me. The workshop is in a quiet Sevenoaks street, machine shop and bench shop on the ground floor, the showrooms above, the neatest and most attractive workshop I know. The instruments just completed at my last visit covered a broad spectrum: a Goujon, a Dulcken; an English virginal in solid oak and a muselar after Couchet, blockpaper decorated; all totally different from each other in every way; a solid walnut English wing spinet; and the harpsichord which interested me most, but is not in regular production, a reconstruction of the John Haward at Knole House. (The name is actually in dispute but it is convenient to continue thinking of it as a Haward.)

Had John Feldberg lived his personality would undoubtedly have been dominant; as things are, the workshop runs as a group effort, and I have therefore included observations from the two craftsmen as well as from Ann Feldberg and Peter Whale. It should not be thought that the other workshops are staffed by production-line workers doing broken-down tasks; in fact those I met were also both competent and articulate craftsmen but, in the Feldberg workshop, these qualities were very apparent.

ANN FELDBERG:

John Feldberg was educated at Blundells School, Tiverton and read Natural Sciences at Christ's College, Cambridge 1949–51. His interest in music predominated, however, and he spent a great part of his time playing the violin, and he also attended the lectures of Thurston Dart, whose harpsichord and clavichord made by Thomas Goff greatly impressed him. I was reading music at Newnham at the same time, and in accompanying him on the piano the conviction grew on us both that I should be using a harpsichord. This conviction was enforced by the fact that we played mostly Handel, Corelli and above all Bach; John's veneration for Bach was total, reinforced by his friendship with Peter Hurford the organist (they were friends at school previously) who was organ scholar of Jesus College at this time.

When John went down in 1951 he eventually took a job with Griffiths Hansen, in London, repairers and experts in Bechstein pianos. This gave him an opportunity to become very familiar with piano actions, also to make in his spare time a pedal piano fitting for Peter Hurford. He went to study the instruments at Fenton House and at the Victoria and Albert Museum when he could get at them, and to ferret out information at the British Museum reading room. He also attended the Northern Polytechnic course in musical instrument technology for eighteen months, until it folded and was eventually to be reorganized as the London College of Furniture. There was a gap, though, into which his course collapsed. Griffiths Hansen was very sound training for him, and a happy coincidence for us, since I was library assistant in the music section of London University Library from 1954 and our tube station for Hampstead, where we first lived, was midway between our two places of work.

John did not intend to remain with pianos, and indeed very early on consulted Tom Goff, who was very kind and helpful but was not able to offer him a job, and eventually recommended that he should go to Germany to learn harpsichord making in the Neupert works in Bamberg. After a trial period he was found to be satisfactory, and our small family removed to Bamberg for a year in January 1957. The Neupert way of making harpsichords at that time meant that he moved through every stage of the work, highly departmentalized, and learnt each section thoroughly. We actually returned to England in December of the same year with an agreement from Neupert and the relevant drawings so that we could make the Neupert designs on licence. In fact, excellent in intent though this was, it was probably a mistaken decision and did neither side much good in the long run. But Herr Neupert was always kindness itself to us and to the workshop.

On our return we rented a workshop in Sevenoaks, which had been used by a furrier. There were high rafters right up to the roof in the main room, festooned with great swathes of cobwebs embellished with greasy fur which had floated up over the years. We got down as much of this as we could and then John put up a false ceiling. That workshop had enormous atmosphere and his dedication to getting the workshop going was absolute. He worked alone and extremely concentratedly, on his own designs and in less than two-and-a-half years he made two very good clavichords and three two-manual harpsichords. In the completion of the last and largest harpsichord, a concert model with

Feldberg Whale: wing spinet in walnut, after the original by Stephen Keene.

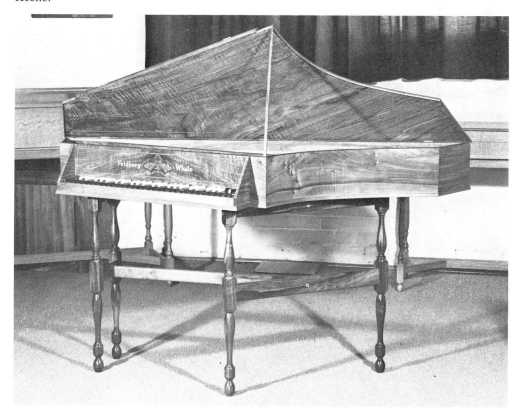

16ft stop he was joined by Peter Whale, who simply walked in, saying, "I heard you needed some help." How true this was. John died in May 1960, three months later.

I had been attending to the office side of the workshop as required and therefore I knew how to proceed. Peter Whale with extraordinary skill and determination applied himself to mastering all branches of harpsichord making. John had just been on the point of launching the schools harpsichord kits; one prototype had been made by him and the instructions were on the way. Peter Whale had to get it off the ground, and this he did while also completing half-finished instruments. Herr Neupert was very generous in sending one of his craftsmen to instruct in the finer points of harpsichord making, and I must acknowledge the understanding and kindness of our customers at that time, who gave us their encouragement by waiting patiently and expressing their confidence in Mr Whale. I remember especially Stanislav Heller and his enthusiasm for his concert harp-

Feldberg Whale: two-manual harpsichord after the Goujon in the museum of the Paris Conservatoire.

sichord, of which John had himself got as far as making the soundboard. He came a number of times to tune for us, while Mr Whale was still learning to tune.

The schools harpsichord *was* launched, and flourished for three years, from 1961–3 or so, petering out in the end as it was not very profitable and, in fact, making it was extremely dull; we wanted to make instruments, not boxes of parts. We kept the original harpsichord and have hired it out ever since to Royal College of Music students as a practice instrument, and it surprises me pleasurably when it comes back for re-quilling. At the same time, John's own harpsichords were making a favourable impression, and were frequently used at Wigmore Hall, then on the South Bank, and of course at the BBC. In our early days, few artists had their own instrument and the concert model was a very good harpsichord for general purposes, and it recorded well. We continued to make the concert models and on similar heavy lines we made for ten years two smaller versions with 8 + 8 + 4 specification designed by Mr Whale as developments of the schools harpsichord. We both felt, though, that the piano-influenced method of harpsichord building must be re-examined, and when we reached the 1970s we were making designs of Mr Whale's box construction built on the baseboard, with plastic jacks. These were lighter and more resonant, but we were still looking for improvements of tone and touch.

We owe a great deal to Jane Clark (Mrs Stephen Dodgson) who introduced us to the Goujon double-manual harpsichord in the Paris Conservatoire Museum, and asked us to make her a copy. This was done in 1971 and it convinced us that we had no alternative any longer but to devote all our time to making copies. I had been chewing over my ideas on the subject for several years, in discussions with Derek Adlam (who worked for us two days a week for several years) and in particular when I tried original instruments, at Fenton House, the Colt collection, and back in Nuremburg. Now we were on the right road at last, and we have made copies since then entirely, concentrating on the construction rather than the decorative details. If the sound and the touch are right, we have succeeded.

In selecting a model that we wish to copy we try to be practical: first it must be a good instrument that we respect and like; then its disposition should be of practical use to the musician, preferably of convenient keyboard compass and acceptable size. We like to be able to offer a wide choice to cover as many styles, periods and nationalities as we reasonably can. There is a challenge in making instruments at a time when the music available in print and on record ranges more widely than ever before, when musicians and the players we hope to serve are more broadly educated in music than ever before, and when there is probably more chance than ever before of being able to inspect European keyboard instruments, or to receive reports of them from travelling musicians and musicologists. It is no wonder that the wealth of materials and the enthusiasm of instrument makers, pitted against universal shortage of cash, makes for workshop headaches. But we all think it is worth the effort.

The original intention of the workshop was inspired by love of music, and I have always hoped that the instruments might be played and enjoyed by large numbers of people. I have had the great pleasure of joining some of the best local musicians in chamber music in the workshop from time to time, and I wish there was more activity of this kind. We have many schoolchildren and students visiting us, and students practising the harpsichord, and I encourage this. The instruments are to be used.

We make fewer instruments than we did, our number of craftsmen has fluctuated, and at the moment we are three men and one apprentice, and all would agree that there is no room for more. The system is that one man makes one instrument from beginning to end; this is in the tradition of the workshop and I am content to abide by it. Financially it is probably not viable, but a craftsman working at his own instrument has a totally different attitude from one on a production line. We moved to our present workshop in 1965, aided by family on both sides, and the fact that I own the workshop gives enormous security to the whole workshop idea. It has been a very personal venture from the start, backed by both families and perhaps with involvement intensified by the early tragedy. The excitement of the early years when it was not certain whether we could survive has given way to the more mundane problems of finance and coping with inflation; all instrument makers must be feeling this.

If my standpoint is that of an amateur I shall have to admit to it, but this is only half the picture. The craftsmen in the workshop are professionals with a great understanding of instruments, to which I hope to supply the love and understanding of music. I can look back to the high points of our workshop's career to date; very early and soon after John's death we had to supply four harpsichords for the Vivaldi-Bach concerto at the Royal Festival Hall, conducted by Giulini, who shook my hand and congratulated me on my husband's beautiful instruments. For this occasion my kind father-in-law had brought over a Neupert "Bach" model to make the fourth, another instance of his generosity. Very much later on, probably in 1976, our Goujon copy joined three other harpsichords by our colleagues in the same work in the same hall and this made another high point as I realized afresh that we had made the right decision in changing to copies. The announcement (to ourselves and to the musical public) that we had in fact made this change, was another high spot, when Kenneth Gilbert played the Goujon copy for its inaugural recital in the Purcell Room in February 1972; this was the grey "workshop" copy, but of course Jane Clark had inaugurated her own, first, example of this in 1971. The older, heavier instruments enjoyed their own moments of triumph, which always gave me great satisfaction. They were at Glyndebourne for seven years, and very often for the touring company in the autumn. This of course had its trials, some urgent call to Leeds or Portsmouth if trouble struck on the tour. And we had some lovely recitals at the Wigmore Hall, usually on the big concert harpsichord, which with the pedal harpsichord made a noble impression, but not one which would be approved of now, at say the Bruges harpsichord week. All harpsichord making is a challenge, and I hope we will continue to meet it. Why do we do it? I doubt whether any maker does it for the money. It is the fascination of aiming at perfection, not just for its own sake but for the music that will be the result.

PETER WHALE:

Cabinet making was my profession from the start, as I was apprenticed to it when I left school at fourteen. The firm made quality furniture, individual pieces for private customers, so it was extremely good training for me. I was just through my apprenticeship when war started, and then followed five years in the RAF. After the war it was back into cabinet making, not with the same firm but with the same cabinet maker, who had started up on his own; then with a firm making kitchen furniture. I had a good deal of control in designing, ordering timber and progressing work through the mill, really organizing the whole factory system. This gave me a wide experience of production and quality control on top of my basic hand cabinet making, but ultimately I became tired of commuting and was seeking a job nearer home when a friend suggested to me that John Feldberg was looking for a cabinet maker. He had not been going very long, and was just beginning to produce instruments and pull in orders. I got on very well with John and the work exactly suited me but very sadly within a few months he died. This was in 1960. At that stage I obviously had not become experienced in the musical side of instruments. There was the question of whether we just folded up or not, but we had orders on hand which had to be completed and delivered. I had to set to and learn rapidly.

Tuning was an essential requirement and I went to the London College of Furniture on the evening course, but once I had the basic knowledge I learned more by practice on our own instruments, and within my first year I was tuning at the Royal Festival Hall. I had a very great interest in music and a natural ear which made it quite easy to learn.

We had some small technical problems at the beginning and I went to take advice from Thomas Goff, who was the master maker of the time. Although he helped in these minor ways, I did not go to study with him: what he gave me more than anything else was encouragement. He said, simply, "You can do it", and coming from Tom Goff that was enough to commit me. John had already contracted with Neuperts to produce some of their instruments on licence and as a result of this I went to Germany to their factory for

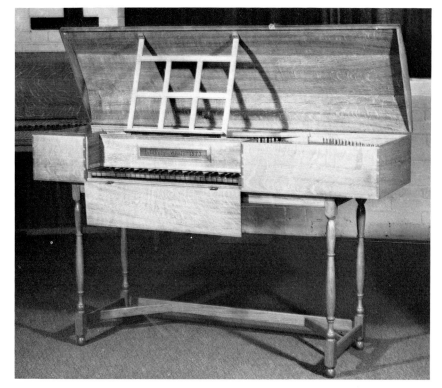

Feldberg Whale: virginal in solid oak, after the instrument "A.H."
owned by the Royal Scottish Museum.

three weeks and worked my way right through their system, picking up any details that I
needed – mostly practice in voicing.

The next thing we undertook was our schools harpsichord, a project which John had
designed and begun to get under way. These instruments were sold as kits, to schools
only, the idea being that they would be made up in the woodwork department, with the
co-operation of the music staff, so that the school would have a useful woodworking task
and end up with a playing instrument. They were small instruments with an 8 + 4 + buff
specification and we sold about sixty of them.

We carried on for a number of years, making the instruments which John Feldberg
had designed, principally the modern, solid frame, open bottom two-manual with
16 + 8 + 8 + 4, the large concert instrument; but we did not have a small single-manual or
a small two-manual, so we designed these and put them into production with the concert
harpsichord. At first they were made after the original Feldberg instruments, but
although they were successful we improved them a little, lengthened them, and then
decided to start again and produce a lighter instrument with a closed bottom. These were
about 6 feet 6 inches long, 5 octaves from either FF or GG as required. We went on pro-

ducing them for a number of years until we realized, from listening to some of the copies which were now being made, that we were not getting the true sound of the harpsichord. While we were coming to this decision we had a professional customer who wanted a copy of an early harpsichord. She had seen and liked the Goujon in the Museum of the Paris Conservatoire. We were able to get permission to take all the measurements we wanted, and a few visits to Paris, together with information available from the time it was restored, enabled a copy to be made. It was so successful that we have made it ever since, at the rate of one or two a year. We make a very close copy, although it has been necessary to increase the width very slightly to accommodate the stop levers. We also fit a music desk, which is not on the original, but have done so without making any alterations to the body.

We needed a single-manual to go with the Goujon, and decided on the Dulcken in the Vleeshuis, Antwerp; since then we have also made copies of the two-manual Dulcken in the Smithsonian.

I believe in copying closely; it does not seem to me very sensible to copy an instrument and then modify it. What is necessary is to try and get inside the skin of the original craftsmen. Although superbly capable, many of them would have been scientifically illiterate, and not familiar with the work of theorists like Mersenne. Early instruments are therefore works of art, developed slowly, not scientifically designed. Their makers would have learned the work as apprenctices and then made small changes, as they thought necessary, to correct some apparent fault or in the hope of some improvement. Although instruments from the same maker usually follow a consistent pattern, so that it is apparent they had standard models, no two are exactly alike.

Dulcken had something very special in mind when he devised his double curved side, with the second (hidden) one supporting the soundboard, and the hitch rail on the outer curve. This occurs on all the Dulckens I know, although the Smithsonian Institute two-manual has been altered; but the Institute plans show the double curved side. I am at a loss to guess what Dulcken had in mind; the only conclusion I can come to is that he wanted to make his soundboard more free to vibrate. But I have heard copies which have been made with the ordinary single curve, and they still have that special Dulcken quality.

As we progressed with making the Goujon, it was obvious we needed a range of copies to make. We were very lucky to be brought a small spinet to restore, and this turned out to be a very early Stephen Keene instrument. It had been badly restored in the past, and fitted with a thick and unsatisfactory soundboard, but when this was removed the original barring could be determined by the notches in the rim. We felt that it was an excellent spinet to copy and so it has proved. The spinet is an ideal domestic instrument, not taking up much space and being simple to tune. The only problem is the difficulty of finding the solid walnut, and the price of the walnut when we do find it. We try now to keep one of these spinets always in stock.

The Dulcken single-manual is a big instrument and expensive to make, and in looking for another single-manual to copy, and one rather smaller, we were lucky to obtain permission from Dr Mirrey to take the details of the Benjamin Slade in his collection. We now have a steady number of these going through the workshop. The date of the Slade is not known, but we think about 1710. There is no very consistent picture available of English harpsichord making about this time. The late and developed designs of Kirckman and Shudi were still in the future, the early Italian influence was in the past, but although still there, had become anglicized. Thus, this instrument has a very English look, but is light and resonant with a tone which springs up with great clarity. With the Slade we make an anonymous Italian, after an original which is also in the collection of Dr Mirrey, and two virginals, one English with the keyboard on the left and the other a muselar after Couchet. Two clavichords complete the range.

We are looking now for yet another single-manual to copy, something which will be a medium size domestic instrument with 8 + 8 + 4. I still toy with the idea of making variations on originals, something I may want to do one day, perhaps after the experience of more restoration. I have completed twenty years of instrument making, now, years of enormous challenge and change, and no other career would have been so satisfying.

TIMOTHY CONSTABLE:

I began my life of harpsichord making in 1962 when I commenced a five-year indentured apprenticeship with Arnold Dolmetsch Ltd, in Haslemere. This provided me with a good grounding in all aspects of the craft with the possible exception of theory.

The Dolmetsch workshop, like John Feldberg, manufactured all their own parts for instruments, such as keyboards, covered strings, metal parts, etc. These activities required a very skilled and imaginative staff. Their craftsmen were always willing to show me how things were done. On many occasions the workshop manager caught me talking with someone in another department, when perhaps I should have been at my bench.

After being with Dolmetsch for a total of eight years I joined the Feldberg workshop, which is smaller and has more individuality. At this time the Feldberg workshop had just started making its "box-type" instruments. They were followed a few years later by the "copy" instruments; these were very interesting times.

Mrs Feldberg kindly allowed me to attend the three-year block release course in harpsichord making, which had been recently started at the London College of Furniture. This provided an opportunity to rectify my earlier lack of theoretical knowledge.

There can be little doubt that the pre-copy instrument, while producing interesting sounds, did not have the free, resonant tone of the original instruments. With the greater interest in authenticity, in both sound and playing technique, came demands for copy-type instruments. This meant that the harpsichord maker was required to abandon his piano making techniques and adapt himself to learning the methods of instrument making used in earlier times.

The copy instrument requires to be made from traditional materials. We no longer need to use some of the modern materials such as plastic and plywood which, although regarded as reliable in use, are as not as aesthetically pleasing as are traditional woods such as lime, walnut, cypress and pear. These will give little trouble if chosen and used appropriately and of course providing that the instrument is suitably cared for. It is more pleasurable to be making a bridge with tapering dimensions and bevelled back, using service or pear, than the plain beech found on pre-copy instruments. An understanding of the qualities and disadvantages of materials such as bird quill and hogs' bristle is also required.

I find that I am far more aware of the detail when looking at original instruments than was previously so. I can only suppose that when one has carried out the processes needed to make a copy instrument one tends to notice which methods were used and to compare these with the ways in which other instruments of a particular period were made.

Although when copying instruments one is limited by the fact that one is reproducing

Feldberg Whale: single-manual harpsichord in solid brown oak, after the "Haward" or "Hazard" in Knole House.

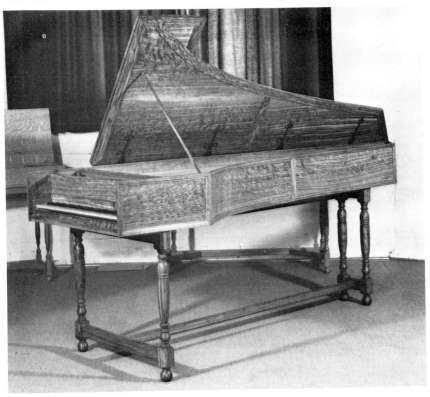

the ideas of another maker, each instrument has an individuality which is difficult to define. This was not so apparent in the pre-copy instruments which, although they may have had the stamp of a particular workshop, gave little indication of the approach of the individual maker.

We are fortunate in this workshop that each craftsman is able to make an entire instrument. This means that he can sense and appreciate the special characteristics of each instrument as he makes it, which leads to a greater understanding of the instrument and, it is to be hoped, is more satisfying for the customer.

It would be nice to think that such accumulation of knowledge and experience would lead to the further development of harpsichords, thus giving artist-craftsmen opportunities to express their own ideas. The stumbling block here, however, is that most of the repertoire dates from early times and therefore requires particular qualities of sound.

I am very satisfied with the way in which my life in harpsichord making has unfolded, affording me an insight into aspects of the instrument which many makers of today do not experience.

CHRISTOPHER JONES:

The first generation of harpsichords built during the instrument's modern revival showed very clearly the influence of the piano. This influence was evident both in the structure of these instruments and in the approach to registration: it seems to have been felt that people accustomed to piano sound would find the harpsichord unexciting and inexpressive unless it could offer a rather wider range of dynamic levels and tone colours than antique instruments had provided. So makers experimented with, for example, 16ft stops and half hooking; at the same time, they sought to produce a more stable instrument by making the action more easily adjustable.

These were the lines along which the harpsichord revival developed until the 1960s. During that decade, however, its direction changed. Interest in authentic performances of early music, and therefore in antique instruments, grew rapidly. Copies of antique harpsichords began to appear, and the ascendancy of this type of instrument was soon established. The piano-orientated builders had been bold and inventive in their approach, and their work had nearly always been distinguished by a high level of craft skill. But their instruments seem less resonant than the copies, and rather lacking in presence, especially for concert or continuo work. Also, the advantages of a regulatable action turn out to be much less obvious than had once been thought. The simpler, unadjustable actions of the copy instruments work perfectly efficiently, and since (unlike more complicated systems) they cannot de-regulate themselves, they present fewer problems of maintenance. Finally, the attempt to achieve expressiveness through elaborate schemes of registration was not really consistent with the nature of the instrument. It seems to have been a wrong turning, analogous to the efforts of some English makers towards the end of the eighteenth century to introduce dynamic flexibility to the harpsichord by means of a swell mechanism.

I think it very unlikely that any second change of course, as radical as that from "modern" to copy instruments, will take place in the future. Unless something happens to dethrone the principle of authenticity in the performance of early music, players will continue to require instruments resembling as closely as possible in sound and touch those for which the music was originally conceived, and this means copies. It would, though, be a pity if authentic building practice were held to rule out all departures from traditional methods, even those which could have no bearing on sound or touch. I think, for example, that modern, square, tuning pins, all machined to exactly the same dimensions, do actually work better than antique flat ones. However, such improvements are marginal. It seems unlikely that more fundamental improvements will readily be made in an instrument which embodies the cumulative experience of more than three hundred years, although the possibility certainly remains that, for example, the application of so far untried materials might provide new sounds for composers to experiment with. For the time being, however, builders will probably be fully occupied in exploring the traditions of the past. Some aspects of this tradition – such as the Italian School – are still relatively neglected.

Harpsichord making offers many kinds of satisfaction. There is the pleasure of working fine wood with a sharp tool. There is the excitement of the moment when, after many weeks of work, an inert assemblage of wood and wire begins to sound, and thus to come alive. And there is the high degree of personal involvement which can come when (as is the case in this workshop) one is responsible for the whole of an instrument. I doubt whether any other occupation could afford me so complete a sense of fulfilment.

The John Feldberg Workshop, 2a Bradbourne Road, Sevenoaks, currently makes the following instruments: A double-strung fret-free late German clavichord. An early German fretted double-strung clavichord. An English virginals after an instrument owned by the Royal Scottish Museum. A muselar after Couchet. A wing spinet after Stephen Keene. A single-manual harpsichord after Benjamin Slade and a single-manual Italian harpsichord (anonymous). The Dulcken single-manual in the Vleeshuis, Antwerp, and the Dulcken two-manual in the Smithsonian. The two-manual Goujon in the museum of the Paris Conservatoire. The originals of the two clavichords, the Slade and the anonymous Italian harpsichord are in the private collection of Dr J. R. Mirrey.

CHAPTER 16

The Adlam Burnett Workshops

The setting for Derek Adlam's workshop is unusual, a Georgian mansion in red brick, of classically balanced proportions and imposing façade. It is not quite the place one expects to find an instrument maker and his being there is because he is in partnership with Richard Burnett, the pianist, who bought Finchcocks to house his collection of early

keyboard instruments. The house (not the workshop) is open to the public during the summer, and not only is the collection on view but Richard Burnett gives inspired lectures and demonstrations in which he plays the instruments in turn and talks about them. The collection is, at heart, one of early grand pianos, perhaps the most important being a number by Muzio Clementi. There are, however, some plucked instruments and a charming little chamber organ of delightful tone.

The workshops are separate from the house, in the stable block and associated buildings. Production is well organized with large stocks of wood drying and maturing. The most important instruments being made are the Ruckers copies and it is interesting to consider how any member of the Ruckers family would have looked at modern copies in general and these in particular. The originals are decidedly crude in parts, very simple, while having a tone which penetrates the conscious act of listening to the music with a second layer of sensual pleasure; this quality is rather like that of admiring a beautiful rose and then being overwhelmed by the scent. Derek Adlam's instruments have this quality but, instead of being in any way crude, are crafted with meticulous care and accuracy; he would have had no difficulty in being admitted to the Guild of St Luke in Antwerp.

Adlam Burnett: single-manual harpsichord after Joannes Ruckers, 1638, with marbled lacquer panels and interior decoration of block printed paper.

Adlam Burnett: fortepiano after Mathaeus Heilmann, *c.* 1785, in walnut.

DEREK ADLAM:

I did not have an opportunity to play an instrument when I was very young, but discovered when about the age of three that the metal fender in my parents' sitting-room had a variety of pitches available; it was possible by tapping from one end to the other to get tunes out of this contraption, and that was my first contact with music making. A relative played the piano and I was quite determined from early on that I would one day play a keyboard instrument; this only came about when I was eleven and started taking piano lessons. My school life was indeterminate; I wanted to take an arts course but my languages were so weak that my headmaster despaired of my having any success, and rather against my will I was pushed into the science side but still studying the piano privately. I was so disgruntled by science that just before A-levels I took myself off and succeeded in getting into the Guildhall School of Music. There I embarked on the graduate course in school music and had the vast good fortune to have as my piano professor Frank Lafitte, a marvellous player of the old school and such a good teacher, whose method is based on the traditions of Clara Schumann and the pupils of Liszt. This sort of classical approach to piano playing coincided with my own preoccupations and interest in music and what I wanted a keyboard to do.

I was also fortunate to be a pupil of Celia Bizony who studied for many years with Edwin Fischer and Gertrude Wertheim, a good pupil of Landowska. At the end of my third year at the Guildhall, just before the final exams when I should have been doing necessary revision, I started working very hard at the harpsichord. However, I passed my finals and stayed another year studying both piano and harpsichord. Celia Bizony's own Neupert harpsichord was at the Guildhall when I was in her class and this instrument eventually became my first harpsichord. I kept it for some years and its sale, later, financed the making of my own first instrument. At first I resented looking after it, but it was invaluable experience; I learnt to tune, and since the instrument needed a great deal of attention to keep in playing order, I became familiar with all the weaknesses that harpsichords and like instruments are heir to. So I gained insight not only into the music but at the same time insight into the technical nature of early keyboard instruments.

After leaving the Guildhall I taught, rather reluctantly, for five years: I was determined to enjoy it and persevered, but in fact disliked it intensely and was very relieved when I was finally able to stop.

While still at the Guildhall I had been encouraged by Ann Feldberg to restore a square piano owned by someone she knew. I was very reluctant to take the plunge on this very attractive late-eighteenth-century instrument but was persuaded, and it did in fact turn out rather well. The restoration was fairly simple and I managed to match ephemeral materials and to get the piano to work mechanically; I found it a most beguiling instrument.

It was during my teaching period that I heard about the Colt collection of early keyboard instruments at Bethersden in Kent and received an invitation to go to see Mr Colt. I suggested that the collection should be catalogued and offered to do this. The collection had been housed during the bad winter of 1963–4 in a "sample" village hall erected by the Colt building firm. It is a handsome building for the display of the instruments and acoustically irreproachable. It was for Mr Colt a period of development and consolidation of the collection. He had acquired a considerable number of instruments over the years, and having this space inspired him to start refining the collection. His preoccupation is with the early piano rather than the harpsichord, mainly, I think, because the period attracts him, and he has a remarkable intuitive appreciation of the finer points of the instruments. It is the extraordinary variety found in early pianos that makes the subject infinitely fascinating. There is a number of approaches to the problems posed in piano construction and the collector who assembles a group of instruments on such a scale can begin to see the lines of development and change, and the methods which were used by talented men to solve all these problems.

It was obvious when I came along to catalogue that the more important job would be getting the instruments into shape. Those which had already been restored needed tuning. Then it was apparent that help was needed with restoration and maintenance. It was invaluable for me to become involved because the whole of the group of instruments became a kind of laboratory for research. I was able to acquire technical information and, more importantly, some idea of the actual standards which have to be brought to bear in musical instrument making. Instrument making is engineering in wood, and I think the thing I appreciated first from my contact with all these marvellous old pianos was how remarkably high were the technical standards to which they were made. This fact began to shape my own ideas and approaches to the design of earlier kinds of keyboard instruments.

It was after I had been teaching for five years that Ann Feldberg offered me a part-time job finishing and tuning harpsichords. I worked at Feldberg's for two days a week while still working at the Colt collection for another two, and so gave up teaching with a great sigh of relief. I moved down to Pluckley, near Ashford, to be near both jobs, one at Bethersden and the other at Sevenoaks. With room for a small workshop at Pluckley and a day a week plus the week-end to myself, I was doing restoration work and also feeling confident enough to begin constructing new instruments. I do not like using the word "copies" of old instruments as it is extremely difficult and sometimes even unrealistic to do accurate copying, but I planned to do instruments which were very closely derived from historical models. It took some time to organize myself because of the sheer range of skills which have to be acquired to build something as complex as a keyboard instrument.

The first instrument I made was a virginal, a muselar. I am not sure if muselars were ever important musically, but they were built in large numbers in Antwerp – they appear in lots of paintings of Dutch interiors and that may have been what attracted me. I thought it might be simpler than a harpsichord but actually soon found that this is not so, it is just as complicated! My first instrument was based on the 1611 Andreas Ruckers in the Vleeshuis in Antwerp but it had not then been restored, and I took a lot of information from the 1650 Couchet. It turned out quite well; Colin Tilney used it for the first time in a recital in the Purcell Room in 1971; it was the sort of instrument which had not been seen before in London and aroused quite a lot of interest.

I had met Richard Burnett a little before this. He was acquiring early pianos especially for concert performance, rather than for a museum collection, and brought me a remarkably fine Graf piano to restore. After some further commissions I finally went into partnership with him while I was still at Pluckley, principally in order to set up a restoration workshop but also with a view to making new instruments. Orders had begun to come in, in embarrassing numbers; the first muselar had been unveiled by Colin Tilney, and on the strength of that Colin ordered one for himself. Another young musician just

Adlam Burnett: muselar after Andreas Ruckers, 1611, decorated with block printed paper.

then becoming well known and whom I had known for many years was Christopher Hogwood; he also ordered a muselar. Colin, on the successful completion of his muselar, asked me to build him a Ruckers style harpsichord. So it went on and, for a number of years, with each new model an order was in hand before the prototype had been built or even before the drawing had been started! So there were a number of leaps in the dark with varying degrees of success. Towards the end of my time at Pluckley the problem was that of too much work and too little space. I had some invaluable part-time assistance from Malcolm Fisk, then still working at Feldberg's, and I also met a remarkable craftsman, Bernard Baverstock, who agreed to come and work for three days a week. Bernard was in fact an important influence on the standard of work in the workshop. A great expert in handicraft techniques and tools he taught me a great deal through example and pointed me in the right direction as far as standards of authenticity were concerned.

This stage had served to show me what was really needed, and Richard and I began to look around for larger premises. It was actually a jump from the tiny to the enormous when we found Finchcocks, an early Georgian mansion in the same park as Scotney Castle and which had in recent years been the home of the Legat school of dance. It needed a vast amount of restoration but had two substantial advantages: there was room to display Richard's growing collection of instruments and in the grounds were some classrooms which, with the stable block, have become the workshops. We came here in '71 and, with Bernard Baverstock for three days a week and Malcolm Fisk joining us full time, we began to get under way.

A great deal of work was done on the house, instruments began to be displayed, recordings were made. Gradually, public access to the house was started, a condition of receiving repair grants from the Historic Buildings' Council. Public access has now developed into our "open days" in which the instruments are not only on view but are explained and demonstrated by Richard. His flair is remarkable, not only because he is a fine pianist but because he has just the right degree of showmanship to make his demonstrations work. It has become an enormous commitment on Richard's part, and takes a great toll of time and energy. It is, of course, increasing: we had eight thousand people this year and expect more next. From my own point of view the commitment became too great: after a hard week making or restoring, a week-end of demonstrating and talking left me exhausted and I had to opt out of many of the open days. And of course the problems of rebuilding, of setting up the workshops, of the open days, were combined with the problems of increasing inflation. I will not say that we have bitten off more than we can chew but, had we known beforehand what would be involved, it might have given us pause.

At one time we had eleven people in the workshop. Some were trainees who tended to unbalance production and were also uneconomic as the cost of training was not recouped; they tended to leave after two or three years. We now plan to keep the staff down to about six experienced workers who will stay with us long term.

We build three basic types of instrument. The Ruckers virginals and harpsichords we

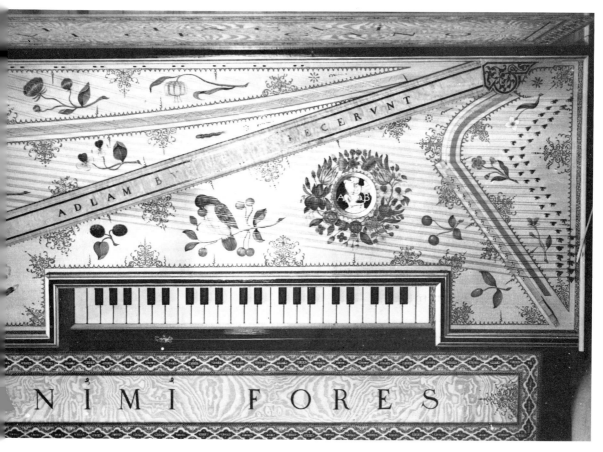

Adlam Burnett: soundboard view of a muselar after Andreas Ruckers,
1611, with painted decoration by Sheridan Germann.

began with are still being made. We follow one model of Ruckers harpsichord derived
from the 1638 transposing double in Edinburgh, a $4\frac{1}{2}$-octave instrument in reality,
although it looks like 4 octaves, and we build it in a variety of dispositions. The simplest is
a single 8 + 8 form, through to a double-manual with four rows of jacks, the second 4ft of
the original instrument being replaced by a third 8ft doglegged between the two
keyboards. In this way it is possible to get the full harpsichord effect of 8 + 8 + 4 and also a
genuine dialogue between the two keyboards in the French manner, but without a
French style shift coupler. It is in fact just like the Kirckman disposition except that there

is no lute register back in the wrest plank; all the registers are together in the main action gap. We attempt to follow all the basic methods of construction and materials in building these instruments and, if the customer requires it, follow authentic schemes of decoration. So they are close to original Ruckers instruments which have been exposed to a *petit ravalement* of about 1640–50.

We also make a copy of a Blanchet of 1730, a standard late French 5-octave instrument, but we do not build many as the fashion for such harpsichords is passing. People are becoming more interested in earlier types of harpsichord which, of course, is where the true centre of gravity of the literature lies.

My own preoccupation is with the early piano and its predecessor the clavichord, so we build a large unfretted copy of a Hass and a smaller fretted clavichord which, actually, is a late instrument, after 1800. The fortepianos are copies of a late-eighteenth-century south German instrument by Heilmann and one after Ròsenberger, a very good Viennese maker, and time has added an additional lustre to his original instrument, which is in Richard's collection. It seems to be facing two ways, very much a classic Viennese forte-piano but also with a prophetic quality in the sheer romantic bloom which it has on its tone.

The impulse behind the workshop is purely musical, perhaps overlaid with my very early obsession with the actual mechanical aspects of musical instruments. Hence the range of instruments, as each represents a high point in musical instrument making, but is also associated with a high point in musical literature, so there is a genuine musical justification for the choice of models made. I have always tried to restore instruments for professionals who want them as the basic tools of their trade, and I feel the same way about making new instruments. We experience music as the product of the musician interpreting the composer; the instrument is the vehicle by which this is done, usually forgotten or ignored by the listener but vital nevertheless. To provide precisely that right vehicle is what I set out to do.

Derek Adlam's workshop is at Finchcocks, Goudhurst, Kent. The house with its collection of instruments is open through the summer for a part of each week and a number of concerts and recitals are also given through the year: a written request should be made to obtain the current details. The new instruments at present being made are: a clavicytherium, late fifteenth century, a fretted clavichord after Schmahl, 1807; an unfretted clavichord after Hass, 1763; a muselar after Ruckers, 1611; a harpsichord after Ruckers, 1638, in both single and double-manual form; a harpsichord after Blanchet, 1730; a fortepiano after Heilmann, c. 1785; and a fortepiano after Rosenberger, c. 1800.

CHAPTER 17

William Mitchell

William Mitchell has as his workshop a deconsecrated church in the little Dorset village of Wool. It is a very small building for a church, just a plain rectangle and porch entrance, a very suitable size for one man working alone. I saw little of Wool, for it was a pouring, sodden day but, inside the workshop, very warm and dry and brilliantly lit. I chose a time, to my regret, when there were no finished instruments to see; instead I was able to look at three under construction. He regards Ruckers as the most important maker to follow and usually bases his work on two Ruckers harpsichords in the Michael Thomas collection. Michael Thomas in fact has been a most important influence on the work of William Mitchell, providing him with the advice necessary to a young maker starting in business and the opportunity to study the instruments in his collection.

WILLIAM MITCHELL:
My father was a farmer, and I have done some farming myself, but my career started out in the sciences and I worked from 1970 at the Ministry of Defence in chemistry research. Music came into my life at school; it started when I became a choirboy but took a more definite shape when I began having organ lessons.

From 1972 onwards I looked closely and seriously at the idea of making harpsichords. Carpentry lessons were followed by building experiments on Italian instruments and clavichords. After distantly perusing the methods and resultant efforts of contemporary builders, I decided the Michael Thomas approach to be best for fine tone. I greatly admired his private collection, which, at the time, I thought to be the most beautiful and historically significant assembly I had encountered. Few approach it, and I still think so.

I went on to establish a small workshop in Dorset, supervised by Michael Thomas, and spent any spare time I had in visiting as many museums and collections as possible. After a while, I decided to specialize in the two Ruckers in Michael's collection: the 1636 double-manual Ruckers–Hemsch and the 1635 unaltered Ruckers by the same Andreas the Younger. The reasons for establishing myself as a specialist builder were first that it seems to me that the total understanding of any one type of instrument, and the gentle and significant improvements in tone which naturally accompany such an understanding, is almost a lifetime's work in itself; and, second, to become involved in copying well the tone of more than one maker seems beyond the scope of both the time available and, in a more practical sense, my particular workshop arrangements. Certainly, not just the first of the Ruckers' family, but all his building descendants seem to have been very single-minded individuals and I am sure that this must have been the case with the successful builders of yore – not forgetting that Ruckers were *the* most successful.

The few other instruments which I may copy from time to time are limited to the 1673 Italian Zenti in the Thomas collection or the 5-octave clavichord based on the classical German design by C. P. Hubert, and I regard them more as interesting academic exercises rather than as instruments for which I hope to be recognized. Having said that, I recently completed, with the help of an organ builder, a claviorganum (combined organ-harpsichord) and I suppose this must represent the biggest academic exercise of my career, although the harpsichord *is* based on the 1636 Ruckers. But more about this later.

In 1976 Michael Thomas dissolved his Harpsichord Centre in London's West End and I became involved with the distinguished teacher, Jaap Spigt of Amsterdam. His whole approach to the interpretation and teaching of Baroque music is unique and I admire his playing more than that of any other musician. This connection with the Netherlands has been of tremendous value, since Holland is certainly the most important teaching country in the world. It has helped me to understand just what it is that players are after, and their patronage has strengthened my faith in the Ruckers and confirmed that I made the correct choice of instrument from the beginning.

In 1977 I attended my first Bruges Festival: a marvellous opportunity for players and builders to meet and exchange thoughts. The only disadvantage to such festivals is that it is almost impossible to listen appreciatively to the music of any instrument while there is

[228]

William Mitchell: two-manual harpsichord after the 1636/1763 Ruckers-Hemsch in the Michael Thomas Collection. Lacquered in white and brown with decoration of flower painting and block printed paper.

so much noise and commotion in progress. Exhibiting leads to loud voicing on many instruments and over-lavish decoration on most. Such factors conflict with my own views
on what a good instrument should be. I prefer an instrument to be voiced so that the
string is plucked firmly enough to bring out the best in a soundboard, so that it "moves"
enough to produce the finest tone of which it is capable, yet stopping just short of making
the string seem as if it were being tugged and forced. Alternatively, too soft a voicing
tends to cause a slight imbalance over the compass. It is often a fact, particularly in
French, Flemish and German instruments, that even with a softly voiced harpsichord the
bass receives overwhelming praise – this being almost inevitable on instruments of such
deep casing. The best voicing is that which I have described and which enables the maker
to bring out the sweetness of the treble and middle regions, while its naturally pleasing
bass is not allowed to put the rest of the keyboard to shame.

Decoration is, of course, a very difficult and personal problem. Those who copy an instrument flower for flower and colour for colour must have clear consciences because any
criticism can be easily axed by reference to the original, which makes decoration
relatively simple. However, an instrument over which the artist is at liberty to roam with
his or her so-called "licence" provides the problem: "what to do?" Here purchasers are
expected to decide, and their feelings should obviously be recognized, but it is the
builder's duty to behave in a strongly suggestive advisory capacity. In my opinion, an un-
painted instrument can be made to look pleasing by subtle use of the grain of the wood in
which it is built. Certainly, veneering has always been recognized as a legitimate method
of improving the appearance of a harpsichord which might otherwise have looked dull.
As for the whole range of alternative methods, my advice would be one of simplicity,
elegance and, above all, restraint. This is virtually parallel to my thoughts on voicing: too
little and it is weak and uninspiring, too much makes for brash lavishness which seems to
shout instead of speak.

From 1977 onwards I took the opportunity to travel as widely as time would permit –
usually coupled with the delivery of an instrument – which allowed me to assess the state
of building and academic interest in the harpsichord and its music abroad. Rightly or
wrongly I am led to the following conclusions.

Western Europe leads the world by virtue of the proliferation of makers in Britain, the
Netherlands, Germany and France, but more importantly by the influence of good
teachers, also found in Belgium, Switzerland, Austria and Spain. Eastern European countries, with which I would include Italy, are quite a way behind in terms of popularity and
teaching. When I took what I understood was the first historically based instrument of its
kind to Hungary in 1979, I was surprised to learn that while there were some willing prospective students, nobody was available to give them lessons. Moreover, my customer

William Mitchell: single-manual harpsichord after the original by
Andreas Ruckers the Younger, 1635, in the Michael Thomas Collection.
Lacquered in white and brown with decoration of flower painting and
block printed paper.

further south at the Venice Conservatoire astounded me when he declared that his colleagues thought him mad to indulge in a serious study of the harpsichord and early music in general. There are pockets of interest developing in Jugoslavia, but these are limited at present to certain festivals which happen to include chamber orchestras and, therefore, harpsichords. The Czechoslovakian situation is even more limited, but a visit by members of the Galpin Society, in 1978, to the Prague Museum, which recently allowed public access to original instruments hitherto languishing in an obscure basement store, may have done something to foster interest. My experience in Eastern Europe is probably similar to that in the Far East, Africa and Australasia, with the possible exception of Japan, although my customers in New Zealand and Australia tell me interest is growing there. The Scandinavian countries have a sprinkling of teachers, and I have sent instruments to Sweden and Finland, but my knowledge of this area is limited.

North America is well served by harpsichord makers. Frank Hubbard, for example, was one of the pioneers of building historical copies and his book *Three Centuries of Harpsichord Making* has done much to assist newcomers. Teachers are in good supply too, but I notice that many students are nevertheless keen to have follow-up lessons with the European Masters. When I attended the Early Music Institute at Indianapolis in 1978, I found that builders were concentrating almost entirely on historical copies. I made the point at one of the evening seminars that it must be to the customer's advantage if the builder is fully acquainted with the original and aspires to emulate its tone, and is thus able to speak authoritatively. The purchaser should be guided by the tone of the original and not by his own ideas of what the tone should be. To my complete surprise this attitude led to something of a stand-up row between me and a famous Chicago academic who disagreed with me. The reason may not have been completely unconnected with the fact that it is not always possible in a country like the United States, where the stock of original instruments is rather thin on the ground compared with Europe, for its builders to work on restorations or to have access to European museums. Hence they are confined to instruments in the Smithsonian Institute or the New York Metropolitan Museum of Art, and some minor collections. This is not really as bad as it sounds; I myself once copied the Thomas Hitchcock mitred bentside spinet in the Smithsonian without even seeing the original, but by following the Institute plans the result was reasonably satisfying.

Certainly the man who has done more than any other to popularize the harpsichord in America, and even the remoter parts of the world, is Zuckermann. He could see the need for a kit instrument as early as the 1960s — an idea much copied by other builders and thus an important American contribution to the harpsichord building scene. Moreover, he was shrewd enough to publish a book on *other* builders which (quite wrongly in my

William Mitchell: single-manual harpsichord after the 1636/1763 Ruckers-Hemsch, in coloured British Columbian pine with block printed paper decoration.

William Mitchell: key-well detail, single-manual harpsichord after the 1636/1763 Ruckers-Hemsch, showing flower painting and block printed paper decoration.

opinion) led many to believe him to be an important authority. The location of most builders in the United States is in the north and along the eastern seaboard. This may be why my own activities are presently confined to the Southern States where there are fewer established makers.

My knowledge of Mexico and South America is somewhat limited, but then I think this could be equally true about any interest there is in these areas. I have a customer as far south as Rio, and the magazine *Ficta Difusora de Musica Antigua* in the Argentine seems to be helping to stimulate people, and so I am planning to visit the area in 1980 and make a personal assessment. From what I can gather, the American influence seems quite powerful, but is limited at present to instruments other than those of the harpsichord family.

In 1978 I believe I had the privilege to be the first builder in modern times to build a claviorganum, or combined organ-harpsichord. It was achieved with the help of John Bowen of Northampton who had previously assisted in the restoration of two old claviorgana: the 1749 Crang in the outstanding collection of Dr J. R. Mirrey of Surrey and the *c.* 1600 French instrument belonging to Michael Thomas, currently housed in the Palais Lascaris, Nice.

I think it is fair to say that the construction of this instrument is the most historically significant accomplishment in the field. The claviorganum was the largest and most complicated of the domestic keyboard instruments. Virtually none have survived in their original state, although there are traces remaining to show that many harpsichords had an organ which has since disappeared, possibly put in a church, while the harpsichord, during its fall from popularity towards the end of the eighteenth century, would have been put away in some obscure place. They seem to have been not uncommon in the sixteenth century: illustrations to the late Raymond Russell's *The Harpsichord and Clavichord* show the Brussels Conservatoire Bertolotti of 1585 and the Flemish maker Ludovic Theeuwes' example of 1579 in the Victoria and Albert Museum, both showing the harpsichord sitting on a large rectangular box which houses the organ. Eighteenth-century examples have, instead of a heavy rectangular box, an organ case which follows the shape of the harpsichord in having a bentside (although this is also true of the Michael Thomas French instrument). A notable player of the claviorganum was Handel; he used this instrument in the opera houses during the intervals and many of his keyboard works suit it eminently. Although Handel's claviorganum was tragically destroyed in one of the fires at Covent Garden, a very fine example remains to represent the century in the instrument belonging to the Earl of Wemyss in Scotland. This has a double-manual Kirckman on a Snetzler organ of 1750 in an exceptionally beautiful case of figured walnut with marquetry in sycamore.

While a detailed appraisal of all extant claviorgana is beyond the scope of this essay, suffice to say that virtually none of them are truly original. Either the organ has been lost or replaced or the harpsichord has been tampered with in some way, and so the design of our instrument was not based on any particular model. Instead, it was decided to incorporate the best of everything — for example, the Dom Bedos facility to remove the double-manual harpsichord so that it can be used elsewhere, yet leave the organ still playable. The harpsichord itself is based on the 1636 Ruckers and has been used because of my specialist knowledge of this instrument. Its disposition is 2 × 8, 1 × 4 and harp, with a compass of GG to g^3. I know that the inevitable "purist" reader will cry out that the original is FF to f^3. The reason I have changed the compass is because I decided to allow a full 5 octaves for the organ and the ability to play below C, which allows the music of the organ to follow that of the harpsichord when playing a piece written to embrace 5 octaves. Now, if we had made the organ FF to f³ we would have had to make two pipes, FF and FF sharp, which are very large on the 8ft diapason stop and would have meant that the organ casing would be that of a large rectangular box and not possess the more elegant lines of the Wemyss or the Thomas instruments.

The organ is built along classical lines with slider wind-chests and tracker action. The disposition is: 8ft stopped diapason, 4ft flute, 2ft principal, sesqui-altera 12th with a 17th mixture from middle C upwards. The harpsichord has a very pleasing distinction of tone between the two 8ft stops, the back 8ft having a round and flutey sound while the front 8ft is more reedy and nasal. The 4ft stop is normally voiced to sound as an echo; that is to say it is not a stop in its own right, but immediately gives more colour and volume when applied. The action, as with all my harpsichords, comprises wooden jacks with wooden registers. The jack tongues are holly with German hogs' bristle springs. Black Russian turkey feathers are specially imported for use as plectra material and in this sense the action is very traditional and the resulting tone much brighter and more pleasing to the ear and touch than plastic.

The claviorganum has many advantages. It can be used as a continuo instrument and allows the player to remain seated in the same place without having to jump from organ to harpsichord as is normally the case. It can be coupled together by simply pushing in the organ keyboard so that the whole instrument sounds together. This is where the claviorganum is unique in terms of the sensation it has on the listening audience: the initial attack of the harpsichord followed by the longer, sustaining notes of the organ make it an unusual and beautiful experience. It can be used for concerto work and made loud and strong enough to balance any orchestra.

Finally, it can be used purely and simply for solo work. By artful manipulation of the five organ ranks and three harpsichord stops with an upper manual coupling device on the harpsichord, a high degree of contrast can be obtained and this provides the competent performer with a tool which will keep any audience spellbound for an evening.

The instrument was exhibited at the Festival Estival de Paris in September 1978 and received praise from Howard Schott. Writing in *Early Music* he observed that the instrument "certainly plays very well". I then took it to Holland where it was used for a radio series and later concerts in Amsterdam. In 1980 I intend to build a portable transposing claviorganum suitable for a player who has much travelling to do.

William Mitchell (workshops: East Burton, Wool, Dorset) currently makes the following harpsichords: A copy of the 1636 Ruckers in either single or two-manual form with 8 + 8 + 4 + buff and a copy of the 1635 Ruckers single-manual with either 8 + 8 or 8 + 4 and optional buff. Both the original instruments are in the Michael Thomas collection.

CHAPTER 18

※

Richard Clayson and Andrew Garrett

Where the North Downs reach the sea at Folkestone and Dover and enclose the flat open grazing land of the Romney Marshes lies the little town of Lyminge, home of Richard Clayson and Andrew Garrett. Lyminge was a market town, the centre of the great sheep sales of the famous Romney Marsh breed; it grew in the nineteenth century with the railway and is now little more than a dormitory for the bigger towns around.

The partners have a workshop which has been used by the Clayson family for three generations, having been built by Richard Clayson's grandfather just after the First World War as a joinery shop for his building business. It is large and spacious, too large probably for this small team of two partners, a cabinet maker and an assistant. Half the shop is given over to the heavy machinery, the other half to construction, with a small room at the end for finishing. When I was there a very important restoration was in progress, the Queen's Ruckers, now on loan to the National Trust at Fenton House. When I was young and first studying harpsichords I loved the tone of this exceptional and magnificent instrument. Now it seemed small and lost and in desperate need of repair. Also awaiting attention was a Shudi–Broadwood from Fenton House, a harpsichord I have always regarded as of deplorably dull tone, while in the finishing room were two new harpsichords.

One was a copy of the Sodi from the Royal Albert Memorial Museum, Exeter, sounding a glorious richness, and the other a copy of the two-manual Dulcken which is in the Smithsonian Institution, Washington. The Sodi had been restored by Clayson and Garrett, and very sensibly they prefer, when they can, to make their copies from harpsichords which have passed through their hands and have thus been properly studied.

ANDREW GARRETT:

Richard and I met at Oxford. He remembers that we passed on the stairs and that I asked what time breakfast was. In the event it was not a meal that either of us attended with conspicuous regularity, except during Schools. Later exchanges were longer and less mundane and it turned out that we shared among other things an enthusiasm for some of the same sorts of music.

Richard had been taught the piano since childhood and was a good organist, too. Both my people sang and played and had sent their children to choir schools: my brother, with a much better voice than I, to Magdalen and me to Christ Church. I still have a soft spot for Stanford and Wesley who made up in those days as much of the repertoire as Byrd and Gibbons. Every chorister at Christ Church had to learn the piano but I took more readily to the violin and the viola which in the event made a music scholarship to Lancing easier.

We both enjoyed part-singing and one way and another made a certain amount of rather poor amateur music. I remember excellent cream teas in Lady Margaret Hall or St Anne's, teas much better than the madrigal singing that served as their excuse.

We listened to a lot of records and made the sweeping criticisms at which the young and uninformed are so good. Some things we loved unreservedly: singers like Deller and Margaret Ritchie; Jennifer Vyvyan and Elsie Morrison. Hearing Alfred Deller suddenly shrank the repertoire for which the contralto voice seemed suitable; Deller supported by Desmond Dupré's busy lute-playing.

Stylistically there was little difference in those days between performances of Bach and

Brahms, not much difference indeed in the resources employed. Four double-basses in a Brandenburg did not raise a single eyebrow in the London concert halls. Recorded performances, too, were thick-textured and heavy compared with what is now regarded as acceptably baroque or classical. Even so, Richard and I found our more certain pleasure in the earlier period. The Romantics were not unregarded but Bach and Handel, Purcell and Telemann had written the music we most wanted to hear and play.

I had joined a couple of Oxford orchestras but Richard was getting no ensemble playing and at some stage during our second year we began to think seriously about buying or hiring a harpsichord. Robert Goble was the nearest builder we knew of and we rang him to get some idea of price. His cheapest harpsichord was £350 (his concert double was £800) and ridiculous though the prices seem now, it meant that purchase was beyond us. We wondered about hiring but that was prohibitive as well.

Kits at that time were a thing of the future but with no clear idea of what we were hoping to achieve we began to wonder about building an instrument ourselves. We knew remarkably little about either the mechanical or the tonal side of things. There was a Kirckman in the Ashmolean but we were not allowed to poke about in it and would hardly have understood what we saw. The only harpsichords we had heard had been those of Thomas Goff and Robert Goble. The instrument was not the commonplace on the concert platform twenty years ago that it is today.

We carried out some experiments with a length of music wire stretched over an open desk drawer. A belief that jack tongues might return by force of gravity if their fulcra were high enough gave way to an appreciation of the necesssity for springs! From such incredibly naïve beginnings a workable action was evolved. The eventual size of the instrument was dictated by the need to get it up and down the staircase. We solemnly carried my wardrobe down into the quad and back up again. The instrument could be no longer than 6 feet 2 inches.

Richard's father owned a building firm in Lyminge and from the original notion of getting timber from him the idea gradually took shape that his joiner's shop should build a case in accordance with our amazingly unhelpful and skimpy plans. The best man – I should think now the only man – to be entrusted with such a commission out of the blue was Ted Burren. A joiner of the first class, he had dealt with enough unworkable architects' ideas to make some sense of plans which told him almost nothing. Surrounded by doors, window frames, skirting, architraves and every other sort of necessary house fixing, Ted started off on a harpsichord.

In the event we ended up with a most handsomely made walnut-veneered case, complete with lid, stand and music-desk, and an action made from modified upright-piano parts. It was an aesthetic, musical and mechanical oddity but for at least a term we were thrilled with it. It seasoned our musical endeavours with a flavour of authenticity and it was a start.

At some stage during our second year we met Meredith Moon who was then Reader at the Bodleian. He was a gifted keyboard player and owned a "B" model de Blaise which he showed us. Any consideration of its tonal quality was displaced by what struck us as its amazing complexity. As an example of mechanical ingenuity we thought it staggering. Meredith had it in mind to build a copy of the virginal in the Smithsonian pamphlet. To need a single-strung short-compass instrument of waif-like frailty when you owned a two-manual, four choir, 6-pedal wonder made some impression on us. Our instrument-building education was beginning. We decided to modify our own instrument. With a new soundboard from Salters' boatyard – that should have made oars for a College Eight – two rows of more recognizably jack-like jacks, a counterchanged keyboard from Pynes and two inches sawn off the case all round, we thought the harpsichord transformed.

Clayson and Garrett: single-manual harpsichord after the Vincenzio Sodi, Florence 1782, in the Royal Albert Memorial Museum, Exeter. Finished in green lacquer with flower painted decoration.

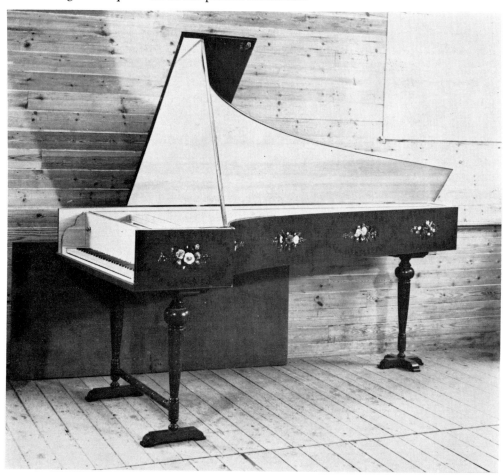

The instrument received a certain amount of publicity. There were a couple of snippets in the press about what was seen as a curious enterprise for two undergraduates. George Malcolm was giving a concert in the Newman Room and we somehow found the nerve to ask him to come and try our own effort. It must have been a shock after the Goble he had just been playing but he was terribly kind and encouraging. Through him, I think, we met Tom Goff, and were most kindly received in Pont Street. Margaret Ritchie came to see us and asked to borrow the instrument for use at her Summer School. In the event the idea came to nothing — we asked for a fee to enable us to be around to look after the instrument — but we were thrilled it had even been thought of.

Somehow Michael Thomas got to hear of us and after we'd visited him he offered to take us on at Hurley Manor. We were in our last term by this time and *Opportunities for Graduates* seemed to offer nothing compellingly exciting for Arts men. I remember, later on, Bill Dowd saying that when people asked him why he built harpsichords his usual reply was "so what else do you do with a Ph. D?" We said we would join Michael in the autumn.

Hurley was fascinating and frustrating, perhaps a little like Michael himself. We were keen but not knowledgeable, enthusiastic but in need of direction. Michael's head was full of knowledge and stuffed with ideas but we found it difficult to abstract the one and grasp the other. Life was pleasant, especially on a converted 75ft Thames sailing barge in the summer of 1962 but the miseries of a very hard winter and a general feeling of not getting anywhere led us to take up Richard's father's offer of workshop space in Lyminge.

Once in Kent we began to sort ourselves out. We rented premises from Richard's father and started building clavichords to Michael's designs. When we could afford it we made use of Ted Burren's knowledge and skill. It was fairly obvious that we stood no chance of learning what he'd already forgotten about wood and the working of wood.

Richard's father insisted on proper book-keeping and proper time-sheets if he was going to assist our enterprise in any way. Life became generally more ordered and it seemed that instrument-making might have a future. Originally we had thought of building Michael's instruments for Michael's customers but gradually we found our own market for our own designs.

The early years seemed to consist largely of restoring square pianos, or spinets as they were confusingly referred to by the antique trade. Certainly we finished work on one every seven or eight weeks but at the same time managed to produce and sell quite a lot of new clavichords and half-a-dozen harpsichords, all much better made than they were designed.

The general musical climate in this country was quite different in the early 1960s.

Hubbard's *Three Centuries of Harpsichord Making* was not published till '65, few collections pursued the restoration of their instruments in an informed way, drawings of originals were not common and people were in any case too sensible to entrust their originals to two young Oxford graduates who might or might not know what they were doing.

Things are very different now. Students in the London College of Furniture's early keyboard instrument department at the start of last year were variously engaged in copies of originals by Ruckers, Hitchcock, Hoffmann, Vaudry, Taskin and Garnier. The harpsichord has reached the stage that the violin reached in the nineteenth century. Fiddles that were not copies of Stradivarius, Amati or Guarneri were not wanted and did not sell. The same thing applies now to the harpsichord: instruments must be copies – Taskin, Ruckers, Dulcken, someone. Partly responsible is the rise in the value of antiques. When you could buy an original instrument as cheaply as a modern one there was little point in makers building copies.

The change is certainly visible in our own instruments. For some years now we have built only copies but our first harpsichords were made to designs dreamt up from very sketchy notions of what musical requirements the instrument should be able to fulfil. Mechanical considerations exercised us as much as tonal ones and the results were far too complex. Actions were pedal-controlled, jacks were of synthetics like Tufnol or Delrin and registers of brass. Everything was adjustable – there were regulating screws everywhere. Eventually we learnt that the more adjustments you build into an instrument the more chance there is that it will be mis-regulated by someone. Nowadays we believe that if everything fits and works to start with there's every chance that it will go on doing so, unless it's subjected to conditions that are as bad for people as they are for instruments.

In 1967 Richard's father's concern ceased to trade and the Clayson joiner's shop came on the market. By our standards it was vast but our accountants seemed to think it would be a sensible purchase. They had no suggestions about what we might use for money. We wrote to a number of acquaintances we believed rich or mad or both, asking for loans at what now seem ridiculously low rates of interest. Amazingly, funds appeared. We bought the shop in April 1967. Quite suddenly we had yards of bench space, woodworking machinery, a vast amount of room, no money but high hopes. Most importantly, Ted Burren agreed to join us, "till Christmas", as he said. Having been with us ever since, he reminds us that he didn't say which Christmas.

Nowadays the building of kits is probably the commonest way to begin an instrument-making career. Established makers are not rich enough to make use of those without perhaps either skill or experience. Beginners set up rapidly on their own. When we began I imagine we were typical in receiving a steady stream of letters from people

Clayson and Garrett: two-manual harpsichord after the J. D. Dulcken, Antwerp 1745, in black lacquer with gold leaf banding and gold leaf interior.

asking for jobs. We treasure one from Chris Hogwood written after he'd finished a year in Prague as a British Council scholar (November 1965). He was probably going back next year, but meanwhile he had so many unpleasant jobs to refuse, could we offer him something more congenial? People used to call on us for the same reason. A titled lady who wanted a temporary place for her son: "Charles made the best mitre joint in Winchester last term". Mostly, would-be colleagues were American or French. We have never been good enough managers to think seriously of expansion but over the years we've had the temporary help of a number of boys and one girl. "Temporary" has meant in some cases four or five years, but understandably people want to set up on their own. Ted contrives to put up with us still and I hope will go on doing so for a long time yet. It's important in a small concern to get on with each other, and we seem to manage to do that.

Whatever the length of the waiting list we will be reluctant to grow bigger but there are snags in the small enterprise. There never seems sufficient money for the economic purchase of materials. We go to Switzerland for our soundboard wood or to Italy for our cypress and it is heart-breaking to part with half the material simply to subsidize the cost of choosing, buying and importing it. We would love to have the funds to commission an English firm to draw brass wire of the tensile strength and ductility that characterizes the eighteenth-century varieties. As it is, we have to buy uneconomically from America.

Government cannot afford to be concerned with us either. We rang the Department of Energy two years ago to ask about grants for Factory Insulation. I think we fulfilled the other conditions but wouldn't be spending enough – only £2,500 it was – to qualify. The insulation had to cost at least £3,000. "What about the small business?" I queried. "Why, how small is yours?" I was asked. "There are four of us," I said. "We don't call that a small business," was the reply. "That's a micro-business." So we borrowed from the bank instead.

We're lucky to have an understanding bank manager. In our sourer moments we thought that with accommodation charges at 20½ per cent he could afford to be. Actually he is on our side and does help, suggesting less expensive ways of making capital investments, for example. For foreign trade perhaps the bank is less helpful. We deal abroad from time to time for hirings as well as sales and Richard once remarked that the local bank's knowledge of international trade seemed to have ceased when the port of Hythe silted up in the fourteenth century. We do seem to end up doing all the paperwork on ATA carnets and things and then paying £25 for the bank to stamp some Indemnity or other for which, of course, we have already counter-indemnified them. We try to operate without agents but do find you have to know your T2L's from your T3L's or you get in a pickle.

Money tends to be a problem. If at any given moment you're engaged on commissions that will bring in £10,000 or so you can have what is nowadays called a cash flow problem. We were unwise when we started to think of a full order-book as a prerequisite for success. In times of inflation you really only need work for as far ahead as you can accurately cost. Customers obviously like to know what they are going to pay and adding on the rise in the Cost of Living Index isn't really an answer – the government's shopping basket is different from ours. It is difficult with new instruments but restorations are even worse to quote for. Only once have things worked out perfectly. We set an instrument to rights for a lady in Usk, years ago now. She gave us a cheque when we delivered and she did seem very pleased. A couple of days later came another cheque. She couldn't pay for such a marvellous job in pounds, here was the balance to make it guineas. We wrote back and said she had just won our Customer of the Year prize.

We are spoilt with restoration at the moment, doing as much work on old instruments as on new. Restoring and building go well together; there is so much to learn. Bill Dowd,

I remember, called in the shop while we were building our first 1745 Smithsonian Dulcken copy. He restored the original and we asked him about the double bentside (the cavity wall arrangement that Dulcken sometimes used). He had supposed the inner bentside to be nineteenth-century work and removed it. "Well, when I first got my hands on the instrument," he said, "it sounded like a strung-up pool table." As we began to think we knew something about instruments it was the sort of thing that helped us to be prepared for surprises: barring systems that were original though odd; FF sharp in evidence when you would not expect it; Italian work that was actually German; dovetails cut the wrong way, patched and cut again; a bentside liner whose dents show that the maker had had the devil of a job getting it back to the bentside.

Our biggest restoration problems come when earlier restorers have assumed that the original maker did not know what he was doing. Nineteenth- and early-twentieth-century "improvements" are a nightmare. When they are simply in the form of structural additions it is not so bad, though their inclusion will probably have imposed the wrong sort of stresses on the casework and done further damage. Worse, though, is when parts of the original have been removed and thrown away. Reversibility is probably the most important factor to consider in working on an original and it is sickening when something or other has been deliberately jettisoned to accommodate new material.

The most straightforward – though still time-consuming – restorations are those of instruments that have just quietly fallen apart. Nikolaus Harnoncourt tells of a violone that was being used by a member of Concentus Musicus. It had been found in the organ loft of a church in Austria as a pile of bits. They were bundled together and taken to the restorer in a parcel which was, as Harnoncourt says, "flat". The restorer laid out the pieces on his bench and examined them. "Excellent," he said. "You have here an early eighteenth-century violone in perfect condition."

Normally we try to restore an instrument to the condition it was in when it left the maker's workshop. Many instruments, though, were altered during their legitimate life, while the harpsichord-making tradition was still alive and before it was replaced by the different techniques of piano-making. We have been working recently on a 1612 Ruckers that, as commonly happened, was gradually altered during its working life from a 1 × 4ft, 1 × 8ft transposer into a 2 × 8ft, 1 × 4ft aligned double with a bigger, fully chromatic compass: obviously we would not think of undoing such a *ravalement*.

Sometimes there is a case to be made for not restoring an instrument. If there is a danger that in spite of photographs and careful documentation organological evidence will be lost, or if because of the replacement of parts of the original there is little reason to think the instrument will sound as its maker intended, it is probably best left alone. As a general rule, though, there seems no reason why instruments should not be restored to playing

Clayson and Garrett: single-manual harpsichord after the original of J. and A. Kirckman, 1776, in mahogany, cross banded and inlaid.

condition and used. Ruskin reckoned art to be a part of life. A musical instrument should be played on, as well as looked at. Some collections have too many instruments to cope with. The Brussels Reserve Collection houses scores of its less exciting examples on shelves like those in a prep. school changing room. The National Trust's policy seems commendable. At Fenton House, for example, the instruments are constantly used by music students and good amateurs, apart from being available for professional concerts on the premises. If the instruments can be kept in condition the idea is good. A Kirckman is a splendid piece of Georgian furniture but it was made to delight the ear as well as the eye.

Our own instruments are now always copies of classical originals. We built the first Dulcken copy in this country from information most generously supplied by Scott Odell before the Smithsonian had produced drawings. At the moment, apart from the 1745 Dulcken, we build copies of a 1776 Kirckman single, of the 1782 Sodi in Exeter Museum

[246]

and of a small Ridolfi. We really prefer to have restored the original before attempting a copy. Very many are first rate but some museum and collection drawings are lacking in detail. There is something to be said for building copies of instruments which are not so commonly reproduced. We have an adequate regard for the later French instrument but I do not think we would ever build a Taskin copy: there are so many. The same goes for the Ruckers family, unless one tried building a copy of the pre-*ravalement* instrument.

The move backwards towards original instruments is a sound one. The Boston school – if one can so refer to Hubbard and Dowd in the early years – did European makers a great deal of good. The instrument was in danger of becoming a competitor to the piano in the way which contributed to its demise at the end of the eighteenth century. We were working on a 1791 Shudi and Broadwood recently and, tonally fine though the instrument is, its complications (Machine stop and Venetian Swell) do not sufficiently increase its musical value. I think when we began we were reluctant to concede that if we built a successful copy the credit would be the original maker's and if it did not come off the fault would be ours. It was Gustav Leonhardt who asked, kindly but tellingly, whether we thought we knew better than the classical builders. I suspect he has put a lot of people on the right lines with the same question. It does seem to us that knowing what was done and why, gaining some insight into the relationship between the materials and proportions chosen and the tonal results, can prevent a lot of disappointing experiment.

Patience certainly plays a part in instrument making. Sometimes it seems a curse that five octaves on a fixed pitch instrument means 61 of everything, or rather multiples of 61. If one is trying to be involved in the whole instrument, everything must be purpose-made: jacks, registers, wrest pins, all of it. This does not make for speed. The finish can take forever, too, if there is to be any depth to it. Whether it is paint and gold leaf or polish, a lot of hours are devoted to preparation and rubbing down. And when it is done, a good finish will only be what is expected. The sound of the instrument is the thing after all. Sometimes, too, you hanker after an instrument you do not have to walk round, something that does not have to be supported on a pair of trestles while work is done. A violin perhaps or a guitar. Then you hear the finished instrument on the platform or on record and you feel involved in the process by which a composer and a performer can delight an audience.

Richard Clayson and Andrew Garrett have their workshop at Lyminge, Kent. They currently make: a two-manual harpsichord after the 1745 Dulcken and an Italian single-manual after Ridolfi, 1665, both in the Smithsonian Institution, Washington; a single-manual harpsichord after the Vincenzio Sodi of 1782 in the Royal Albert Memorial Museum, Exeter; and a copy of a J. & A. Kirckman single-manual of 1776 in a private collection.

CHAPTER 19

✺

Peter and Ann Mactaggart (Decorators)

Peter and Ann Mactaggart are a husband and wife team with an unusual business, that of providing a specialist service in decorating musical instruments. They live in a large Edwardian red brick house in Welwyn village; Ann's studio is in the house, Peter's workshops are in a run of buildings across the yard, converted from the original garages.

Peter's rôle is that of marquetry cutter and technical assistant to Ann's restoration activities, but he has also started to deploy his talents in producing block-printed papers for Flemish instruments. These require the pattern to be cut in relief on the surface of a block of long-grain box or pearwood and from this the printing is done on hand-made paper using traditional inks. Ann is a painter of diverse talents who makes her own paint and has learned to work in many of the various styles and techniques which have been used in harpsichord decoration in the past. Together they have made a number of valuable contributions to the study of decorative painting, pigments and pigment vehicles – the papers they have published are listed in the bibliography. Among the things they have established is that soundboard painting, so long described as being in tempera (a paint made by grinding pigment into egg yolk) was probably always done in water colour.

ANN MACTAGGART:

One morning, early in 1975, we called at Dennis Woolley's workshop. We had been cutting marquetry for about eighteen months and were attempting to build up some contacts. It was only after Dennis had ordered some panels for spinet nameboards that I noticed he had just been painting a garland of flowers around the rose of a partly finished harpsichord.

"You don't need anyone to help with decorating then," I commented.

"Well," he said, "I do it, but I don't like it. Can you do that sort of thing?"

"I've never tried a soundboard," I replied, "but I did train as a painter."

Such are the chance beginnings from which a whole new business can arise.

When we married, Peter's parents ran an antiques business and he worked with them in the firm. It was inevitable that I should become involved, and so I learned to restore paintings and in a fairly short time had put together a studio of equipment for the purpose, including a vacuum hot-table for relining. We did quite a lot of furniture restoration as well, and not infrequently I was called into the workshop to help. Peter did beautiful woodwork repairs but hated finishing surfaces, and it was in this way that I learned to grain and marble, gild and french polish.

The sixties saw the beginning of the vogue for stripped pine. At that time there were still nice little pieces of eighteenth-century decorated furniture about, and occasionally we managed to rescue one of these before it reached another dealer's stripping bath. Quite often it proved possible to recover the original decoration from beneath layers of varnish and graining, using cleaning methods normally applied in painting restoration. We became interested in the decoration of these pieces and spent many satisfying hours attempting to reconstruct surfaces and effects, partly from the evidence provided by the pieces themselves and partly by digging about in eighteenth-century books on applied art practices. All this proved to be valuable background experience when later on we began restoring painted decoration on harpsichords.

Almost by chance during the early seventies we got to know Bill Dow – I think he came into the shop one day – and when he went to work at the Russell Collection for a while we visited him there and met the curator, John Barnes. By 1975, when the first commission to copy a Taskin soundboard for Dennis Woolley arose, we were already acquainted with the Russell Collection instruments and the visit to study the Taskin was a welcome excuse to return. It was during this visit that John Barnes first talked to us about

Ann Mactaggart: chinoiserie and lacquer decoration on a copy by David
Rubio of the 1681 Vaudry in the Victoria and Albert Museum.

restoring the soundboard paintings on the Taskin and the, newly attributed, Goermans harpsichord in the Collection. These discussions eventually resulted, in 1976, in our cleaning the soundboards of both harpsichords as part of a programme of restoring and restringing the instruments. To the best of my knowledge these restorations were among the first in which painting and musical-instrument restorer worked side-by-side in a fully integrated manner. The more or less instant exchange of information and evidence which resulted was tremendously valuable. It was this work which firmly directed our steps towards restoring painting on instruments, and we are very conscious of the debt we owe to all those at the Russell Collection for their confidence in us and for their encouragement, both then and since.

For these restorations, the National Gallery provided invaluable assistance by carrying out the analyses of pigments and mediums, but this information only became available after the work was completed, as the samples had to be fitted into their schedule. However, it made us realize the advantage that could be gained from carrying out identifications of pigments, particularly if they could be done on the spot, and we resolved to install our own facilities for this as soon as possible. Eighteen months of concentrated work saw us in possession of both the necessary equipment and the expertise to make use of it. The outlay and effort has since been amply rewarded by the new dimension that has been added to our restoration work.

For us, the seventies were a period of intensive activity, with a new business arising phoenix-like out of the ashes of the old. At the beginning I mentioned Peter's marquetry. This was initiated partly by a desire to concentrate on highly specialized forms of restoration so that our energies were not dissipated across too wide a front, and partly by another of the series of incredible coincidences which happened to us at that time. We had met an old marquetry cutter – Andrew Oliver – while attempting to trace a supply of obscure veneer for a restoration job we were doing, and he agreed to show Peter the basic techniques of cutting if Peter was prepared to build his own "donkey" (the chief tool of the marquetry cutter). The work of making it coincided with a very cold winter, plagued with industrial action in the form of power cuts. I clearly remember Peter in the workshop slogging out by hand six-inch-square beech uprights and, later on, his using the donkey in the sitting-room because it was the only place we could heat.

The first person to commission marquetry from us for stringed instruments was David Rubio. Getting to know him was part of another chain of coincidences. On our first visit to Edinburgh, John Barnes had shown us an elaborately marquetried harpsichord which, at the time, he had in for restoration. One of the problems was how to repair the lid, which was of thin, brittle mahogany and had four splits running down its length. Peter made some suggestions based on a method we had developed for repairing Georgian table tops, and after admiring the harpsichord we departed and thought no more about it. A year or more later we were rung up by someone who said he had a harpsichord lid which needed repair. Of course it was the same one. Some to-ing and fro-ing ensued, and when the lid was finished the owner came to collect it. Apropos of the marquetry on his harpsichord we showed him some of Peter's marquetry over lunch, and it turned out that he was on his way to see David Rubio who happened to be looking for a marquetry cutter. It was not long before David had become one of our most stimulating and rewarding customers, and some of our most elaborate designs have been executed for him.

A microscope of one sort or another had always formed part of Peter's equipment, ever since the shop days when it had been one of the tools he used for checking gemstones, and restoring marquetry gave him another opportunity for putting it to good use. Shortly after becoming involved in marquetry restoration we went to a lecture given by Jo Darrah of the Victoria and Albert Museum on wood identification. We had been interested in the possibilities of identifying timbers positively for some time, but lacked the necessary encouragement, which she provided by making the work sound not impossibly difficult. In most cases the woods which we needed to identify came in the form of fragments of veneer – certainly not the one-centimetre cubes preferred by the authorities – and we had to find methods of cutting and staining them reliably. The techniques we developed came into their own when people started to bring us pieces from antique instruments to identify. Little slips of soundboard wood, bits of hitch-pin rail and hammer shanks were all made to yield up their secrets in the interests of accurate restoration.

We seldom become directly concerned with restoring marquetried instruments – probably because there are not a lot of them about. One of the most interesting involved returning the marquetry fingerboard of a Barak Norman viol to its full width. In this case we designed and cut the extra pieces of marquetry, which had to register – exactly – along the whole length of the fingerboard, and Michael Heale performed the delicate task of fitting it and the original parts together. Quite recently our prolonged study of marquetry on Kirckman harpsichords was at least partly justified when Dennis Woolley commissioned complete sets of marquetry for two Kirckman copies.

Dennis's original commission to copy the 1769 Taskin soundboard was followed by one to paint a muselar with a decorative scheme based on the 1650 Couchet in the Vleeshuis. After this the word began to get around and orders, mainly for painted soundboards, rolled in steadily from a small but very loyal group of builders. As early as 1976, David Rubio commissioned a copy of the decoration of the 1681 Vaudry, the original instrument having been only shortly before acquired by the Victoria and Albert Museum. On that occasion the copy was completely painted in our studio, and we used genuine vermilion for the interior so that we could get exactly the right kind of sympathetic

PETER AND ANN MACTAGGART (DECORATORS)

surface for the gold and bronze powder decoration. Experimentation with old processes is a continuous part of our studio work. Most frequently we are concerned with reconstructing seventeenth- and eighteenth-century casework finishes, basing our ideas on discoveries made as a result of examining antique instruments. We were recently given just such an opportunity when a French harpsichord of *c.* 1700 from the Villa Medici in Rome was brought to our studio by Mark Stevenson for restoration of its painted surfaces. The way in which the case was marbled proved to be comparable with the method used on some Flemish harpsichords, and supplied useful information on which to build marbling techniques for new instruments.

Ann Mactaggart: detail of soundboard painting copied from the Pascal Taskin of 1769 in the Russell Collection, for an instrument made by Milan Misina.

When taking our marquetry round in the early days we had visited the Goble workshops and had met Robert and Elizabeth Goble with their son, Andrea. It was only then that we discovered that Andrea was quite capable of producing his own marquetry, but the contact persisted and he was the first builder to commission from me a sound-board painting based on that of the 1745 Dulcken in the Smithsonian.

Being a craftsman painter and restorer I naturally tend to concentrate on copies. Years spent restoring paintings taught me to get myself out of the way as much as possible, to be a chameleon, absorbing the style and techniques of the original painter and recreating the work from within, consciously and critically, rather than attempting to reproduce it superficially by slavish copying. At a time when there was so much interest arising in authenticity it seemed natural to carry this approach over into instrument decoration. To me, restoration and the painting of copies are two sides of the same coin. The restorations allow me to study the original far more closely than would be possible in any other way. I can examine and analyse, and try to understand the original craftsman's technique and his attitude to the painting. The copies allow me to try out at full scale what I think I have discovered. It is all too easy to create difficulties for oneself by altering some apparently insignificant detail of technique, or even the order in which parts are painted. Having reconstructed schemes at full scale I have developed a considerable respect for the achievements of the old decorators. Their work, despite, and not because of, the scratches and abrasions, the damage and repairs, can still have a positive quality, directness and unity which is seldom equalled by the modern decorator. One also appreciates their problems, both practical and artistic, such as not getting one's hand lacerated by hitch pins, and the difficulties of composing within a shape which bears no resemblance to a rectangular canvas. However, the layout of a soundboard presents few difficulties compared with creating a design for the inside of a lid. This is probably because the scattered flowers which constitute the chief idiom of soundboard painting can be arranged to fill any irregularly-shaped area, whilst in the case of lids, the decoration is adapted from forms which usually have their foundations in architecture or conventional pictorial representations. I consider that to design a successful, balanced, formal composition for a lid is one of the most challenging tasks with which the harpsichord decorator can be faced.

In our work we find we need to understand not only the techniques of the craftsman but also the qualities of his materials. Although in painting restoration one seldom uses the same pigments, and certainly not the same mediums that were used originally, mainly for the sake of reversibility, it is of inestimable value to know what pigments were used as well as how the decoration was built up. It would be useless, for example, to attempt to repair a translucent colour layer with opaque pigment or to build up relief decoration without a proper foundation.

There are a number of factors which combine to make the reconstruction of old techniques and effects difficult for present-day decorators and restorers. Firstly, many old pigments are no longer available, either because manufacture has been discontinued as is the case with smalt and blue verditer, or because the mines have been worked out, as has happened with Oxford ochre and the best terre verte. Old paint, particularly when bound in oil or varnish, is likely to darken with time and also to become more translucent, so that in copying a surface one can be struggling to achieve an effect which was not present originally. For example, the borders around the marbling on the Villa Medici harpsichord referred to earlier, consisted of a mixture of lead white and lamp black applied over a ground of red ochre; but it proved impossible to match the colour when retouching the case using these pigments alone without the addition of others to modify the colour because of the darkening which had occurred in the original paint. The opacity or translucency of a paint depends on the relationship between the refractive index of the pigment and that of the medium. This is well demonstrated by chalk, which has very little covering power in oil because its refractive index and that of linseed oil are very similar, but which is quite opaque in gum or glue. Modern pigments are usually very finely ground and often have much greater staining power than the old, more coarsely ground colours. We have found that nineteenth-century samples of Prussian blue for instance, have considerably less tinting strength than modern Prussian blue. On the whole old colours were softer and they did not become uncontrollable in mixtures in the way that some modern pigments do. Perhaps one of the most significant indications of the change is the way in which the early painters used their colours pure and went to great lengths to keep them that way, while today we constantly mix tints and use pure colour only on a very restricted scale.

The fineness, opacity and chemical stability of most modern pigments means that paint made with them gives flat, even coats, with excellent covering power; but these surfaces usually lack the interesting qualities of the old ones. The old decorators knew how to use their pigments to the best advantage, building up the surface with a series of layers if necessary. This in turn gave the paint surface a depth and subtle variety quite unobtainable with a one-coat application. Examining a documented piece of Chippendale furniture recently we found that the pink paint of the original decoration had been applied in two stages. The lower one consisted of red lead with a little madder lake, and the upper one entirely of madder lake. By using red lead, which is very opaque, the decorator had provided a foundation coat which would cover the gesso beneath, and had economized on the expensive madder which, being a lake, also had less covering power.

The more one can understand about the materials old decorators used, the more intelligently one can re-apply their techniques in new work and reconstruct the effects they obtained when it comes to restoring missing sections of a design. The constant interchange of information between old and new is a principle which we also applied to our most recent venture – that of printed papers for copies of Flemish harpsichords. This got under way for two reasons, the first being that one of our builder-customers – Milan Misina – ran out of lid papers and asked us to produce some in a hurry. Almost at the same time we were asked if we could provide replacement papers for a Ruckers harpsichord undergoing restoration. We knew what the patterns should have been and also that they

Ann Mactaggart: painted soundboard and trompe l'oeil case decoration
on a muselar by Dennis Woolley.

were not commercially available. We set to and cut the blocks, and almost before we knew what was happening we had embarked on yet another voyage of exploration, this time about paper fibres and the ingredients of seventeenth-century ink, how the tools used to cut a block influenced the appearance of the print and the type of press that would have been used.

I suppose if we have a secret formula for our modest success, it is that we always work together. I do Peter's marquetry designs for him; he photographs soundboards for me.

On restorations we usually collaborate, with Peter providing the technical back-up while I remove layers of varnish. For us, the last ten years have been action-packed and full of thrills, to borrow a current phrase; we could not possibly have worked any harder, but neither would we have missed a minute of it.

Peter and Ann Mactaggart live and work at 19 Mill Lane, Welwyn, where they cut marquetry, decorate soundboards and casework of musical instruments, print traditional Ruckers papers and also restore decoration on instruments. Their services are available to builders, private owners, other musical instrument restorers and museums.

CHAPTER 20

John Paul

John Paul lives in a house in the Sussex countryside with his workshop adjacent. He works alone and is married with two teenage daughters.

JOHN PAUL:

Harpsichord making started for me quite out of the blue. I had no musical background when I was a child, my parents were not interested, nor did I hear any music at school. My father was an enthusiastic amateur carpenter, and I still use his tools. I think I must have been seized with a love of music from listening to the Proms on the wireless and I can remember sitting night after night with my ear close to the set. I have a vivid recollection of the broadcasts of a Toscanini season before the war, when the papers were filled with critical acclaim. I grew up in the depression, in the thirties, and left school at fourteen to take a series of dead-end jobs, but the war brought a great change to me as to so many. Chance put me into anti-aircraft radar and in due course I found myself at the

Royal Military College of Science doing general physics as well as electronics, and this was to prove of immense value in instrument making.

The war left me with a disability that was an employment handicap and so I became self-employed. At first I worked in photography, making cameras and trying to invent better systems of colour photography, until I realized that I stood no chance competing with Kodak. I had bought and enjoyed records by Wanda Landowska, without knowing anything about harpsichords, when one day a little spinet turned up in a local auction. It was a late instrument, made in London about 1770 by a German immigrant named Schöne who had anglicized his name to Shean. My library had just sufficient information for me to make its identity certain, and I acquired it for £10 and set about restoring it. Such small chances condition our lives and I have been a harpsichord maker ever since.

There was no harpsichord industry then, as there is now, just a few scattered makers. There were no books on the subject, no information available other than the most trivial, and I think I am right in saying that the only collection of harpsichords in England where the instruments were kept in playing order was the Benton Fletcher, then in Cheyne Walk. I visited this collection several times, making careful notes and measurements, and decided that one of the Kirckman instruments was best.

The scaling and measurements of this harpsichord are still to hand in my notebook and frequently referred to, and I still like to work in the tradition of eighteenth-century English cabinet making with rich polished woods, veneered panels, inlays and cross banding.

I needed basic instruction which was very hard to find. The firm of Arnold Dolmetsch at Haslemere was taking apprentices and I would have liked to work there, but they required pupils to have the ability to play the instrument they were being taught to make and I did not play at all. One source of help was Henry Tull, retired and living near me, one of the rare first-generation harpsichord makers of modern times. I talked to him several times and looked at his instruments, which I did not really like, and came away with some important information, the string gauges of his regular scale. For lack of a micrometer I had not been able to measure the string sizes of any of the Benton Fletcher instruments. This data was vital and I doubt if I could have started without it; unfortunately he was stringing his instruments too heavily which led me astray for some time.

The way I overcame the lack of information was by experimenting on several c. 1800 grand pianos, also bought for a few pounds each, using them as test beds for soundboards, string scaling and experimental actions. In retrospect it was obviously the wrong thing to do; restored as pianos they would have been worth a great deal today. It is rather shattering to realize that I threw away a small fortune in valuable piano actions. However, not only did I learn something about harpsichord making from those

John Paul: English virginal in walnut and rosewood with satinwood interior and flower painted decoration.

experiments, I also learned a lot about early grand pianos and have since restored about a dozen of these lovely instruments by Broadwood, Stodart and Clementi.

My first completely new harpsichord was quite simple and small, $4\frac{1}{2}$ octaves compass with just two unisons, and only 5 feet long. To my great satisfaction it was tonally delightful and, thinking that I now knew everything, I developed from it an elaborated design in which the compass was taken down to FF, and added a lute stop, a 4ft and a second manual. All this, crammed into a little instrument under 6 ft long, was too much and I have not again built such a specification into anything so small. Although it is possible to make short pianos by using wrapped strings in the bass, in harpsichord making the bottom notes of the full compass require length and there is no way round the fact.

At this stage I was not yet making harpsichords full time but was planning to do so and phasing out my other work of making cameras. In the early 1950s, post-war recovery was still very slow in England but the demand for harpsichords was growing in the USA. I was living and working in a tiny flat in Eastbourne, making harpsichords in total chaos, planning to get married and not having any idea whether I could support a family by instrument making. I had no savings and the work I had done had required too much research to show a profit. In such circumstances there is no substitute for that peculiar gift known as luck, and I can claim with some justification that I have survived by a Micawber-like quality of something, at the very last moment, turning up.

Halfway between Eastbourne and Tunbridge Wells I found a beautiful building site, nearly ten acres of Wealden countryside, at the extraordinary price of hardly more than £50 an acre. It was so suitable that I took it immediately and designed a house to live and work in. The girl I was to marry felt it could not possibly be real and declined to cast her eyes over the plans, something she now deeply regrets for I provided her with a laundry room hardly big enough to stand up in. She did, however, have savings in the bank and so did her mother and my parents. I borrowed shamelessly from all of them and went ahead. There would have been no point in approaching a building society; such organizations are realists and require the assurance of a regular income as a fundamental condition for parting with their money.

It was apparent that we could not afford to have a complete and immaculate home ready to move into, and so I had a builder construct the shell, while I did the wiring, plumbing, carpentry and decorating. My intention was to carry on finishing at weekends what could not be done immediately, but I failed to take into account that I would have to work a six-and-a-half day week to survive in business. It is only now, more than twenty years later, that I am getting it finished.

At first I could not have both a house and a workshop and so two incomplete rooms were left, to make one large room in which I worked. This was excellent for three or four years but then the arrival of our second daughter showed that it was a temporary expedient which could not continue. By this time land prices had risen considerably, and the sale of an odd half acre of garden which was hardly missed made it possible to build a substantial workshop which has served me well ever since.

In my early days it was possible to buy an old harpsichord for less than a maker could produce a copy, and this inevitably led makers to try and produce better instruments than the old ones, otherwise they would not have sold anything. There was little point in setting out to make a copy of a Kirckman when one could buy the real thing for £100 or so. "Better" could mean a number of things, perhaps modern-looking, but generally bigger and more complex, with more strings, more stops, pedals and half hooking. I had a

John Paul: single-manual harpsichord in mahogany and satinwood, after
two different instruments by Pascal Taskin.

request to quote for a harpsichord with four sets of strings, a lute and two buff stops, with half hooking on each pedal, but as I could see no practical way of half hooking a buff stop I heard no more. The big selling point was reliability, the really weak area of old instruments, and one searched for ways to make harpsichords stay in tune longer, to ensure that they would never warp and that the action was efficient and easily regulated.

The winners in this race were Pleyel, who made what were large complex grand pianos with harpsichord actions, and Challis in the USA who made his harpsichords with aluminium soundboards which he claimed sounded just like the real thing and hardly ever went out of tune. I was extremely curious to know how effective they were and wrote to ask him how he made these boards. His reply was that he had experimented long and hard to find out and I could do the same. Such a reply surprised me considerably as I enjoyed giving away information. I, too, experimented and made a little harpsichord with an aluminium soundboard. It sounded quite well, but stayed in tune no better or worse than any other I have made. My intention was to make a harpsichord that would travel anywhere abroad without damage, and I think this one could have, but in the way such things happen it was sold to a lady living a mere four miles away and happily she has it still. I made another major soundboard experiment: by laminating one from spruce veneers. It would have been the answer to a lot of stability problems if it had been satisfactory but the tone was poor and I took it out again.

I have also tried out the various sources of spruce which have been available, American Sitka spruce and the European from Roumania and Switzerland. The Swiss product proved best without any doubt, although it needs careful selection to get the right stock. There is a great deal of mystique surrounding soundboards and a general belief that an extremely close grain is best, although I have seen some magnificent old instruments with soundboard grain which would have been more appropriate on a kitchen table. I like to have a tight grain in the treble and a more open grain and thinner section in the bass. More important is the feel of the wood when I handle it, a recognition of quality which comes with experience. Such wood is light in weight and rings clearly when tapped, and will be wide enough to come from a large old tree. When I need to make a board I select the planks from my store and put them in a conditioning cupboard where the humidity is controlled and there they stay for several months while all the other work goes ahead. At intervals they are planed and jointed and have the bridges fitted, then I proof the made-up board with a mixture of linseed oil and preservative. This is an insurance policy against possible worm or fungal attack and also seals the grain and has a stabilizing effect on the fibre structure. If I am going to decorate the soundboard I do so before it is fitted, putting it back in the conditioning cupboard between painting sessions so that it is kept stable, ready to be glued into the instrument.

At first I made only the soundboards, rim and action, putting out the cabinet work, the keyboards and employing a tuner. Then I learned these skills one at a time, and it was not until I could do everything that I felt I had become a real harpsichord maker. Doing everything, from the design to the finish, is now so important to me that I could not employ staff and put my name to anything someone else had made. The very last skill I have acquired, and only in the last year, is to paint so that I can decorate my nameboards and soundboards.

By the time I was moving into my new house orders began to come in from the USA and for a number of years this was my main market. There was a demand for large concert harpsichords, with 16ft as well as the usual two-manual specification, big heavy instruments with eight pedals. I liked to make these with as wide a variety of tone as possible and did so by putting quill plectra on the upper manual jacks and leather on the lower, and having the 16ft quite different in tone from the unisons by having all of this set of strings lightly wrapped. These instruments were an enormous technical challenge and I found it very rewarding to overcome all the problems that arose in such a complex specification and to ensure that everything worked with precision. But once I had conquered the design they became less attractive to me and I ceased to make them. The last one took me sixteen months to make and then was damaged on the way to the USA, and the thought that so much effort might have to be written off deterred me from making any more.

The era of the bigger and better harpsichord was anyway coming to an end, and authenticity was becoming the important concept. Naturally, I have been influenced enormously by this trend, but for a number of reasons I have not taken entirely to making copies, and I still spend about half my time doing original work. In the old instruments I happen to have restored, the casework was distorted and to have copied the construction would have been foolish. In fact I have already seen modern copies as bent as instruments more than two hundred years old. Also, I regard myself to some extent as an artist, and this side of me can only be expressed by doing original and creative work. The man who tackles only copies acquires a very limited knowledge of harpsichord making. The good harpsichord maker needs to be a designer, one who can determine the reason for, and the result of, doing something in a particular way. He must be prepared to accept mistakes and be most critically observant to recognize when he has done so.

In practice, the original work I am doing now is largely derived from several different early makers, choosing the best features from each. My case construction is based on that of the early English makers, Hayward and Hitchcock, in which strong framing runs diagonally across the bottom boards. Hubbard describes this as "a design much superior to that used in mid-eighteenth-century English instruments" and I would agree with

John Paul: upright harpsichord in rosewood and satinwood with flower painted decoration by Shelagh North.

him. I start by putting down a full length baseboard and building up on that, in the Italian manner. The late English and French method of adding bottom boards to a completed rim is little more than an exercise in neatness. It is my belief that early makers approached the stress problem as one of propping up the hitch rail with battens or knees and failed to give enough consideration to taking the strength over the action gap to the wrest plank. I like to look at the whole length of the structure as a girder of mainly U-section created by integral sides and bottom, and see that there is balanced strength the whole way.

For appearance I still prefer the style usually referred to as late English, made in solid mahogany or a similar fine hardwood, and relieved with an inlay decoration. The current fashion for lacquered finishes does not appeal to me and it may be ephemeral because of the difficulty of keeping the surface in pristine condition.

Harpsichords of course stand or fall on their tone. The Hitchcock construction is acoustically sound and can be used with soundboard and scaling systems from all the late makers, so that I have a wide range of sources to choose from. At the moment I am working after Taskin and Kirckman but I also find it of value to read what has been said in the past, instead of going only to the instruments. I have never, for example, used a just scale for my own designs in the way most modern makers do. Instead of doubling the string length for each octave, I follow the recommendations of Van Blankenburg (who wrote in the early eighteenth century) and shorten (taper) my scale as it goes down, so that I can bring the brass strings up as high as possible. This gives richness both to the bass and the lower tenor, especially when combined with a Kirckman soundboard; a solo, not an ensemble instrument, but it is the solo instrument that I like to make.

When I make copies, it is very largely with the intention of finding out what the maker was trying to do, rather than imitate his result. The next copy I would like to make is of the Russell Collection Hass, a very fine, simple, single-manual instrument and I am hoping that they will soon release plans of it.

We are still trying to find our way to an understanding of the factors that create harpsichord tone. It is apparent that the tone as a whole results from the complex relationship between strings, soundboard and case, and one of the interesting things about this job is discovering how small changes in any part can affect tone without it being very clear why they have done so. There is quite a lot known about the effect of the various parts looked at in isolation, but the art of the maker consists of intuitively understanding the whole. The string plan, of course, is of the greatest importance; the type of wire, the tension, whether the scale is just or tapered. The modes of vibration of the wire, the long strings in the bass much more flexible than the treble, control the harmonic content. The long bass strings are strong in harmonics and weak in fundamental, the treble strings weak in harmonics and strong in fundamental, and this basic pattern is further controlled by the soundboard behaviour.

There are many physical characteristics of soundboards which affect tone but most are fixed effects. The maker has to be concerned with the variables under his control and the one I regard as important is the soundboard size and shape and the way it is barred. For maximum efficiency as a radiator of sound the area of board controlled by any note would need to be equivalent in size to the square of the wavelength of that note but, in practice, this is nowhere near achieved, except in the high treble. In fact, harpsichord soundboards are very restricted in size and this restriction greatly controls the tone. The soundboard is hardly capable at all of radiating the fundamental in the bass but it can radiate the plentiful harmonics; ascending the scale more fundamental is radiated, until in the treble it is all there. Luckily, the volume output right through the compass closely matches the level of hearing efficiency of our ears so that the average instrument sounds perfectly balanced, while our hearing recreates for us the fundamental missing from the bass notes.

One of the principal differences between harpsichords is the way in which the vibrating region round the bridge is hemmed in by the curved side and boudin and the way in which the soundboard is unbalanced, so that there may be more area on one side of the bridge than on the other, while part of that area is modified by the effect of the barring. These different constricting influences control the efficiency of the soundboard as a radiator of sound. This means that at any point on a bridge every soundboard has a selective action in the way it emphasizes harmonics and therefore a substantial controlling effect on tone colour.

When it comes to the case, virtually every maker will say that it is vital to copy not only the shape and dimensions of an early instrument, but also the species of wood used in every part. If one looks at old case woods the variety is considerable: fir, spruce, cedar, cypress, lime, poplar, oak, walnut, to name those usually found. There is no common factor here, while trying to divine the intention of early makers is further complicated by the way they used mixtures of species, for example some north European makers commonly used pine for the long side and oak for the curve. One must logically recognize that they used oak for the curve because it will bend easily and pine will not, and this further suggests that they had no acoustic intention in their choice. But, intentional or not, the choice of timber has some effect because wood varies in the extent to which it absorbs sound. All species tend to absorb and kill sound, the loss being greatest as the frequency rises and this high frequency loss is the reason wooden instruments are rarely harsh. This is an area of harpsichord construction which has not been properly investigated, but I feel that of equal importance is cavity resonance, the resonance of the column of air contained within the body.

The effect of cavity resonance is to reinforce some harmonics at the expense of others and thus again modify what the soundboard is doing to the basic string tone. The cavity feedback tends to fluctuate in and out of phase with the soundboard and this is the main

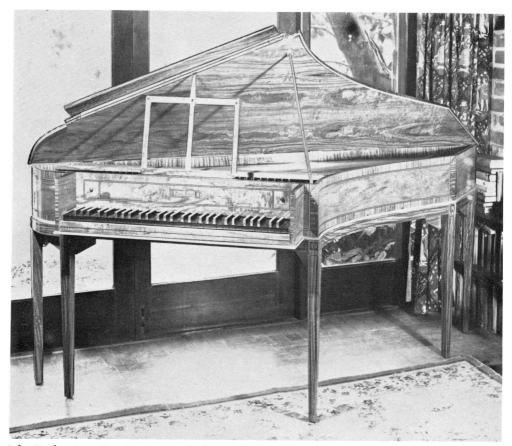

John Paul: wing spinet in satinwood after an anonymous late English instrument.

cause of the vibrant quality of a good instrument. The phase drift is due to the fact that the velocity of sound differs in air and wood. One of my interests is to do research on cavity resonance by altering the shape of the cavity, which can be done by designing the structural members to act also as baffles. After building harpsichords for a lifetime the hope emerges that one can control tone. I regard this as a more realistic aim than trying to copy the tone of an old instrument, which is nearly always doomed to disappointment. As I work I carry in my head an image of the tone for which I am aiming; usually a clear piping treble matched to a shimmering reverberance in the bass and tenor.

There is still no clear picture of the aims and intentions of musical instrument makers of the past. I certainly doubt if many of them had some vision of the kind of tone they were seeking (as I do), or if they balanced and considered each piece of wood in the way of violin makers. They certainly must not be compared with the modern makers, many of whom are graduates and are a remarkable breed of bench-working intellectuals. The makers of the past probably cannot be classified in this way because they number hundreds or thousands spread over more than three centuries, an extraordinarily disparate group of men. I do have a general picture of some of them, possibly even the majority, as being bourgeois artisans, about on a social par with bootmakers (and if this seems unfair, remember Mozart relegated to the servants' table). Customers might order an instrument much as they might order any other furniture, paying a good deal of attention to the size and finish. They would only buy a harpsichord if the tone and touch suited them but they would not expect it to be constructed with mysticism and artistry, to have special tonal qualities over which their friends would rhapsodize or which would illuminate the work of one school of composers rather than another. The makers who stood above this level, men like Shudi and Kirckman, were factory owners, buying their wood in bulk from their nearest wharves and sawmills and processing it through a production line.

Among these makers were those of seminal importance who introduced new concepts in the way they made their instruments, but their intention is, in many cases, unclear. It is flattering to musicians to say that the demands of art prompted the technology and equally flattering to instrument builders to say that their technology prompted composers to write for their instruments. Actually, that musical quartet, composer – musician – instrument builder – audience, work together in a way we do not understand. We still make value judgements on insufficient evidence when we assign music to a harpsichord having particular tonal qualities; what we are then really doing is to make a statement about our own taste.

I look back at how the old makers worked, and believe that instruments in the past were largely made "off the cuff", whereas the present generation tries too hard. This produces instruments which are very good but a bit too precious, and we may not yet have got it right. Does it matter? Probably not, for the simple reason that we have no choice but to be of our own generation and we cannot escape from that.

Recently I received a grant from South East Arts towards the work of designing and painting an instrument, and this gave me time to experiment.

The traditional painting of harpsichords has mostly been that of landscape scenes with figures on the insides of lids, combined with flower painting on the soundboards. Landscape decorated lids would have been out of keeping with my inlaid finish, but I found that I could paint flowers. It has always seemed sensible to me as a business attitude, not to do what everyone else is doing and this rationalizes my personal wish to be original. Thus I felt that I had to avoid painting soundboards in the French and Flemish manner and look for a different and attractive use of flowers. The Clementi-painted nameboard, with its stylized posy which caught the eye and directed it to the nameplate, became my choice.

John Paul: nameboard detail of virginal; satinwood with tulipwood
inlay and oil painted decoration.

These nameboards were of inlaid satinwood with the painting in oil colour. I soon found that I would have to follow Clementi and use rich oil colour in exactly the way he did. The water-based colours of traditional soundboard painting, heavily broken with white to produce pastel shades, looked grey and lost on satinwood. Quite a lot of interesting research was needed to find the best preparation of the satinwood so that the paint keyed properly and yet was suitable for taking polish on the finished surface. One polishes by cutting back each layer with glasspaper and pulling over again, but this is impossible once the flowers are painted. I found it best to grind my own paint into an oil vehicle which was resistant to polish and dried quickly.

Once I had established a painting technique in oil I carried the same method over to soundboard painting. There is less difference between paints than is usually imagined. Oil, tempera, water colours, contain the same pigments; the difference lies in the optical quality of the dry vehicle and the handling qualities the different vehicles present to the artist. The adoption of any unfamiliar technique results in additional decisions having to be taken, and I had next to change my soundboard preparation and varnishing. It is interesting that there is a myth in violin making that oil varnishes are better than spirit while, in harpsichord making, it is believed that oil varnish is fatal; in fact harpsichord soundboards were rarely varnished. I have not been able to find any effect on tone from using any varnish, provided it is applied thinly. Oil paint requires the protection of a varnish, usually one based on turpentine, and this is what I now use. I would always use a varnish, anyway; a dirty soundboard which could not be wiped clean would be anathema to me.

The really big problem which has dominated my career has been how to produce work which will not suffer when transported from my workshop environment to a new home, especially if abroad or in a difficult climate. One harpsichord I sold to an American consular official years ago went to Tunisia, whence he subsequently moved to a number of different areas of India and ended up in Amman. When I last heard, it was doing well, but it may have been more the quality of his care than the way I built it that has enabled it to survive these climates. Changes of humidity are stressful to harpsichords, and as I cannot match all foreign climates easily the solution I have adopted is to concentrate on English conditions by building my workshop with the same construction as the average English house. It has the standard cavity walls, brick outside and insulation block inside, with an insulated roof, while the humidity is maintained by air conditioning at 60% RH. This figure is a median one between the humidity of unheated summer air and the average centrally-heated winter conditions in an English home. If my customers take the trouble to keep a check on their own room humidity they should have no problems.

When I review my working life and add up the instruments I have made the total in numbers is quite small, about thirty harpsichords, twenty clavichords, and also some thirty early instruments restored, mostly pianos. Each harpsichord has been different, in some respect, as I either tried to make each succeeding one better or tried to arrive at some fundamental truth about harpsichord acoustics. I am therefore a mixture of researcher and artist, not a production man except as a means to those two ends. I am often asked how I can bear to part with my work, but as soon as I have finished an instrument I dislike it and want to start on a better one. Actually I am now at a level where I have almost ceased to experiment and am building on experience, making instruments which are relatively simple in design but as beautiful in proportion and execution as I can manage. Had I been asked a year or two ago how I saw my future, I would have regarded it as unchanged. Writing this book, though, has made me look critically both at my fellow harpsichord makers and myself; I realize that I am standing on the edge of a vast field of knowledge and experience that I have yet to explore, a challenging prospect.

John Paul has his workshop at his home, Parkway, Waldron, Heathfield, Sussex, and is currently making: a late-seventeenth-century English virginal, harpsichords both single- and double-manual to his own design after Kirckman and Taskin, and can occasionally accept commissions.

GLOSSARY

ACTION: The assemblage of mechanical components which sets the strings in motion.

ANNEAL: To soften a metal, usually by heating followed by controlled cooling. Such softening is usually total, as opposed to tempering, which is partial.

ANTINODE: Position of maximum displacement along the length of a vibrating string or maximum or minimum pressure in a vibrating column of air.

ARCADE: A decorative finish on the vertical fronts of keys, shaped like an arch.

BALANCE PIN: The pin which supports the key at the fulcrum and keeps it upright. It is driven into the centre bar of the key frame or key bed.

BEAT: Two frequencies sounding together will add together, resulting in new tones being created which are the sum and difference of the original two frequencies (and of their harmonics). The difference note, if low enough, will be heard as a beat. An interval tuned until the beat note disappears is tuned exactly.

BELLY: The soundboard.

BELLY BARS: The bars of wood glued to the underside of the soundboard, either as support or to restrict the vibrations.

BELLY RAIL: The bar of wood immediately behind the action of a harpsichord and which supports the front of the soundboard.

BENTSIDE: The curved side of a keyboard instrument.

BOUDIN: (Fr.) The hitch rail of the 4ft strings.

BOX SLIDE: A type of register or jack guide which is deep so that it serves the purpose of both top and bottom ordinary jack guides.

BRIDGE: The strip of wood attached to the top of the soundboard and over which the strings pass. It conveys the vibrations of the strings to the soundboard.

BRIDGE PINS: Pins driven into the bridge which both locate the strings and hold them tightly to the bridge.

BRISTLE: Hogs' bristle, the original return spring material of the tongue, or a substitute.

BUFF STOP: A row of pieces of buff leather (originally buffalo hide) which can be pressed against the strings to cause a partial muting.

CENT: One twelve-hundredth part of an octave. There are 100 cents to an equal tempered semitone.

CHEEKS: The sides of the case at the keyboard end.

CHOIR: All of one set of strings.

CHROMATIC: Having the quality of colour. The name given to the scale of twelve semitones to the octave.

CLAVICYTHERIUM: Upright harpsichord.

COMMA: The difference between two sets of just intervals or between combinations of just intervals. It is possible to invent commas indefinitely; the two most important are the ditonic or Pythagorean comma which is the excess of twelve fifths over seven octaves (approximately 24 cents) and the syntonic comma, which is the excess of four fifths over two octaves plus a major third (approximately 22 cents).

COUPLER: The mechanism by which the upper manual is operated from the lower manual.

COURSES: Two or more strings on a musical instrument producing the same note. Modern terminology uses the word "unisons" when the strings are at the same pitch, but courses has a wider meaning and includes strings at octave or sub-octave pitch.

CUT-OFF BAR: The large, long, belly bar which runs approximately parallel to the line of the bridge.

DISPOSITION: The way the stops of a harpsichord are disposed or arranged, e.g. the order of the registers from front to back and the way they are split between the manuals.

DOGLEG JACK: A jack with a stepped tail so that it can rest on both the upper and lower manuals.

EXPRESSIVE TWO-MANUAL HARPSICHORD: An instrument in which the two manuals control different tone colours or different dynamic levels.

FORMER: A pre-fixed shape over which wood is bent or formed to that same shape.

FRAME: The body structure of an instrument.

FREQUENCY: The measure of the number of complete vibrations which occur each second. At one time defined as cycles per second, now known as Hertz, abbreviation Hz.

FRET: A bar placed across the fingerboard of a stringed instrument so that when the string is pressed down on to it the speaking length is reduced and a note of higher pitch can be sounded. Fretted, applied to a clavichord, indicates an instrument in which some of the strings are struck by more than one tangent; a fret-free clavichord has one string, or one course of strings, for each note.

GROUND: A first or under-coating of colour.

HARMONICS: Every musical note has a recognizable pitch, the fundamental, plus a series of overtones or higher frequencies which are (in theory precisely, in practice not always) $\times 2$, $\times 3$, $\times 4$, $\times 5$ the fundamental and so on up. The proportion of overtones present constitutes to a large extent the tonal quality of the note. The fundamental is the 1st harmonic, twice that frequency is the 2nd harmonic and so on.

HITCH PINS: The pins to which the strings are attached at the remote end.

HITCH RAIL: The bar of wood into which the hitch pins are affixed. The 8ft hitch rail is usually attached to the inner surface of the curved side and tail. The 4ft hitch rail is a bar attached under the soundboard and the pins driven into it through the soundboard. Alternative term for the 4ft hitch rail is boudin.

HOOK: A mechanism to keep a pedal engaged by retaining it by spring pressure in a stepped metal plate.

ICTUS: The audible quality of the starting transient of a note.

IMPEDANCE: A resistance which alters with frequency. First used in electrical theory where it is the effective resistance to alternating current of a capacitor or inductance or an equivalent circuit. Applied to wave transmission in wood it can best be considered in terms of inertia or resistance to being moved. The soundboard is an impedance matching device which is capable of being moved by the strings and is in turn capable of moving the air.

INTERVAL: The aural appreciation of the relationship between two notes. The traditional name, [of] third, fourth, fifth, etc., is given to the distance apart of two frequencies when the ratio of the frequencies can be expressed in simple figures. The most important are:

$$1:2 \text{ octave}$$
$$2:3 \text{ fifth}$$
$$3:4 \text{ fourth}$$
$$4:5 \text{ major third}$$
$$5:6 \text{ minor third}$$
$$3:5 \text{ major sixth}$$
$$5:8 \text{ minor sixth}$$

These are known as the harmonic intervals, meaning that they are harmonious to the human ear.

JACK: The action component of the harpsichord.

JACK RAIL: A cushioned bar of wood which limits the upward travel of the jacks.

JUST: Exact. Just intervals are those exactly in tune, or perfect.

JUST SCALE: The scale of an instrument in which the length of the strings is doubled at each octave.

JUST TUNING: A system of tuning in which the intervals are perfect.

KEY: The wooden lever which conveys the touch of the player to the action.

KEY BED or KEY FRAME: The frame of wood into which the balance and guide pins are driven, and on to which the keys are fitted.

KNEE: A wooden brace which supports the inside surface of a curved side in the manner of a buttress.

LINER: A strip of wood attached to the inner surface of the case and to which the soundboard is fixed.

LOCKBOARD: The front panel of the harpsichord body, which is removed to reveal the keys.

MACHINE STOP: A mechanism usually operated by a pedal which changes several stops at once.

MORTICE: A hole, usually rectangular, in a piece of wood and into which another part is fitted, e.g. the female half of a mortice and tenon joint. Also the slot in a jack guide in which the jack will slide.

MOTHER-AND-CHILD VIRGINAL: A combination of a standard rectangular virginal and a small octave virginal (one at 4ft pitch). The octave virginal fits into the larger instrument, under the soundboard, in the manner of a drawer. It can be withdrawn to be played separately, or placed on top of the main instrument over the row of jacks (with the jack rail removed) and in this position it becomes coupled. The jacks of the main section will activate the octave jacks, so that the combined instrument becomes a two-manual, the lower keyboard an 8 + 4 and the upper at 4ft only.

MOULDED KEY FRONT: An alternative key front design to the arcade, a decorative finish of horizontal lines incised or shaped.

NAGS-HEAD SWELL: A variation on the Venetian swell, in which part of the lid can be raised while playing to provide a crescendo. The name comes from the shape of the mechanism.

NODE: A point of a vibrating body or string or column of air which is relatively motionless.

NUT: The name given to the bridge which is on the wrest plank.

PEDAL-BOARD HARPSICHORD: A complete harpsichord with pedal operated keys; it is placed flat on the floor and the manual harpsichord stands on top of it.

PHASE: The relationship between two oscillations of similar frequency expressed as a fraction of a cycle and measured in degrees. When the peaks and troughs coincide the waves are in phase; if they alternate they are out of phase by 180°. Our left and right ears translate phase differences between them into a sense of direction but, in an instrument, phase differences affect the sum of two vibrations added together. In-phase vibrations add completely, out of phase by 180° they cancel out, and intermediate phases add or subtract proportionately.

GLOSSARY

PITCH: The audible sensation of a particular frequency. Standard pitch: the frequency of one note agreed as a tuning standard, currently a¹ = 440 Hz. Quint pitch: a fifth higher. Quart pitch: a fourth higher.

PYTHAGOREAN SCALE: A form of just tuning or a scale. Not necessarily evolved by Pythagoras, as it developed over hundreds of years. Originally a tuning for the Greek lute, it became, in mediaeval times, a diatonic scale for the keyboard, but problems arose as the accidentals were added. The Pythagorean interval is a ratio between a power of two and a power of three. The fourths and fifths are the same as in the harmonic set but the major third ratio is 81:64, making it sharper than the harmonic major third (5:4 or 80:64) by a syntonic comma, while the minor third is 32:27, flatter by the same amount than the harmonic minor third.

QUARTERED TIMBER: Wood cut from the trunk along the radius. Such wood will expand or contract equally on both surfaces and should therefore have a minimum tendency to warp.

RACK: A board behind the keys with vertical slots cut in it; each key has a pin in the end running in its own slot. Thus a guide to keep the keys in line.

RAVALEMENT: (Fr.) Enlargement of a harpsichord.

REGISTER: The slip of wood with slots or mortices cut in it which guides the jacks and keeps them in the correct position.

RESONANCE: Sympathetic or induced vibration at a particular frequency or frequencies. Resonant: having the ability to vibrate when stimulated.

RESONANT FREQUENCY: The natural frequency or frequencies at which an object will vibrate; e.g. in an instrument the strings have a natural frequency and so does the casewood and the contained volume of air.

RIM: All the inner part of the case to which the soundboard is glued, i.e. the liner plus the belly rail.

ROSE: A soundhole modified to provide an ornament or a maker's insignia. Usually of cast metal, carved wood or cut parchment.

SCALE: In music, an ordered and repeated series of notes. In instrument making, the measurements of the string lengths, usually given shortly as the measurement of the c² string.

SCANTLING: The size to which wood is to be cut; in an instrument, the sizes of the various structural pieces of wood.

SHORT OCTAVE: The bottom octave of a keyboard from which several keys are omitted, commonly the bottom four, C to E♭. This is designated C/E as the apparent E plays C, while apparent F♯ plays D and apparent G♯ plays E. The bottom octave is then C–c in naturals plus the B♭. The broken octave takes the compass lower. The bottom note is

[277]

an apparent BB but plays GG, C♯ plays AA and D♯ plays BB, and the F♯ is the first actual accidental.

SHOVE COUPLER: Also, sliding coupler. The French type of manual coupler which is operated by sliding the upper manual in and out.

SLIDE: A movable jack guide or register.

SPINE: The straight long side of a harpsichord.

STOP: In a harpsichord, any register, including the buff batten, which can be brought into, or out of play.

STRINGING: A narrow band of patterned inlay; the plain strip of inlay, usually box or ebony, is called a line.

TEMPER: To moderate. To partly soften in a controlled manner, as in to temper steel. In tuning, to soften dissonances by spreading them over several intervals.

TEMPERAMENTS: Systems of tuning in which some of the intervals are adjusted in order to increase the number of keys in which music can be played. Meantone temperament: commonly accepted as being the 1/4 syntonic comma temperament published by Pietro Aron in 1523. Well temperaments; also "good" temperaments: embrace a number of temperaments in which the fifths are not all the same size and which have no distinction between sharps and flats and can be used for modulation between all keys. Equal temperament: Any system of temperament that divides the octave into equal-sized units. Our standard equal temperament divides the octave into twelve equal semitones.

TONALITY: The quality of relationship to the tonic, i.e. to the key scheme of music.

TONGUE: The little pivoted insert in the jack which holds the plectrum.

TRANSPOSING DOUBLE-MANUAL: A two-manual harpsichord in which both keyboards pluck the same strings, but an interval apart, usually a fourth.

TRANSPOSING KEYBOARD: A keyboard which slips sideways by one semitone distance so that it can play at a pitch of either A 415 or A 440. Immediate transposition is only possible if the instrument is tuned to equal temperament; in any unequal temperament, re-tuning is necessary.

TROMPE L'OEIL: Deceiving to the eye. In decoration, painting on a flat surface in a way which simulates bas relief.

TUNING HAMMER: The key used to turn the wrest pins when tuning. Called a hammer because it sometimes incorporates a hammer head for tapping the wrest pins down to tighten them.

UNISON: Together. One of two sets of strings at 8ft pitch.

VENETIAN SWELL: A cover over a soundboard consisting of a set of openable slats. Designed to control the volume and provide a crescendo.

WOLF INTERVAL: The audible quality of a mis-tuned interval. Dissonance great enough to be painful.

WREST PINS: The tuning pins, round thin rods with square or rectangular heads to which the strings are attached and which can be turned by the tuning hammer.

WREST PLANK: The block of hardwood into which the wrest pins are set.

BIBLIOGRAPHY

General

Apel, Willi, *The History of Keyboard Music to 1700* (Indiana University Press, 1967).

Bedbrook, G. S., *Keyboard Music from the Middle Ages to the beginning of the Baroque* (DaCapo, 1973).

Benade, A. H., *Fundamentals of Musical Acoustics* (Oxford University Press, 1976).

Boalch, Donald, *Makers of the Harpsichord and Clavichord* (1956, 2nd edition, Oxford University Press, 1974).

Campbell, Margaret, *Dolmetsch: The Man and His Work* (Hamish Hamilton, 1975).

Dolmetsch, Arnold, *The Interpretation of the Music of the 17th and 18th Centuries* (Novello, 1916, 2nd edition, 1946).

Dolmetsch, Mabel, *Personal Recollections of Arnold Dolmetsch* (Routledge and Kegan Paul, 1958).

Ford, Charles, Ed., *Making Musical Instruments, Strings and Keyboard* (Faber and Faber, 1979).

Harding, Rosamund E. M., *The Piano Forte* (2nd edition, Gresham Books, 1978).

Hirt, Franz Joseph, *Stringed Keyboard Instruments* (Boston Book and Art Shop, 1968).

Hubbard, Frank, *Three Centuries of Harpsichord Making* (Harvard University Press, 1965, 3rd edition, 1970).

James, Philip, *Early Keyboard Instruments* (Peter Davies, 1930, reprinted Holland Press, 1960).

Jeans, Sir James, *Science and Music* (Cambridge University Press, 1937, Dover Paperbacks, 1968).

Kirkpatrick, Ralph, *Domenico Scarlatti* (Princeton University Press, 1953).

Montague, Jeremy, *The World of Baroque and Classical Musical Instruments* (David and Charles, 1979).

Neupert, Hans, *The Harpsichord Manual* (Bärenreiter, English translation).

Ripin, Edwin M., Ed., *Keyboard Instruments* (Edinburgh University Press, 1971).

Russell, Raymond, *The Harpsichord and Clavichord* (Faber and Faber, 1959, new edition revised by Howard Schott, 1973).

Schneider, E. Harich, *The Harpsichord* (Bärenreiter).

Schott, Howard, *Playing the Harpsichord* (Faber and Faber, 1951).

Scientific American, The (from), "The Physics of Music" (W. H. Freeman & Co., San Francisco, 1979).

Wood, Alexander, *The Physics of Music* (Methuen, 1944/65).

Yates, Peter, *An Amateur at the Keyboard* (Allen and Unwin, 1965).

Tuning

Barbour, J. Murray, *Tuning and Temperaments* (Michigan State College Press, 2nd edition, 1953).

Di Véroli, Claudio, *Unequal Temperaments* (Buenos Aires, 1976).

Jorgensen, Owen, *Tuning the Historical Temperaments by Ear* (Northern Michigan University Press, 1977).

Kellner, H. A., *The Tuning of My Harpsichord* (Das Musikinstrument, Frankfurt/Main).

Lloyd, Ll. S. and Boyle, H., *Intervals, Scales and Temperaments* (Macdonald and Jane, 1978).

Articles and pamphlets

Barnes, John, "The stringing of Italian harpsichords" (Paper given at the Internationale Arbeitstagung des Instituts für Aufführungspraxis der Hochschule für Musik und darstellende Kunst in Graz, 1971).

Barnes, John, "Bach's keyboard temperament" (in *Early Music*, vol. 7, no. 2, April 1979).

Blood, William, "Well-tempering the clavier: five methods" (in *Early Music*, vol. 7, no. 2, October 1979).

Mactaggart, Ann and Peter, "Some problems encountered in cleaning two harpsichord soundboards" (*Studies in Conservation*, 22, 1977).

Mactaggart, Ann and Peter, "Refiner's Verditers" (*Studies in Conservation*. 25, 1980).

Mactaggart, Ann and Peter, "Tempera and decorated keyboard instruments" (*Galpin Society Journal*, XXXII, 1979).

O'Brien, Grant, "The stringing and pitches of Ruckers instruments" (*Colloquium – Ruckers Klavecimbelo en copieen*, Antwerp, 1977).

O'Brien, Grant, "Some principles of eighteenth century harpsichord stringing and their application" (*Organ Yearbook*, 1980).

Shortridge, John D., "Italian harpsichord building in the 16th and 17th centuries" (*United States National Museum Bulletin*, 225, Paper 15, Smithsonian Institution Press, Washington, D.C., 2nd edition, 1970).